About this book

This work looks at how contemporary global economic policies are made: by which institutions, under what ideologies, and how they are enforced. The author reveals the central roles played by organizations such as the IMF and the World Bank in supervising the livelihoods of over 2.5 billion people. He shows that neoliberal economic policy is enforced by a few thousand unelected and un-accountable experts in the North and has failed to deliver tolerable living conditions for the poor.

The book argues for a new geographic theory of power, exercised through dominant institutions, concentrated in hegemonic power centres. It seeks to transform the existing geography of policy-making power by exposing its structures, centres and mechanisms, critiquing its intellectual founda-tions, uncovering its un-democratic justifications, and passionately supporting its opponents. The conclusion makes a further positive contribution by exploring policy alternatives that point the way forward.

About the author

Richard Peet is Professor of Geography at Clark University in Worcester, Massachusetts, USA. He obtained his BSc (Econ) at the London School of Economics, his MA from the University of British Columbia, and his PhD at the University of California. He was the Editor of the radical geography journal, *Antipode*, from 1970 to 1985 and Co-Editor of *Economic Geography* between 1992 and 1998. His published books include: *Radical Geography* (Maaroufa Press, 1977), *Global Capitalism: Theories of Societal Development* (Routledge, 1991), *Modern Geographical Thought* (Blackwell, 1998), *Theories of Development* (with Elaine Hartwick, Guilford Press, 1999), *Liberation Ecologies* (with Michael Watts, Routledge, 1996 and 2004) and *Unholy Trinity: The IMF, World Bank and WTO* (Zed Books, 2003). *Unholy Trinity* has been translated into Spanish as *La Maldita Trinidad* and is being translated into Arabic and Korean.

Richard Peet

Geography of power: making global economic policy

Zed Books

LONDON · NEW YORK

Geography of power: making global economic policy was first published in 2007 by Zed Books Ltd, 7 Cynthia Street, London N1 9JF, UK and Room 400, 175 Fifth Avenue, New York, NY 10010, USA

<www.zedbooks.co.uk>

Copyright © Richard Peet, 2007

The right of Richard Peet to be identified as the author of this work has been asserted by him in accordance with the Copyright, Designs and Patents Act, 1988.

Cover designed by Andrew Corbett
Set in Sabon and Gill Sans Heavy by Ewan Smith, London
Index: <ed.emery@britishlibrary.net>
Printed and bound in Malta by Gutenberg Press Ltd

Distributed in the USA exclusively by Palgrave Macmillan, a division of St Martin's Press, LLC, 175 Fifth Avenue, New York, NY 10010, USA.

A catalogue record for this book is available from the British Library.
US CIP data are available from the Library of Congress.

ISBN 978 1 84277 710 7 hb
ISBN 978 1 84277 711 4 pb

Contents

Figures

Tables

Preface

I began this book in Christchurch, New Zealand, at a time when that
deeply social democratic country was recovering from a bad bout
with neoliberalism. The New Zealand Labour Party renationalized
the railways and declared a new incomes policy that gave income and
services to poor families. This revived my sense that change was possible and could be made through policy. My time in New Zealand was
supported by an Erskine Fellowship at the University of Canterbury,
and this, in turn, was made possible by Ross Barnett and Eric Pawson.
I gave early versions of Chapter 1 to audiences at the University of
Waikato and the University of Otago, where I received good com-
ments and lots of encouragement. Phil O'Neil, of the University of
Newcastle, went out of his way to make my family's visit to Australia
particularly memorable. When I returned to Clark University in
the United States, my home base now for more years than I can
remember, my work on the book was rendered more enjoyable by a
group of graduate students who are as politically committed and as
intellectually competent as any I have known: Waquar Ahmed, Ipsita
Chatterjee, Mohammed Eskandari, Kendra Fehrer, Jayson Funke,
Mazen Laban, Sagie Narsiah, Thomas Ponniah, Janet Redman and
Deb Singh were all supportive and each has contributed to the ideas
in this book. Waquar Ahmed graciously agreed to draw the diagrams
two days after flying back from India and did a super job. I have
always been impressed by the sense of moral justice that comes from
the undergraduate students at Clark University, and my recent years
teaching Global Society and Political Economy of Development to
large, enthusiastic and vociferous classes have stimulated my intellect
and reinforced my hope for social justice in the future. In 2005 I spent
time in São Paulo State, Brazil, where my encounter with the militant
activists of the MST rejuvenated my lagging sense that fundamental
social change comes from the bravery of ordinary people – Cliff
Welch and Bernado Fernandes were my friends and guides. But most
of all, as source of support, there is the love and the pleasure of being
with my family as I try to find the time to write. Lukas, Eric and
Anna are fun and loving kids. And my wife, Elaine Hartwick, was
constantly supportive of a project she admired and shared. Elaine,
you are the source of my inspiration and the centre of my affection.
You made this book possible. – *Leominster, MA, September 2006*

For Hugo Chávez, Juan Evo Morales, João Pedro
Stédile and the millions of brave people who fight,
with them, for a far better world

*Para Hugo Chávez, Juan Evo Morales, João Pedro
Stédile y milliones de personas valientes que luchan
con ellios por un mundo mejor*

*Dedicado a Hugo Chávez, Juan Evo Morales, João
Pedro Stédile e milhões de brava gente que lutam,
com eles, para um mundo melhor*

ONE
Introduction: concepts for a geography of power

§ Power means control, by a person or an institution, over the minds, livelihoods and beliefs of others. Power accumulates into systems. With the term 'geography of power' I refer to the concentration of power in a few spaces that control a world of distant others. My argument is that a new kind of economic power system has arrived on the world scene. Power has increasingly been accumulated at the global level by governance institutions – the G7/G8, the European Union, the Bretton Woods Institutions and the United Nations. These institutions control the economies and livelihoods of people the world over through policy devices like structural adjustment, the 'conditionalities' accompanying loans or debt relief, annual inspections by teams of experts, and other similar strategies. This book looks at types of power accumulation – economic, ideological, political – and the forms taken by power in global space. And the book examines popular resistance to concentrated power by alternatives constructed by social movements and organic intellectuals.

Let me begin by dissecting the term 'global governance institution'. 'Global' implies that governance power transcends national commitment in favour of some kind of 'universal interest'. On the surface, this interest is humanitarian concern about global poverty. Yet global institutions condition 'aid to poor countries' on their adopting a set of neoliberal policies. These insist on an exaggeratedly market-organized, export-oriented economy. Such an economy is said to produce the economic growth that creates jobs and reduces poverty. Yet these policies also favour free enterprise, private capital investment and the extraction of profit from poor countries. Global governance institutions therefore act, at least in part, in the interests of global capital. Humanitarian governance has a class bias. It favours private investment and global financial integration. And, while 'global' in their sphere of operations, governance institutions cluster their headquarters in relatively few places. The resulting centres of global power are exclusively cities in Western capitalist countries: either the capitals of leading national powers, overwhelmingly New York (for example, the United Nations) and Washington, DC (the International Monetary Fund and World Bank), or definitely Western, but officially neutral, political spaces, as with Geneva, Switzerland (the World Trade Organization and many UN agencies). So in terms of its geography, 'global' has come to mean the spatial expansion of the field of the exercise of power accompanied by the spatial concentration of control in a few Western cities. In the twin terms of class and space, a few thousand people, clustered in a small space, control the lives of billions of others, the world over.

In this light too, 'governance' in the above phrase ('global governance') means regulation, management and control of national economic policy by institutions that are, at best, indirectly elected (i.e. *through* governments). In this undemocratic context, policy is legitimized as true and correct more by science and expert opinion than by electoral consent. This may sound fine – a kind of global Plato's Republic, wisely directed by modern-scientific, rather than classical-philosopher, kings. More critically, scientific, humanitarian governance may be read as a new, kindly faced version of Western imperialism. Global governance and expert-designed economic policy have a power-geography in two of main senses of this originally Foucauldian term. First, the world cities where governance institutions congregate, and experts co-mingle, display landscapes imbued with the trappings of Western power – locating the headquarters, and much of the bureaucracy, in such centres lends the policies they prescribe the aura of Western authority. Second, this ambient content is released as 'power effects' as policies extend over space, from power centres to dependent peripheries, and are adopted, under varying conditions of compulsion, in capital cities all over the world. The two power-geographies, place and space, reinforce each other in symbiotic embrace. As a result, the main international financial institutions (IFIs), the International Monetary Fund (IMF) and the World Bank, have become powerful institutions indeed. This book describes the geography of the power system formed from the undemocratic concentration of power over others in a few small spaces.

Understanding the sources, mechanisms and relations of power with any degree of adequacy requires a set of analytical concepts. My idea, in this book, is to resuscitate some existing concepts, reorient others and add new versions of still more. But as Marx may once almost have said, new theoretical approaches are sought not to further knowledge for 'its own sake', whatever that might be. Rather, the objective is to develop concepts whose logic, style and passion are so appealing, at least to people of conscience, that merely encountering them is an inspiration to resistance. The book examines power at a number of levels, from the abstract to the concrete, and a number of scales, from the global to the national to the local. But I favour an intermediate level of analysis, an institutional geography of power, drawing on broader concepts – ideology, hegemony, discourse – to give critical thinking more accuracy and believability. To this end, I try to specify: what kinds of institutions, in what arrangements, bound by what power relations, produce what specific kinds of global economic policy? I try to break power into its main types, as with economic power, ideological power and political power. And I look at the main groupings of power: hegemonic, sub-hegemonic and counter-hegemonic. The book's general, political objective is to uncover the interests served by global economic policy. Those of the super-rich global elite, who already have so much money they do not know what to do with it, except reinvest and accumulate even more? Or those of the masses of poor workers and peasants, who have so little that they must watch, helpless, as their children fade and die? Should it be the case that the poor die because the rich get more, then I believe we must advocate fundamental change, no matter the forces against us – 'we' and 'us' meaning people who care about others, close or distant, like us, or not. We must open the possibility for the peoples of the world to theorize their own economic destinies. And we must offer our help in formulating their wishes without imposing our own policy designs. In the end, issues of global economic policy are questions of political ethics and humane values.

What are concepts?

Thinking deeply about complex issues requires minds filled with insightful, analytical concepts. Let me begin, therefore, by saying (very briefly!) what I think an analytical concept is. The notion of a 'concept' is best understood in the semiotic tradition, as a signifier (a combination of idea, model, picture and words) that represents a signified (a piece of the presumably separate, material world) in a certain way (within a political stance). *Theoretical* analytical concepts differ from most other signifiers in that they are denser (represent more reality in fewer terms) and more rationalized (components of the sign-concept are arranged in defendable, logical sequences). For reasons that will soon become clear, this book does not assume that theoretical concepts are scientifically accurate in anything like the positivist sense of representational truth – that is, the analytical terms correspond exactly to identifiable, bounded pieces of a separate reality. Even a moment's thought shows the impossibility of anything

3

like this kind of 'accuracy'. For reality is originally physical, while concepts are ideational. And the conversion of the real into the ideal is little more than a modern form of intellectual alchemy, despite the pretensions of scientific method. In saying this, however, I do not abandon hope that, occasionally, fragments of analytical reasoning may bear the imprint of truth in two of the other ways that word is used: as deep insight into causal mechanisms; and therefore as a base for taking ethical, normative, political positions.

Questions of accuracy and truth become murkier when we analyse the economic policies prescribed by experts. For then we deliberately use theoretical concepts to critically examine concepts that also were consciously theoretical as they were expertly elaborated. In this instance, critical analysis becomes the collision of theoretical consciousnesses. In effect, concepts developed already, as summaries of understanding from the vantage of one political tradition in thought (critical social theory), are employed to criticize concepts from other political traditions (mainstream economics, for instance). I should repeat that this is essentially a political, rather than a scientific, exercise. And I need to say, from the beginning, that I take a pretty dim view of conventional economic theory. Indeed I will demonstrate, with some validity, that classical, neoclassical and mainstream economics, and the policies based on these theories, are fundamentally flawed – with disastrous results for the peoples ruled by expert opinion, and with rich rewards for the rulers and the experts.

Policy regimes

In this book I am not so much interested in particular economic policies, such as 'fiscal responsibility' or 'lower marginal tax rates', as in more general 'policy regimes' formed in centres of global power. What is a policy regime? Let me start by comparing the term to similar, existing ideas.

The concept of 'policy regime' proposed here resembles a concept used by the French Regulation school. My notion of 'regime' is similar to the 'mode of regulation', understood as a *situated rationality*, illuminated by a dense network of institutions' (Boyer and Saillard 2002: 41) that influences the trajectory of an economy, or what the regulationists call 'accumulation'. This is a little dense. What I am alluding to, with the regulationists, is the notion that economic growth is directed by an institutionally produced rationality, rather than growth being 'natural' or 'endemic'. Of particular interest is one aspect of regulation, the 'regime of economic policy', defined by the regulationists to include: the specific forms of state intervention in an economy; the institutional frameworks of intervention (national, international or supranational); and the conditions of validation of policy by private economic agents, such as investors (Lordon 2002: 132–3). In other words, economies are directed by policies, policies reflect rationalities, and rationalities are developed through the quest for power. The notion of 'policy regime' is also similar to that employed by neo-Gramscian international relations theory, in the sense of: social, cultural and political structures of accumulation (Cox 1987); cemented together by a post-war 'international historic bloc' of social forces centred on the USA (Gill 2003); and led by a new congruence of ideas, institutions and policies in a system of 'embedded liberalism' (Ruggie 1982). Again, these are similar ideas to my own. But both lines of thinking are vague about: the connections between accumulation and regulation, such as the social, political and economic forces producing new modes of regulation (as with the people thinking up neoliberalism); and the geographic location of the sources of economic transformation (as with power centres, with their clusters of institutions). Clearly policy regimes are political-economic mechanisms of power through which governmental and governance institutions direct economic growth. Less clearly, and more controversially, policy regimes are interest-based *interpretations* of the contradictions and problems experienced in earlier phases of growth, stagnation or decline which then redirect the economy, in a system that combines structural necessity with political-economic agency. I apologize if this is dense. But what I am saying is that policy regimes are innovative responses to past problems, innovations in thought that create somewhat new futures. This ability to redirect the economy is the source of expert power.

Thus a policy regime indicates: a systematic approach to policy formation by a set of government or governance institutions, dealing with a definable, limited range of issues, which prevails, as the dominant interventionary framework, over a historical period lasting at least several decades. Policy regimes, I argue, are lent coherence by an underlying political-economic interpretation of the causes of a set of related socio-economic problems. This interpretation is not scientifically neutral. Instead it represents the interests of a certain element of power, such as a fraction of capital, as with a set of financial institutions, and a certain group of people, such as investment bankers. Further, the ideologies that lend consistency, cohesion and believability to policy regimes are constructed over long time periods by experts residing in geographic centres of ideological power, with new regimes thought up in prestigious, elite institutions. There is, however, considerable freedom of the proximate agency and the space of ideological power in the reconstruction of regimes. Change often comes from elite institutions that were previously peripheralized – as with the Chicago School of Economics. Then again, several policy regimes may coexist in time, as past, present and future versions of a given approach to solving a limited range of problems. Regimes may coexist in space, as regionally variant approaches to somewhat differently experienced problems, with relations of dominance and subordination between the approaches. Indeed, the coexistence in time, but separation in space, of more than one policy regime makes the dominant dynamic and coherent – any effective policy regime contains elements of its alternatives as co-opted, but potentially conflictive, elements – the concern for poverty in contemporary neo-liberalism, for instance. All this produces a policy regime that has been well described, in the case of neoliberalism, as a contradictory process, existing in historically and geographically contingent forms, produced during a period of institutional searching (Peck and Tickell 2002: 383; Tickell and Peck 1995).

Since the Second World War, the capitalist world has seen two main political-economic policy regimes: Keynesian Democracy, pre-dominating between 1945 and 1973; and Neoliberal Democracy, predominating between 1980 and the present; the years 1973–80 represent a transitional period, when the two regimes contended for dominance. The Keynesian policy regime was characterized by counter-cyclical macroeconomic management by an interventionist state committed to achieving full employment and high incomes for everyone. This regime responded to the Depression of the 1930s, a crisis that delegitimized the theoretical rationality and the persuasive claims of the previous, long-lasting Liberal (free trade) regime, by using state authority to stabilize accumulation and democratize economic benefits. Regional differences in theoretical-interpretative and political-economic tradition informed three main variants: Social Democratic Keynesianism in western European countries and their former settler colonies; Liberal Democratic Keynesianism in the USA; and Developmental State Keynesianism in Japan and many industrializing Third World countries (Chang and Rowthorn 1995; Kohli 2004). The convention is that in the 1970s Keynesianism entered into a crisis characterized by problems associated with stagflation – high rates of inflation coinciding with high rates of unemployment (I discuss this in Chapter 4). Its successor, the Neoliberal policy regime, revives late-nineteenth-century, free-trade Liberalism by partially withdrawing the nation-state from macroeconomic management within an upward displacement of power to the IFIs, yet with an increased reliance on market mechanisms. Neoliberalism employs monetarist economics under the conceptual belief that macroeconomic problems, such as inflation and debt, derive from excessive government spending (fiscal deficits). While regional variations in speed of adoption, and level of commitment, persist, the neoliberal regime responded positively to the globalization of economy, society and culture of the late twentieth century. Indeed, neoliberalism helped to organize the emergence of a particular kind of globalization that benefits a newly re-emergent, super-wealthy, financial-capitalist class, mainly living in the leading Western countries, especially the USA, but operating transnationally in terms of investment activity.

What happened to the global economy under these two policy regimes? The measure used by conventional economists to measure economic well-being is economic growth – let me, for a moment, accept this measure at face value – i.e. 'growth is good'. Economic growth in the OECD countries, the richest countries in the world, averaged 3.5 per cent a year in the period 1961–80, basically during Keynesianism, and 2.0 per cent a year in 1981–99 (basically during neoliberalism). In developing countries excluding China, the equivalent figures were 3.2 per cent and 0.7 per cent (Pollin 2003: 133). In other words, Keynesianism vastly outperformed neoliberalism. At the same time as economic growth slowed under neoliberalism, global inequality increased. In 1960 the 20 per cent of the world's people living in the richest countries had thirty times the income of the 20 per cent of the world's people living in the poorest countries; in 1973 the ratio was 44 to 1; and in 1997 74 to 1 (UNDP 1999: 36–8). According to the World Bank (2004a: 246–7), 971 million people living in the 'high-income' countries and making up 15.5 per cent of the world's people now receive $27.7 trillion in income, or 80.4 per cent of the global income of $34.5 trillion, while 2,310 million people in the 'low-income' countries, making up 36.8 per cent of the world's people, receive $1.04 trillion, or 3.0 per cent of global income. Putting this a little differently, the 'average person' living in the high-income countries receives 63.5 times as much as the 'average person' living in the poor countries. National poverty rates in the low-income countries are in the range of 45–70 per cent of the population, while the percentage of people living on less than $2 a day varies from 50 to 90 per cent, depending on the country.

Yet geographic inequality only begins this sorry tale. Class, ethnicity and gender distribute incomes extremely unequally *within* countries. Of the 80 per cent of income going to rich countries, 50 per cent typically goes to the highest-income 20 per cent of the people, while the lowest-income 20 per cent in the rich countries receive 5–9 per cent, again depending on the country. At the other end of the world, in the low-income countries, the richest 20 per cent typically receive 50–85 per cent of national income, while the poorest 20 per cent typically get 3–5 per cent … of the 3 per cent of global income that these poor countries receive (World Bank 2004a). One of the unmentioned facts about global income distribution is this: poverty results from inequality. Poverty increases as the world becomes a more unequal place. So, what has been happening to inequality under neoliberalism? Take the case of the leading capitalist society, the USA, 'neoliberal model for the rest of the world'. Between 1947 and 1973, under the Keynesian policy regime, every income category of people experienced real income growth, with the poorest families having the highest rate of growth of all. After 1973 average real income not only remained stagnant, but that average reflected high-income growth for the top 20 per cent of families, and significant income decrease for the poorest 20 per cent, so that almost half of all families received lower real incomes by the mid-1990s than they had in 1973 (Leone 1996). The key factor causing these secular changes in class incomes was an even greater divergence in the ownership of wealth, especially financial wealth – that is, bank accounts, ownership of stocks and bonds, and life insurance and mutual fund savings. Particularly important is ownership of stocks and mutual fund shares. Despite 'democratization' (retirement savings invested in mutual funds, etc.) only 27 per cent of US families own stocks. While 78 per cent of the richest families own stocks and mutual funds, 3 per cent of the poorest families do so. The equalizing trends in wealth ownership of the entire state interventionist period between the 1930s and the 1970s (New Deal, War Economy, Keynesianism) reversed sharply in the neoliberal 1980s, so that by 1989 the richest 1 per cent of households owned almost half of the total financial wealth of the USA (Wolf 1996), a concentration of ownership that has only become more extreme since (Harvey 2005: 16–17). Within this rich 1 per cent, the super-rich – that one-thousandth of the population (145,000 people) making an average of $3 million a year – doubled its share of total national income between 1980 and 2002, to 7.4 per cent, while the share earned by the bottom 90 per cent fell (Johnston 2005: 1; see Figure 1.1). Or putting this more starkly, the assets of the 200 richest people are greater in value than the assets of the 2.6 billion poorest people on earth.

What can we learn from this? The general message is that economic

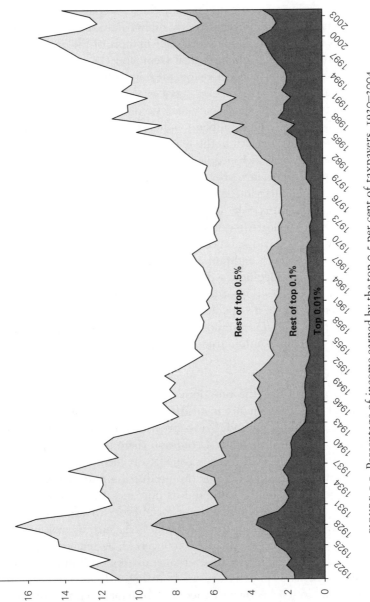

FIGURE 1.1 Percentage of income earned by the top 0.5 per cent of taxpayers, 1920–2004
(*statistical source*: Piketty et al. 2004)

policy makes a real difference in people's lives, through the mechanism of economic growth, obviously yet superficially, and through the distribution, in class and geographic terms, of the benefits from economic activity. During Keynesian state intervention, the rate of economic growth was significantly higher than under neoliberalism. More importantly, under Keynesianism more of the income went to the poorest people – under Social Democratic Keynesianism this was accompanied by the extension of state-subsidized healthcare, free education and other social services to working-class people. State intervention, for all its bureaucratic deficiencies, was good to the working class. The neoliberal policy regime, by contrast, has concentrated global wealth in the hands of a few hundred thousand, mainly Western, very rich people. Let us take for granted the (mad) desire of the super-rich to become even richer, in the sense of 'all wealth corrupts, but a lot of wealth corrupts absolutely'. The more interesting question is: why do so many non-rich people support a neoliberalism that clearly is good mainly for the rich? A policy regime, legitimized as producing an economy that benefits everyone, but in fact benefiting the rich and famous more than anyone else, has to be understood as an ideology, a discourse of power and a hegemonic rationality. Ideologies do not arise from nothing, but are crafted by talented people, experts operating in the interests of concentrated economic power. To understand this we need critical concepts. In the following sections, I outline some of these concepts.

Ideology

Such concepts link the economic policies prescribed by governments and global governance institutions to the basic interest of protecting and legitimizing underlying structures of political-economic power. In the critical theoretical tradition there is only one place to begin this analysis – Karl Marx's concept of 'ideology'. The Marxist concept of ideology refers to the production and dissemination of ideas, primarily by the state and its bureaucratic apparatus, that support and legitimize the prevailing social order (Marx and Engels 1970). The ideas behind institutional practices, such as making and enforcing policies, are not neutrally conceived, as science pretends, nor thought in the interests of everyone, as modern humanitarianism hopes. Instead, policies are made to serve dominant political-economic interests. In Marxist theory, dominant interests are those of the richest people in society, powerful because they possess capital, defined as ownership of productive wealth, and typified by the shareholders and upper management of companies and corporations. In

Marxism, capital is the fundamental source of economic and political power. The state supports an economic system founded on private ownership of socially produced capital through ideological devices that impart legitimizing characteristics to the resulting social order. This 'legitimization' takes several forms. Naturalization presents the social order as resulting from natural processes, as with competitive 'man', or survival of the fittest individuals or economic systems. Historicization suggests that capitalist social relations have been immanent in the long-term evolution of society. Eternalization makes the existing social and economic system seem to last for ever. And universalization makes the economic system, its elected government and the policies it favours seem equally good for all humankind. Fundamental opposition to a social order is therefore deemed to be: unnatural, anti-historical, pointless and undemocratic. Protesters are misguided fools.

There are several different versions of the Marxist theory of state and ideology. Two seem germane here. In structural dependence versions of the theory of ideology, states serve the interests of capitalists because private owners of productive assets impose binding constraints on the effectiveness of governmental operations – Offe (1985) emphasizes the power of capitalist refusal to comply with state policy, especially through 'investment strikes' – for example, investors refusing to invest in a country whose policies they do not like. Power elite theory, by comparison, argues that governments act on behalf of capital because state managers have similar interests to capitalists and share many of the same values, often because they move back and forth between the corporate, financial and government worlds. So, for Miliband (1969; cf. Poulantzas 1978) capitalists are able to control state institutions, and use them to realize their interests (Przeworski et al. 1990), because capitalists, elected representatives and high state officials are all the same elite people. (Who can forget that video clip in Michael Moore's 2004 film *Fahrenheit 9/11*, where President George W. Bush, addressing what is clearly a very rich audience, says: 'This is an impressive crowd – the haves and have mores. Some people call you the elite. I call you my base'.) In the Marxist tradition, then, the policies made and enforced by governments (and governance institutions) are ideologies, produced in the interests of dominant political-economic elites, but posited as good for all. Marxists are dedicated to producing alternative, socialist policies in the interests of working-class, peasant and poor people. No wonder Marxism has a bad name in conventional media that rank among the biggest of businesses!

Hegemony

While the Marxian notion of ideology founds a critical analytics of power, we can hardly stop there. For one thing, governance institutions engage somewhat different institutional mechanisms and strategies of ideological power than the governments of nation-states that Marx was originally thinking about. Moving 'up' the institutional hierarchy towards global governance institutions seems to be paralleled by 'ideological deepening', from the state's production of persuasive ideas to a broader, sociocultural construction of logics, or ways of thinking. One concept dealing with 'sociocultural construction' is 'hegemony'. This concept was derived from Marx's theory of ideology by the Italian Marxist Antonio Gramsci (1971), writing from prison in the 1920s, with important additions coming later from the French philosopher Louis Althusser. Gramsci thought there were two levels of political control over people: 'domination', which he understood only too well to mean direct physical coercion by the police, the army and the courts – what Althusser (1971) would later term the 'repressive state apparatus'; and 'hegemony', which referred to ideological control and the production of consent by non-physically coercive means and institutions – what Althusser would later call the 'ideological state apparatus'. 'Domination' we know only too well – torturing prisoners, clubbing demonstrators, detaining people at airports and so on down a frightening list. By 'hegemony' Gramsci meant the cultural production of systems of values, attitudes, beliefs and morality so that people supported the existing social order and the prescribed way of life. Hegemony, for Gramsci, was an 'organizing principle' diffused, through socialization, as common sense, into every area of daily life. Or in Althusser's typically even stronger version, for he was a man of extremes, the ideological state apparatus instilled systems of meanings in people's minds which placed them in 'imaginary relations' with reality – the social construction of the imagination precludes anything like a true understanding of the real. What these theorists have the audacity to suggest is that the philosophy, culture and morality favoured by the ruling elite are made to appear as the natural way of thinking, believing and creating of entire groups of people – national pride and prejudices, for example, or even, in advanced versions, a specification of the good of global humanity, as with philanthropic neoliberal reform. More precisely for the present topic, hegemony is constituted by a set of related ideologies that include, in advanced liberal capitalism, the validation of competitive individualism and the fetish of expertise resulting from technological rationality (Boggs 1976).

Furthermore, while Marx had stressed the role of the political, coercive superstructure (basically the state apparatus) as the maker of legitimizing ideologies, Gramsci looked more closely at the roles played by supposedly non-coercive social institutions, such as churches, schools, trade unions and so on, institutions that he collectively designated 'civil society'. (Within this, Althusser thought that the dominant role in the construction of minds was played by the 'educational ideological apparatus' – that is, the schools and universities.) Also, Gramsci paid more attention than Marx to the specific people actually thinking up, supporting, elaborating and spreading hegemony – the ideological agents, so to speak. Each social group, Gramsci said, organically creates a stratum of intellectuals that lends meaning to that group's collective experience, binds the group together and helps it function effectively – that is, without too much stress. Hegemony, for Gramsci, was produced for the ruling class by the civil servants, managers, priests, professionals and scientists of his day. For us it is produced by movie directors, scriptwriters, talk show hosts, investment analysts, think tank experts and superstar professors. In other words, there is a special class thinking up and spreading dominant modes of thought. We should know who they are.

Clearly the world is not a homogeneous space, in class, ethnic or spatial terms. Hegemony conceived in the centre has to be creatively 'translated' to fit many local contexts. The term 'sub-hegemony' refers to the semi-autonomous strata and locations that translate broad hegemonic ideals into particular ideologies suited to more discrete audiences. This can be thought of in terms of class, as with priests translating the Pope's encyclicals (written in Latin) for the Catholic faithful. Or it can be thought of in terms of space, and often ethnicity, as with local intellectuals translating the latest ideas from New York, London or Paris into languages and terms that regional peoples can understand. Then too, this whole process of hegemony construction and translation is not a smooth operation whose end is known from the first instance. The great thing about ideas is that they can always be countered. The great thing about thought is that it can be silent. Specifically, countering the hegemony of a broadly defined ruling class meant, for Gramsci, constructing a 'counter-hegemony' as part of class struggle. That is, Gramsci did not believe in structural contradictions playing 'themselves' out automatically in social transformation. He thought instead that activists had to seize moments of structural crisis by employing powerful counter-ideas conceived in advance by people who thought differently. In all these struggles over ideology and hegemony, intellectuals play leading roles. For Gramsci, upsetting consensus, and countering 'common' sense, meant not only convert-

13

ing traditional intellectuals to the revolutionary cause – by posing more compelling logics, or prodding conscience. It also meant the production, within working-class movements, of organic intellectuals engaged not just in consciousness-raising but in consciousness-making. Gramsci thought that workers and peasants could actually think! This was not an easy process if, indeed, as Marx said, the ruling ideas are everywhere those of the ruling class. In brief Gramsci, and others of his persuasion, see hegemony as a site of conflict over the cultural-ideological construction of sense and mind.

Interpretation

My own analysis essentially adheres to a kind of Gramscian project. But adherence comes with a few words of criticism, and with something of a redirection. First the criticism, though I venture it reluctantly. While Gramsci points to the social construction of common sense, and Althusser takes this farther (perhaps too far) with his notion of the sociocultural production of imaginary relations to the world, neither theorist quite gets to the heart of the matter, at least to my mind. The great puzzle, surely, is how society manages to produce a safe, system-supporting, *common* sense when many people commonly experience a horrific everyday world of poverty, hunger and death? To get to the root of this social constructionism, we have to repeat Gramsci's original question: 'what prevents miserable life experiences from forming mass critical consciousness?' The answer, I think, involves re-examining the relations among material reality, collective and individual experience, and the making of consciousness. A complete answer to this is a task beyond the confines of the present book! But let me offer a few words, anyway. Material events do not form experience directly, nor does experience flow into consciousness as photographic memories. Instead experience passes through what might be crudely termed the filter of socialized beliefs. Beliefs, in turn, are best thought of as interpretive devices so interventionary that what one person sees as mere coincidence, another finds to be definitive evidence of divine intervention. In other words, experience is lived belief, rather than material existence lived directly. So, the key to hegemonic domination is the social production of tradition, especially the collective beliefs that people live their lives through. Rephrasing Gramsci and Althusser, with this kind of existential emphasis on interpretation in mind, civil society institutions, such as the Church and the mass media, create hegemony by deeply embedding belief-structures into mentalities so that they direct the interpretations of class, gender and ethnic experiences in essentially safe ways. (Notice that I am avoiding here the original construction of beliefs, most of which I think are fundamentally mistaken – God, for instance.) Bringing this back to the topic at hand – that is, the formation of economic policy – we need to look at the great modes of interpretation of modern life, including the theories behind policies, as 'belief structures' produced by social institutions. In this book I take an unusual stance on this. I argue that the most important product resulting from biased interpretation is the dominant rationality. That is, I do not think that conventional rationality is some kind of perfect reflection on the world, but rather that the rationality that dominantly prevails is a socially produced mode of careful thought based on beliefs conceived and perpetuated in the interests of elite power. (I am thinking particularly about economic rationality and economic theory here.) Control the belief system and you control the interpretive frame in which social life occurs.

Discourse

In modernity, the policy arena is populated by highly trained and fully experienced individuals – 'experts' – and well-established, abundantly financed institutions – government departments, think tanks, banking associations, etc. – that are more economic-institutional than civil-institutional in character. This high-level, economic-institutional thinking employs a kind of symbolic representation for which the Gramscian term 'common sense' is insufficient, and something else, 'expert sense' perhaps, is involved. Examining this expert sense requires grafting on to a Marxian-Gramscian-existential base Foucault's (1972, 1973) notions of discourse, discipline and expert. Foucault claimed to have discovered a previously little-noticed kind of linguistic function, the 'serious speech act', or the statement, backed by validation procedures, made from the standpoint of experts and developed within communities of experts (Dreyfus and Rabinow 1983: 45–7). Serious speech acts, for Foucault, exhibit regularities as 'discursive formations' with internal systems of rules determining what statements are taken seriously, and what objects are included in discussions deemed important or responsible. Foucault thought that these regularities of presence and absence could be analysed archaeologically (identifying the relations that bind statements into whole arguments) and genealogically (how discourses were formed within institutions claiming power). Therefore, as Best and Kellner (1991: 26) summarize, discourse theory analyses 'the institutional bases of discourse, the viewpoints and positions from which people speak, and the power relations these allow and presuppose ... [and] ...

discourse as a site and object of struggle where different groups strive for hegemony'. Discourses assume, as one, particularly significant propositional form, the shape of policies suggested by experts to governing bodies, who use them as instruments of power ('political technologies' in Foucault's terms). Political technologies rephrase essentially social, cultural or political problems in the apparently neutral language of science to gain the adherence of people convinced that science benefits humanity. The effectiveness of this manoeuvre depends on a combination of external objectification, typical of science, and internal subjectification, the production of mentalities governed by, and thinking through, scientific concepts (Rabinow 1984).

Here again, however, I need to add more in the way of critical conceptualization. What is it that is being socially constructed? Behind a discourse we find a set of concepts with labels on them – theories with analytical terms that a discourse subsequently employs. Particularly important are the originators of a line of interpretation, thinking and discussing – in what might be called the construction of a theoretical memory. At the other end of a discourse lies what Cornelius Castoriadis (1991: 41) calls a social imaginary, a system of significations that organizes the (pre-social, biologically given) natural world, institutes a social order (articulations, rules and purposes), establishes ways in which socialized and humanized individuals are fabricated, and saturates consciousness with the motives, values and hierarchies of social life. While this sounds interesting, I find it a bit vague. I like the term 'social imaginary' because it places imagination at the creative edge of hegemonic culture, while still rooting the imaginary in the social – in other words, it combines the social construction of ways of thinking and believing with the mind's creativity. Social imaginaries, then, are collective forms of consciousness, structured by specific social environments, that make people not only think in similar ways, but imagine similarly. Imaginaries take class and regional forms: that is, the imagination uses materials (images, memories, experiences) from the familiar to project imaginative versions of the already known. There is a limit on what we can think about formed within the prison cell of our experiences and interpretations. Despite such structuring, however, the word 'imaginary' clearly implies imaginative interpretation and creativity – projecting interpretations into the scarcely known – so that social imaginaries are vital sources of transformational, as well as reproductive, dynamics. This is what I meant earlier when talking of transitions between policy regimes. So the imaginary realm has to be seen as tension-full, between visionary and more grounded logics, between received wisdom and new interpretations, between fundamental beliefs and practical forms of consciousness, between alternative ways of knowing and different ways of envisioning. The connection between memory and imaginary is a set of ideas running through the entire ideological formation. The people who originally think these up, and lend them terms to speak with, originate a system of discursive and imaginary power. A good example is the discourse of classical-neoclassical-neoliberal economics – hence the power of Adam Smith, David Ricardo and others in forming the collective memory, the social imaginary of contemporary mainstream economics.

Returning to the topic at hand. For some time now experts have been trained as intellectuals primarily in universities, where they learn to think theoretically – that is, employing theories to understand and change natural and social reality. Theory is the quintessential form taken by serious thinking at its deep level of contemplation, when the mind seeks the original, causal sources of events. Theory restructures the mind to think in deeper, more powerful ways. A persuasive general theory, learned at school or university, becomes the imaginary base for hundreds of expert discourses that structure thousands of policies, that affect billions of people. Theory structures the expert imaginary by forming the concepts through which even creative thinking reaches into the scarcely known. (I do not say 'unknown', because I do not know what that is.) Thus in modernity hegemony is produced as dominant theoretical imaginaries in disciplines claiming power by presuming to the status of science. Putting this slightly differently, hegemony means controlling what is taken to be 'rational'.

Governmentality

Some recent readings of Foucault's work have placed his discourse analysis within a broader social analytic he termed 'governmentality' (Foucault 1991). Govern*mentality*, as it might be written, refers to the mentalities of modern government – governors and governed. The term refers to the shaping of human conduct for definite ends by authorities and agencies broader than the state, particularly by institutions that invoke truth through the use of scientific resources, means and techniques. As Dean (1999: 11) puts it: 'An analysis of government … is concerned with the means of calculation, both qualitative and quantitative, the type of governing authority or agency, the forms of knowledge, techniques and other means employed, the entity to be governed and how it is conceived, the ends sought and the outcomes and consequences.' Understanding governmentality involves an analysis of 'regimes of institutional practice'. Here 'regime' denotes the forms of knowledge and truth that define the fields of institutional practice by codifying what thoughts it is possible to have, and what objects it is possible to recognize. (In many ways post-structuralism was concerned with the social means of limiting knowledge and controlling experience in the interests of power.) Four dimensions of 'regime' are recognized by these Foucauldian scholars: fields of visibility, which emphasize some objects and relations while obscuring others; the *techne* of government, or the mechanisms, procedures and vocabularies that constitute ruling authority; the *episteme* of government, emphasizing the expertise, strategies and rationalities employed in governmental practices; and the identities through which governing operates – that is, the forms of person (statuses, capacities, attitudes, etc.) assumed by the politicians, bureaucrats and professionals exercising authority, and by the workers, consumers and pupils who are authoritized (ibid.: 29–33). In brief, governmentality explores how governing authorities exercise power through regimes of institutionalized thought and practice.

This set of ideas elaborates the notion of the rationalities of government in a direction that is compatible with the previous notions of ideology, hegemony and interpretation, and I think adds to the notion of policy regimes explored earlier. In terms of Marxist notions of the legitimizing effects of ideology (naturalization, historicization, externalization and universalization), it adds new dimensions, as with the professionalization of elite, expert practice and the scientization of ideas in modern societies persuaded by the power of representational 'truth'. In terms of the relation between ideology and state, it rephrases power elite theory to say that the business class, the politicians and the upper echelons of the state bureaucracy are bound into a class because they think within the same mentality or imaginary – that is, collectively forgetting or de-emphasizing the same topics, problems or classes of people, as well as thinking the same way, having the same obsessions, and so on. Governmentality rephrases structural dependence theory to say that some discourses – neoliberalism with its enhanced power of capital to move at will – are backed by compelling economic power, as with accumulated capital, but also by theoretical, imaginative power, as with the notion that foreign investment is crucial to development. Further, governmentality also means using the same key words in a shared agreement to think optimistically – so problems are always 'challenges' (does the World Bank have a programme that automatically changes 'problem' into 'challenge' in all the texts they release?), while approved growth is inevitably 'robust' and fiscal stinginess is 'prudent'. In general power is exercised by interest groups in proportion to the resources they command, the money that they have, the access and political influence that campaign contributions can buy, but also the ideologies and hegemonic discourses, and the deep imaginaries and mentalities, that money can buy. Minds can be like commodities – thought for sale.

Institutional geography

Perhaps the main problem with notions like these – ideology, hegemony, discourse, imaginary, mentality, rationality – is their tendency to float in the structural stratosphere. Vaguely defined 'capitalists' or 'state apparatuses' produce ideologies that are inevitably believed by cultural dupes. Some might say that this is convincing only to the leftist dupes who already believe! The way out, surely, is to add an intermediate-level analysis that focuses on the exact agencies that produce definite ideologies as specific discourses – that is, a critical institutional analysis. In this section of the book I review some ideas from contemporary institutionalism and point these more towards critical policy analysis.

A few exceptional, usually critical, economic theorists have long been interested in institutions (Veblen 1912; Polanyi 1944). But interest in institutionalism has more recently been revived in a number of academic disciplines (Hodgson 1988; Samuels 1995; Metcalfe 1998). Many institutional economists share the dominant (and safe) convention with mainstream economists, that economics is the study of the efficient allocation of resources. But they no longer see the market as the economy's sole guiding mechanism. Instead, they argue, the structure of society organizes markets and other institutions (Ayres 1957). For these institutionalists, the optimizing results of neoclassical economic theory could be realized only in an institution-free environment, where transaction costs are minimal. By contrast, an exchange process incurring transaction costs implies significant modifications in economic theory and has different implications for economic performance (Williamson 1985; North 1990, 1995). Institutional economics therefore has a broader set of interests than conventional economics, being more concerned with power, institutions, individual and collective psychologies, the formation of knowledge in a world of radical indeterminacy, and the relations between culture, income and control in societies: in other words an economic universe that begins to look like that envisaged by social theorists like Gramsci or Foucault, except that institutionalists are not usually social critics – they just want to make a more inclusive, conventional economic theory that serves existing power.

In the discipline of geography, similar arguments have been made – that conventional economic geography abstracts economic action from its contexts, whereas in reality economic activity is socially and institutionally situated (Martin 1994; Scott 1995; Sunley 1996; Martin 2000). Institutional economic geography looks at the shaping of space economies by environments of institutions characterized by path-dependency. One main strand of institutionalist interest focuses on social regulation, governance and the effect of policies in shaping national, regional and local economies (Amin 1999). This kind of thinking comes more easily to geographers because of the discipline's environ*mentalism*. But the problem with the term 'institution' is that no one is sure what it means – organization, as with a corporation or a bureaucracy, or values, such as efficiency or benevolence? Let us explore this a bit further in the context of economic policy. At base, the institutions effecting policy might be conceptualized materially, like North's (1990) 'institutional arrangements' of organizations, with the less tangible conventions, norms, rules and (in this case) discourses, mentalities and imaginaries conceived as 'institutional products' made by organizations. Simply put, in what follows 'institution' initially means an organizational entity, located in a space, with a mission and declared purpose, backed by command over some kind of resource (ideas, expertise, money, connections). But additionally 'institution' is used in the Foucauldian sense of a 'community of experts', an elite group controlling an area of knowledge and expertise, and forming the base for a policy regime, similarly understood as a discursive formation. This community of experts shares the same ideas and ideals. Most importantly a community of experts takes the same things for granted – indeed, that is the meaning of 'consensus'. There are basic ideas and methods that they do not have to be discussed, so debate focuses 'productively' on slight differences within a meaning structure that is assumed, within a set of institutions, as with government, governance and elite academic institutions. Membership in such a community is the main source of an expert's power, status and income. Saying something outside the accepted discourse can lead to banishment from the inner, institutional circle to the outer fringes of quasi-responsibility, or even, perish the thought, to the desert of nutcase irresponsibility! Institutions as communities of experts are self-policing. Of course, the main problem is that the institutionally taken for granted may be the main cause of the problem that the expert community is supposed to be addressing – indeed, the main message of this book is that economic policy does not address poverty in a fundamental way, but always in a superficial way. Community

20

discourse therefore takes the form of perpetual variations on the always-irrelevant. But do not be the one to point this out! Even when intellectually bankrupt, the kings of theory have power.

These communities of experts can be 'mapped' in the sense of analysing the arrangement of institutions within a space – with 'arrangement' being formative, rather than derivative, of policy power – and examining the power relations among these institutional complexes. This concept of 'mapping' is similar to the notion of 'policy networks' used in political science to connote the 'structural relationships, interdependencies and dynamics between actors in politics and policy-making' (Schneider 1988: 2). In political science, policy networks are understood as 'webs of relatively stable and ongoing relationships which mobilise and pool dispersed resources so that collective (or parallel) action can be orchestrated toward the solution of a common policy' (Kenis and Schneider 1991: 36). Policy elites circulate within the institutional complex – from Harvard to the Treasury, from Treasury to think tank, with time spent at the IMF, or from Congress to lobbying firm … it's a great life if you can get it. Well paid, too. In effect, the institutional mapping I have in mind realizes the 'networks' and 'webs' of policy network analysis in a spatial matrix composed of points (institutions), clusters (power centres) and flows (power relations). The essential idea of mapping from a critical perspective, however, remains to trace the discourses and imaginaries produced in institutional complexes to underlying class interests.

Geography of power

In other words, I contend, mapping institutions as they are located in space is a productive approach to understanding the generation of power. Clusters of power-generating institutions, I propose, make up a power centre. In advanced modernity governance policies and practices are conceived by experts in institutions concentrated in only a few power centres, global cities that exercise power in world space. Each power centre can be thought, in and of itself, as a place, in the sense of a cluster of interconnected institutions, or what might be termed an institutional complex. Furthermore, centres of power can be classified as belonging to three main types, according to the dominant purpose of their leading institutions and the type of power they initiate: economic, meaning that their leading institutions deal primarily in money, as with financial markets, investment banks or corporate headquarters, and transmit power as control over investment and financial expertise; ideological, meaning that institutions deal in ideas produced at the level of theory, as with universities, research institutes and foundations, and transmit power as scientifically justified ideas, rationalities and discourses; and political, meaning that institutions construct and enforce ideas in practical formats, as with government and governance centres that transmit power as policy. Power, then, takes three forms: ideological, meaning control over rationalities; economic, meaning control over capital; and political, meaning control over practice.

Power centres composed of complexes of institutions can also be mapped by looking at power relations or as power transmitted across space. To begin with, each power centre concentrates resources (capital, ideas, expertise) from a broader 'field of power'. This field may be physically contiguous, in the sense of a hinterland. It may consist of networks among widely separated centres. Or it might be 'virtual' in the sense of position in a worldwide web. Experts clustered in power centres process intellectual, theoretical and practical resources drawn from fields of power by applying their own concentrated knowledge and expertise. My argument is that power centres formed by institutional complexes can be classified as hegemonic, meaning that they produce ideas and policies with sufficient theoretical depth and financial backing that they dominate thought over wide fields of power; sub-hegemonic, referring to peripheral centres of power that translate received discourses, modify and add to ideas, and provide evidence of their validity through regional practice; and counter-hegemonic, meaning centres, institutions and movements founded on opposing political beliefs that contend against the conventional, and advocate policy alternatives. Furthermore, in the modern world, ideas backed by political, cultural and economic resources are transmitted among power centres in the specific ideological form of discourses that are legitimized as scientific, and backed by resources that are recognized as productive, such as capital investment. At the receiving end, in sub-hegemonic centres, discourses release their contents as 'power effects', as with theoretical persuasion. Even so, this explosion of persuasive content should not be seen as a one-way movement of uncritically received power but, rather, as an articulation in both senses of the term: as creative combination with ideas and expertise originating in local institutions; and therefore as a process of rewriting and modification, but also independent discovery and creative adaptation. Peripheral power centres are sub-hegemonic in that they basically support, while modifying, the ideological positions taken by central institutions. But they may also be counter-hegemonic in that they differ fundamentally by offering alternative ideas backed by their

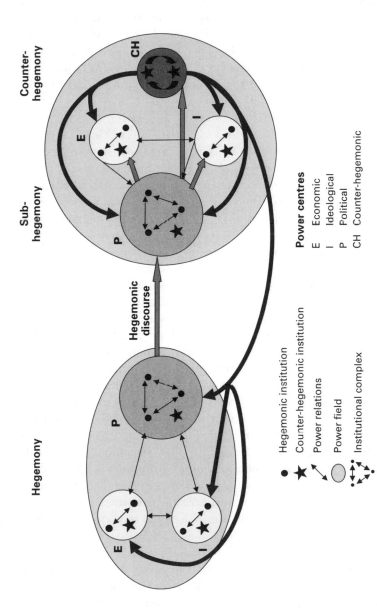

Hegemony

Sub-
hegemony

Counter-
hegemony

**Hegemonic
discourse**

Power centres

E   Economic
I   Ideological
P   Political
CH Counter-hegemonic

• ★   Hegemonic institution
• ★   Counter-hegemonic institution
↔   Power relations
⬭   Power field
⋰⋱   Institutional complex

FIGURE 1.2 Power, institution, discourse

own varying constellations of experiences, modes of interpretation and intellectual, if not financial, resources. Formed into alternative discourses by organic intellectuals, peripheral experiences contend against policy in sub-hegemonic, hegemonic and (though they are rare) counter-hegemonic centres of power. Power of even the most apparently solid, indisputable kind is ever destabilized by class, gender, ethnic and regional differences in experience and interpretation. Figure 1.2 portrays some of the main elements in this simple model of the institutional geography of power.

Global governance

The global capitalist economy is made up of thousands of specialized components tied physically together by flows of products, resources, people and money, and tied together organizationally by markets governed by governmental, inter-governmental and governance institutions. In neoliberal theory, governmental intervention in market mechanisms is unnecessary. Indeed, in extreme (Hayekian) neoliberalism, government is harmful to economic efficiency and dangerous to political liberty, because it constrains the freedom of individual action. But in practice, all market systems are embedded within institutional contexts that include state legislation, governmental intervention and, increasingly governance regulation. When market systems were primarily national in geographic scope, the necessary institutional framework could similarly be limited to the nation-state. With regionalization, such as the partial integration of the western European economies, governance expanded to the international scale, as with the European Union. But the globalization of capitalism has long required and, indeed, has been led by the parallel globalization of institutional regulation. In the first globalization of the late nineteenth century, British national institutions precariously managed international economic relations, with sterling as the agreed-upon currency of account, and London as the global, hegemonic centre of political-economic power. Pax Britannica was challenged during two world wars, with Britain demoted in their aftermath to the status of sub-hegemony – although remnants of the previous hegemony remain, for example in London's strong position in global currency exchange and the international bond market. In the second globalization of the late twentieth century, US institutions have come to precariously manage international economic relations, with the US dollar as the currency of account, Wall Street as the main centre of political-economic power, and Washington, DC, as the corresponding centre of political power. The second globalization learns, however, from the collapse of the first globalization in the Depression of the 1930s, that nationally based institutions cannot suffice, no matter how powerful Pax Americana may be. Hence Bretton Woods, the IMF, the World Bank and the WTO, the OECD, the G7 and later, with the addition of Russia, the G8 using, as well as US dollars, the yen, Deutschmark, pound and euro in a spectacular array of regional, supranational, international and truly global institutions, greatly influenced, but only partly disciplined, by American political-economic and political-militaristic power.

Power and policy

I have outlined in this introductory chapter a set of concepts that might facilitate a critical analysis of global power. Thinking back against global institutions requires an array of analytical concepts derived from several disciplinary and political traditions, but organized as a coherent theoretical system by similarities of critical content and intent. All the ideas I presented are critical of existing forms of knowledge – even new institutional economics began as trenchant criticism of an overly abstract, neoclassical economics. Nearly all the ideas I presented are politically critical of capitalist globalization and the neoliberal policy regime. Note that much of this criticism is not 'anti-global' in nature, as its counter-critics often contend, as though it were a new kind of Luddite opposition to 'inevitable progress'. Instead most critics in the traditions I looked at want a different *kind* of globalization based, for example, on fair trade rather than free trade, on partial protectionism, on combinations of strong, interventionist states and reformed global governance institutions, and so on. The ideologues of neoliberal globalization have been able to get away with such mischaracterization (that we are anti-global ... and violent too) because they control the conventional media. Discussion of economic policy in the business pages of leading newspapers, on serious talk shows or as expert commentary built into television news reports is exclusively 'responsible' in the way I have defined it – that is, taking for granted the dominant system of ownership and control of economies, the existing distribution of income and the prevailing policy regime. In other words, 'responsibility' means support for capital. This makes for a constrained 'public' discussion of economic policy characterized by slight differences of viewpoint and limited consideration of alternative policy directions – a boring discourse avoided by most readers, listeners, watchers and especially thinkers. I suggest breaking in to this discourse: by deconstructing it – that is, taking it even more seriously than its proponents; tracing its leading themes to their interest base; and by countering it with far more appealing alternative ideas, imaginaries and policies – appealing, that is, to people of conscience, people who care about the world, people who abhor a system in which the rich can squander their money while the poor must watch, horrified, desperate, in tears, powerless to prevent the lives of their gaunt, empty-eyed babies slipping away into … nothing. This book is an attack on a global capitalist system that is so callous it is perverted, uncivilized and not worthy of humanity.

Towards this end, what have I said so far? In summary it is this. Economic policies are instruments of collective power exercised by governments and governance institutions in the interests of capital – what I later characterize, in Chapter 2, as global finance capital. Policies propagated by modern institutions appeal to science as source of legitimization – so economic policies are based in mainstream economics, an ideological process I look at in Chapter 3. In modern democracies policy has to appear to be in the interests of everyone, because people can vote – see Chapter 4. So policy has to be garbed in humanitarian clothes – 'debt relief', 'ending global poverty', etc. Policy is spread around the world under coercive pressures that are both open and obvious and subtle and hidden – see the case study of South Africa as sub-hegemony in Chapter 5. Neoliberal policy is increasingly resisted by real alternatives, particularly in Latin America – see Chapter 6. And neoliberal economic policy is one component of a complex of new means of global domination, the three 'neos' outlined in the concluding Chapter 7. For me, the vital question is how to get to the essence behind the various appearances or disguises assumed by policies. The analytical concepts I outlined in this first chapter elaborate an essentially Marxian position – policies are ideologies meant to support continued domination by elites. But this is not simple conspiracy – big, fat guys, smoking cigars, getting together with corrupt politicians and telling them what to do – although something similar to this occurs every year on the ski slopes of Davos when the World Economic Forum brings the captains of industry together with the leading academics and prime ministers and presidents … all under the charitable rubric of improving the world! Instead, I argue, in late modernity, ideology is produced as hegemony – that is, as leading, 'cutting edge' ideas or, more deeply, as logics, rationalities, mentalities and imaginaries. Control over policy is exercised as control over the theoretical imagination, by technically sophisticated economists, by clever bankers, by persuasive stock analysts, by writers of elegant opinion pieces, by well-financed think tanks and superstar-studded universities. The idea is to render impossible different thoughts, and should these begin to occur, the idea is to relegate alternatives to the never-never land of utter irresponsibility, where misinformed idealist zealots rage madly, inspiring only the easily misled. But there is more. This level of control over imaginaries and their discourses can be possible only when the interpretive schemas, the beliefs people use to derive meaning from experience, are employed in the service of power. For otherwise, on seeing those little kids die pitifully, and those elderly people lose all respect as they beg for one more moment of life, people of conscience would become persons of consciousness with its rage of criticism, anger and desperation for the world to achieve something finer. So the centres of power, the cities packed with fine institutions, inhabited by men and women of learning, by experts backed with decades of accumulated expertise, the cities of millions that make, through policy, the lives of billions, are by necessity centres of the creation of meaning. They are places where theorists and policy analysts imagine a world that they themselves re-create. For otherwise these cities of meaning would be torn apart by the 'angry mob' that persists, no matter what, in thinking differently.

Please re-read the book's dedication with this in mind.

TWO
Economic power

§ Let me start with a simple thesis that derives from the arguments made in Chapter 1: economic policy is made in the interests of dominant economic power. In capitalism, economic power is concentrated in the hands of a class of rich people owning large blocks of capital. Decisions made by this class to invest, or not, in a country or economic activity bring intense pressure to bear on policy formation. In effect, investors simply refuse to go along with a policy regime, or a policy proposal, they do not like. Usually it is enough for the media to signal that 'The Market is not happy' and the policy is dropped or changed. ('The Market' is spoken about as though it is a collective imaginary, or even a person, to lend it the appearance of rationality.) If The Market (essentially the New York Stock Exchange and associated commodities and futures markets) does not like a policy, prices respond negatively. In the USA, even a slight modification of policy, such as a change in the interest rate, can make the Dow Jones go down, the dollar sink, money be lost, investor incomes fall. Elsewhere, in more dependent countries, currencies can be devalued by 20 per cent overnight by waves of selling on the world's intersecting currency markets, investment dries up, unemployment rises.

Within the class of private owners of the corporate production system, which fraction influences public policy-making most? Specifically, what fraction of capital favours and implements the global neoliberal policy regime that we have shown to be disastrous for working people? Let us review a recently proposed theory. In *A Brief History of Neoliberalism*, David Harvey (2005: 31–8) argues that ownership (shareholders) and management (CEOs especially) of capitalist enterprises have fused together as upper management is paid with stock options. Increasing the price of the stock becomes the objective of corporate operations. Additionally, Harvey says, corporations heavily involved in production – automobile or steel makers, for example – have become increasingly financial in orientation, diversifying into credit, insurance, real estate, etc. All this, Harvey says, is connected to a burst of activity in an increasingly unregulated, and rapidly globalized, financial sector in a process he describes as 'the financialization of everything', meaning the control by finance of all other areas of the economy. Neoliberal states, individually (as with the USA) and collectively (as with the G7/8), have to support financial institutions and the integrity of the financial system, for that is what keeps their economies going. Within this rearranged capitalist system, Harvey finds the power of shareholders declining, while that of CEOs, key members of corporate boards and financiers increases. He sees this new class changing as quick fortunes are made by entrepreneurs like Bill Gates, or people connected to corrupt states, especially when government-run activities are privatized, as with the telecommunications system in Mexico. The tremendous economic power of this new entrepreneurial-financial class facilitates vast influence over the political process. Is this class basically national or transnational in orientation? Harvey's answer is a little complicated. He says that the loyalty of the capitalist class to the nation-state has always been fragile. Globalization has deepened, and widened, transnational connections. Individual capitalists tend, however, to attach themselves to specific state apparatuses, because this lends advantages and gives protection to the corporation. So it still makes sense, as a kind of shorthand, to speak of US, British or Korean capitalist interests. And while there are tensions and rivalries within fractions of the new capitalist class, there is nevertheless an accordance of interests around neoliberalization that can be coordinated by meetings such as those of the World Economic Forum. Harvey links this with the capitalist notion of 'freedom'. Karl Polanyi (1944), he says, differentiated between good and bad freedoms, including, in the bad, the freedom of the individual to exploit others, or to make inordinate gains without commensurate service to the community. Planning and state control are seen as enemies by those who benefit from this latter version of freedom. President Bush speaks of 'freedoms' such as these when he says that the USA has the obligation to help the spread of freedom. Thirty years of neoliberal freedom for the market, Harvey says, turn out to be little more than the spread of corporate monopoly power, while disproportionate influence over the media enables the message to be propagated that everyone is better off under neoliberal freedom. Even so, the question for Harvey remains ... why have we so easily acquiesced to all of this?

Global finance capital

This quick summary of the notion of economic (class) power points the discussion in a useful direction, which I intend to pursue. In terms of the changing composition of the capitalist class, as with Harvey, I would add the following. The period of the last quarter-century, when neoliberalism has prevailed, has seen the emergence of a new form of capitalism. This new form comes from the intersection of three main tendencies. First, economic power has been deflected upwards, from the individual corporation to the capital that finances all corporations. That is, corporations compete for the investment attention of accumulated capital by offering not so much high dividends as a rapid rise in the price of the corporation's stock. CEOs and corporate boards come and go, prosper or not, largely on the basis not so much of how well they run the corporation, but how much they can run up the price of the corporation's shares. Furthermore, even investing in the equity market (the stock market) in such a temporary way (i.e. making a quick profit and then selling) competes for other, even more speculative, 'investment opportunities', such as futures, derivatives and currencies. Second, economic power has expanded outwards, from its original, capitalist bases in the advanced industrial countries, on to a global playing field, where trillions (thousands of billions) of dollars range with ease and speed in search of high returns. Clearly, this global playground for capital is still lined by political boundaries. But increasingly, within the established investment space, countries are adjudicated merely as risk/benefit ratios and, by being included that way in the profit calculus, reduced in significance. Third we find capital, government and governance merging into a single political-economic formation. Within this institutional complex, elites move with ease and grace from investment banks to the upper echelons of government and governance bureaucracies. We might call the form of capitalism resulting from the interaction of abstraction upwards, expansion outwards and fusion inwards *global finance capital*, meaning that finance is the leading fraction of capital, that finance normally operates on a global scale, including through global governance.

The term 'finance capital' comes originally from Rudolf Hilferding (1981), an Austrian Marxist theoretician writing in the early twentieth century. Hilferding was talking about the increasing concentration and centralization of capital in large corporations, cartels, trusts and banks, together with a change in the structure of the capitalist economy towards the export of capital from the industrial countries in search of higher rates of profit elsewhere. Flows of investment capital served to integrate the nascent global economy operating predominantly under the control of the City of London. The term has been revived more recently to refer to a broadly similar globalization taking placed in the late twentieth and early twenty-first centuries. This new version of finance capitalism is centred on the deployment of large accumulations of wealth by specialized institutions, such as investment banks and risk assessment firms, primarily located in New York, but also in London, Frankfurt, Tokyo, Hong Kong and Singapore, that have connections with governments and governance institutions. New York has changed from being a port for commodities flowing in and out of the USA to a centre of financial control over flows of money. In the early 1980s total annual US trade in goods and services and total US trade in long-term securities had the same approximate value of $1,000 billion. By the early 2000s, trade in commodities had risen to about $4,000 billion; but annual trade in securities was $15,000 billion (Steil and Litan 2006: 3). Control over sums like this gives finance capital and its banking representatives tremendous power – over policy-making, over economies, over employment and income ... over everything. Bankers rule. And despite its global deployment, finance capital still has a home base in the oldest capitalist countries, where wealth accumulated most, particularly the USA, and especially New York. Let us look at the history of the development of US finance capital.

Fordism and capital

Contemporary American economic power is based fundamentally on a system of production and consumption relations that might be termed 'Fordism'. The term Fordism as a description of the US socio-economy comes, yet again, from that tragic fount of originality, Antonio Gramsci. Comparing America with his native Italy, Gramsci (1971: 285) wondered about the 'formidable accumulation of capital' that was occurring in the USA 'in spite of the superior living standard enjoyed by the popular classes compared with Europe'. He found the answer in experiments conducted by Henry Ford, patriarchal head of the Ford Motor Company in the early twentieth century. Ford reduced the costs of producing automobiles and, even more importantly, paid higher wages to workers so they could buy what they made. Gramsci thought that American high-waged industry was a temporary phenomenon resulting from a monopoly over new production techniques which would eventually be broken by the diffusion of the new methods within and outside the USA. (Gramsci was right, but it took a while.) And he was particularly interested in the social production of American-style hegemony over workers that skilfully combined force (the destruction of trade unionism) with persuasion (high wages, social benefits and subtle ideological and political propaganda). This whole system of technology, economy, society and culture Gramsci called 'Fordism'.

To further understand Fordism we draw again on the French Regulation School. As I mentioned in Chapter 1, this school divides the history of capitalism into regimes, based essentially on the prevailing labour process. These regimes are: manufacture, dominant in the capitalist countries between 1780 and 1870; machinofacture, dominant between 1870 and 1940; Fordism, beginning at the turn of the century, but dominant from 1940 to the late 1970s; and flexible accumulation or post-Fordism, beginning with the economic crises of the 1970s and expanding rapidly in the late twentieth century (Dunford and Perrons 1983). The regulation school theorizes society in terms of development models, their parts, and their transformations: 'regimes of accumulation' describe the main production–consumption relationships; 'modes of regulation' describe systems of cultural habits and institutional rules (Lipietz 1987; Aglietta 1979).

In a little more detail, the regime pioneered by Henry Ford was developed in Detroit in the immediate pre-First World War years, and became generalized in the United States starting in the 1920s. Ford linked two innovations: the semi-automatic assembly line, adopted between 1910 and 1914; and the $5, eight-hour day, inaugurated on 5 January 1914, whereby workers were deliberately paid more than the wage rate prevailing at the time (around $3 a day). As Gramsci (1971) says, Ford's goal was to create a new kind of worker, thoroughly Americanized, committed to conventional morality, who would never join a union. Paying workers well was a way of doing two things simultaneously: making workers into consumers; and creating mass markets for more than the simple commodities (clothing, hardware, bicycles, etc.) that most working people had been able to afford up to then. Fordism entailed standardization of production and separation of conception, organization and control from manual work, producing a rapid rise in the volume of goods produced per person. This expansion in productivity was counterbalanced by an equally massive growth in consumption, first by unionized wage earners, later by many other sectors of the population. In the Fordist mode of regulation the conflictive, competitive mechanisms of the nineteenth century declined in favour of compulsory agreements between capital and labour (collective bargaining) and an increasing concentration of productive power in the hands of large corporations. Regulation of the population was also achieved by advertising and the control of imagination through media, popular culture, spectator sports, and so on. Fordism can be seen as a species of democratic capitalism that provided high wages and mass consumption to people who had never had much before. And it can be seen as temporarily resolving the central problem of mass-producing, industrial capitalism – what to do with all that product.

Fordism was only partly in place, however, and only in the USA, when its further development was interrupted by the Depression of the 1930s. At first the political beliefs of the time precluded state intervention in the economy, even at times of crisis. This had to change. For practical, political reasons – to mitigate massive protest by the unemployed – states began to intervene in the economy far more than before. As the 1930s went on, these practical interventions were bolstered by a rethinking of economics and economic policy led by Keynes. Informed by Keynesian economics, the state used monetary and fiscal policies to smooth out cycles of boom and bust, to provide basic social services and to redistribute income in what had previously been extremely unequal societies (see Chapter 4). The resulting mixture of Fordism and Keynesianism proved spectacularly successful. The generalization of Keynesian Fordism after the Second World War produced economic growth rates typically of 4 per cent a year, essentially because more income went to those who spent it – the working class. Increasing numbers of working-class people became union members, and unions wielded economic and political power, within the capitalist system, rather than against it. Under Keynesian Fordism, wealth continued to be amassed by the already rich, as high salaries, dividends and rising share prices, but also wealth was accumulated by unionized workers, in the form of pension funds saved for retirement, houses bought with mortgages, and so on. The resulting mass of stored wealth forms the basis of contemporary US-led global finance capitalism.

Money/power

The Fordist/Keynesian system, articulating mass production, mass consumption and mass marketing, proved to be the most success-ful social, cultural and economic system of the twentieth century. US-based corporations, skilled in Fordist techniques of production and persuasion, and wealthy beyond their competitors, led the sec-ond globalization in the late twentieth century. As a result of the Fordist connection between increasing productivity and rising mass incomes, one-third of global GNP is earned in the USA alone – the annual GNP amounts to $11,000 billion in a global GNP of about $34,500 billion (World Bank 2004a: 256–7). This fundamentally Fordist productive–consumptive power base intensifies, however, to become more exaggeratedly powerful with the move from industrial capital to finance capital. Even moving from money to credit increases the importance of the USA – so US credit card holders generate 51 per cent of worldwide purchases of goods and services (Nilson Report 2003)

– Americans love that plastic. The important thing about moderately high incomes earned by tens of millions of people is that these allow a lot of people to save, they produce bank accounts and pension funds, and savings promote investment. The important thing about the very high incomes received by a few hundred thousand extremely rich people is that these compel investment, because incomes in the order of tens and hundreds of millions of dollars a year cannot possibly be spent, and must be invested. As a result, in terms of the equity market, domestically listed companies in the USA have a market value of $15,000 billion, 49 per cent of global market value of companies listed in all countries. The the annual value of shares traded on the US exchanges (i.e. stock markets) is $32,000 billion, 74 per cent of the global total of $47,000 billion a year. In the debt market, all outstanding debt securities issued in the United States amount to about 40 per cent ($15,000 billion) of the global total of $52,000 billion. And in terms of more exotic financial instruments, 72 per cent of the $43,000 billion worth of derivatives (futures plus options) traded on all global markets are traded in North America (BIS 2004).

Financial power accumulates disproportionately in the leading Fordist industrial capitalist countries, especially the USA, but also the United Kingdom, Germany and Japan. Furthermore, this financial power is centred in a few 'global cities'. Saskia Sassen (1991: 4) points out that these cities accumulate the capacity for widespread political-economic control by serving as concentrated command points in the organization of the world economy, and as key locations for finance and specialized service firms (see also GaWC 2006). Control is centred in the few cities that move from being company and corporate headquarters into being 'capital markets', financial organizational centres for the national and international economies. Global cities are characterized by international financial institutions, law firms, corporate headquarters and stock exchanges (the New York Stock Exchange, NASDAQ, Bourse de Paris, Tokyo Stock Exchange, London Stock Exchange) that lubricate the world economy through finance. These cities also have advanced communications infrastructures on which modern transnational corporations rely. And they have influential media outlets with international reach. The globalization of the late twentieth century saw increased concentration of capital at the top of this global hierarchy, especially in New York, London, Tokyo and Frankfurt, with one city, New York, consistently presiding over the rest (Poon 2003). The dominance of New York comes from the amount of capital the city controls and the technological sophistication with which money can be moved from Wall Street to anywhere in the world

(Warf 2000). Essentially this kind of global power is exercised by controlling access to the biggest capital accumulations in the world and directing flows of capital in various forms – as equity purchases, bonds and direct investment – to places and users that are approved by Wall Street banks and investment firms. Capital markets are filled with financial experts making money from the uncertainties that arise in the normal operation of capitalism – which, after all, is a system whose overall 'rationality' emerges from the collision of millions of self-interested actions motivated only by profit. Uncertainty is partly overcome by collecting and applying financial and technical information that is combined with subjective judgements based on practical experience. The result is financial expertise. Financial cities are centres of intellectual and experiential power. They are like big money-egos written into space. The annual passage, through a global city like New York, of documents controlling billions of dollars in commercial and financial assets leaves, as its institutional residue, a system of thousands of specialized companies filled with connections, knowledge and expertise. The combination of expertise, concentrated in specialized institutions, with real physical control over substantial capital investment, is the basis of the political economic power exercised by global centres of financial power. This power takes many forms.

One of these powers is the influence of capital markets on the making of global development policy by government and governance institutions. The most important actors in international capital markets are corporations directly investing in foreign countries and 'professional' or 'institutional' investors, financial institutions that invest the savings of wealthy individuals, pension and mutual funds, and invest for non-financial companies, such as insurance companies, in the forms of bonds, equities and loans (Blommestein and Funke 1998). In making these decisions, corporations and investment professionals assess countries and companies using a range of consultancies and specialized institutions, especially national credit ratings made by agencies like the Economist Intelligence Unit, Business Environment Risk Information, International Country Risk Guide and Euromoney Institutional Investor. Professional investors in capital markets look at the economic policies of governments as signals of the investment risk involved in buying sovereign debt in the form of government bonds (a sovereign bond, issued particularly by the national governments of countries with high or unpredictable inflation, or with unstable exchange rates, and denominated in more stable foreign currencies. Nations cannot file for bankruptcy in the event of default; instead the defaulting borrower presents an exchange offer to its bond holders as part of a restructuring effort.) An assessment that a government bond issue carries a high risk of default or rescheduling, or that the inflation rate will rise, or the exchange rates might become volatile, means that investors demand higher interest rates, increasing the cost of debt service, or that bond issues will be under-subscribed or, worse still, withdrawn from the market. The capital market, acting through institutional investment decision-making, influences government policy-making via bond interest rates, through decisions on direct investments and by speculative trading in national currencies.

Versions of structural dependence theory dealing with international capital markets argue that globalization accompanied by increased market openness and greater capital mobility has increased the power of capital over government policies (Obstfeld 1998; Simmons 1999). This is particularly the case for the fiscal and monetary policies of governments that are quickly and efficiently punished by reactions from the international bond and currency markets (Garrett and Lange 1991). More broadly, during the transition period of the 1970s, financial markets punished governments that persisted in following Social Democratic Keynesian policies that investors believed led to state deficits that would impede repayment of borrowed funds (Germain 1997). The paradigmatic case was the disciplining of the British Labour Party in 1976 (Harmon 1997). The terminal case was the Mitterrand government in France, elected because it was committed to economic expansion combined with income redistribution, but forced by bond interest rates of 17.4 per cent to reverse course in 1982 and 1983. Since then, developed countries have converged on a neoliberal policy model preferred by the market, consisting of smaller governments, lower deficits, less state provision of social services, lower levels of taxation, less regulation and smaller unions (Dryzek 1996). Since the middle 1980s international investors have had a high degree of confidence in the policies of what became liberal, rather than social, democracies in the developed world. Financial markets retain a strong influence on government policies but now consider only a limited set of policies in assessing risk premiums, leaving some room for policy manoeuvre and choice (*within* a basically neoliberal policy regime) in national economic policy decisions. By comparison, in the case of 'emerging markets' (low- or middle-income countries) investors retain a strong and broad influence on governmental policy. As Mosley (2003: 103) puts it mildly: 'although emerging market governments are not always constrained to follow the dictates of global capital markets, the cost of defying [them] is often high'. In summary, private capital markets pressure elected governments to adopt 'pro-investor' economic policies.

Wall Street influences

New York's leading position in global finance capitalism translates into coercive political-economic influence on development policies. Influence is exerted along the lines of a number of power relations linking Wall Street to governments and governance institutions. Standard and Poor's and Moody's, two powerful credit rating institutions, assess the bonds and loans of over a hundred sovereign nations, as well as thousands of corporations the world over, to ratify their eligibility for purchase by global investors – this 'rating' includes examining the country's economic policy regime – according to 'objective criteria', established on Wall Street. A low rating sends a signal to governments that economic policies should be changed. This kind of indirect influence might be termed Wall Street's influence on the 'investment climate' within which nation-states, corporations, municipalities and others determine policy direction, knowing that some policies are more costly than others. Finance capital also directly affects the economic policies of governments through the persuasive influence of Wall Street on the IFIs involved in global economic governance, especially the IMF and the World Bank, institutions that in turn coerce governments forced to borrow outside the private capital markets. The trade economist Jagdish Bhagwati calls this institutional connection the 'Wall Street–Treasury Complex' (in Wade and Veneroso 1998: 18). Joseph Stiglitz (2002: 230), former chief economist at the World Bank, says the IMF follows 'an ideology ... broadly consonant with the interests of the financial community'. My own previous research calls this the 'Washington–Wall Street Alliance' (Peet et al. 2003).

More exactly, the main line of influence, the power relation, connecting Wall Street to the IFIs passes through the investment banks. Investment banking is a specialized part of US finance capital created by the Bank Act of 1933, more commonly known as the Glass-Steagall Act. The Act was designed to separate banking from the securities business, and divide commercial banking, taking deposits and issuing short-term loans, from investment banking, concerned more with corporate finance, mergers and acquisitions. Glass-Steagall restricted the primary market, involving the 'floating' of publicly traded corporate securities, to investment banks – 'floating' means setting the price and terms on initial public offerings (IPOs) of stocks and bonds that are later traded on secondary markets (such as the stock exchange). In particular, one of a small number of investment banks, the 'special-bracket firms' (traditionally Merrill Lynch, Goldman Sachs, Salomon Brothers, First Boston and Morgan Stanley), takes the lead in forming a larger syndicate of banks that underwrites major

37

issuances of corporate stock and bonds and handles the intricate connections with regulators (as with the Securities and Exchange Commission), the specialized accounting and legal service firms, and potential buyers in the secondary market. Here the connection with large blocks of capital is crucial because underwriters have to 'take up' any unsold shares or bonds in any new issue (Bloch 1986). Since repeal of Glass-Steagall in 1999, commercial banks, such as Chase Manhattan Corporation and Citibank, have developed, or acquired, investment banking facilities, as well as a range of insurance and stock brokerage services, to produce gigantic, enormously profitable financial conglomerates. Of the 100 biggest global corporations, one-fifth are banking, insurance and other financial service companies. These financial institutions essentially control access to the New York capital market and its accumulated expertise. Through this they exercise control over global development. The 280,000 workers in New York's financial sector make an average of $8,323 a week and collect more than half the wages made in Manhattan (*New York Times* 2006).

In the post-war period, especially as the neoliberal policy regime was established, many of the key posts in the US government and in the global governance institutions involved with the financial aspects of national and global economic policy were occupied by experts from the investment banking industry. The change in direction of economic policy, from an essentially Keynesian to a neoliberal regime, begun during the US Nixon and Ford Republican administrations, solidified in the 1980s, under the Reagan and (first) Bush Republican administrations, and continuing in the Clinton and second Bush administrations, was overseen by investment bankers (Peet et al. 2003). A corps of elite policy-makers circulated between investment banking and the highest levels of governmental and governance institutions. Some of the key players making policy at the time were:

- William E. Simon, Deputy Secretary and later Secretary of the Treasury in the Nixon and Ford administrations, US Governor of the IMF and the World Bank, the Inter-American Development Bank and the Asian Development Bank. Simon had previously been a partner at Salomon Brothers, a prominent Wall Street investment banking firm, and was active in the Investment Bankers Association of America.
- James A. Baker III, Secretary of the Treasury in the Reagan administration between 1985 and 1988, previously with the Houston, Texas, law firm of Andrews and Kurth from 1957 to 1975 and,

after public service, senior partner in the law firm of Baker and Botts and senior counsellor to the Carlyle Group, a private global investment firm.

- Richard Darman, Assistant Secretary of Commerce for Policy in the Ford administration and Deputy Secretary of the Treasury (1985–87) in the Reagan administration. Darmon was a graduate of the Harvard Business School and had been a partner and managing director of the Carlyle Group and managing director of Shearson Lehman Brothers, a Wall Street investment banking firm. After public service he returned to the Harvard University Kennedy School of Government in 1998, where he had previously been a lecturer from 1977 to 1980.
- Nicholas F. Brady, appointed Secretary of the Treasury by President Reagan in 1988, and continuing in office throughout the Bush administration, was former chairman of the New York investment banking firm Dillon, Read and Co.
- David Mulford, Under-Secretary for International Affairs, and senior international economic policy official at the US Treasury under Secretaries Regan, Baker and Brady, was a lead actor in the Republican administration's international debt strategy and was formative in the development and implementation of the Baker and Brady Plans dealing with Third World debt relief. He had been managing director and Head of International Finance at White, Weld & Co., an investment banking firm. After public service he became vice chairman of Credit Suisse First Boston and a member of its executive board.
- Robert E. Rubin, Secretary of the Treasury for much of the Clinton administration and previously co-senior partner and co-chairman of Goldman Sachs and Company, a Wall Street investment banking firm. After public service Rubin became a director at Citigroup Inc., a New York commercial bank, and a member of the Citigroup management committee. Citigroup owns Citibank, a commercial New York bank, Salomon Smith Barney, an investment services company, together with insurance companies and many other financial service corporations.
- Lawrence H. Summers, who followed Rubin as Secretary of the Treasury, had been President of Development Economics and Chief Economist of the World Bank. Previously he was Professor of Political Economy at Harvard, to which he returned as controversial university president, and faculty member of the Economics Department in 2001 – he resigned as president in 2006.

George W. Bush tried a different tack, using CEOs from the (non-financial) corporate world.

- Paul H. O'Neill, Secretary of the Treasury from 2001 to 2003, had been chairman and CEO of Alcoa (an aluminium company) from 1987 to 1999, and was previously president of the International Paper Company from 1985 to 1987, where he was vice-president from 1977 to 1985.
- John Snow was Secretary of the Treasury between 2003 and 2006. Snow had been CEO of CSX Corporation, a transportation company, and chairman of the Business Roundtable, a business policy group comprised of 250 chief executive officers of the largest US corporations, where he played a major role in supporting passage of the North American Free Trade Agreement. He also served as a Visiting Fellow at the American Enterprise Institute and as Distinguished Fellow at the Yale School of Management.

Yet despite these backgrounds, neither O'Neill nor Snow was smooth enough for the job of US Treasury Secretary – they were 'too outspoken'. Bush reverted to the previous pattern in 2006:

- Henry Paulson, appointed Treasury Secretary in May 2006, had been sole chief executive officer of the Goldman Sachs Group, an investment banking firm, and before that co-chairman and chief executive, with Jon Corzine – now a US senator (D-NJ). Previously he was at the Pentagon as Assistant Secretary of Defense during the Vietnam War. He was educated at Dartmouth, and has an MBA from Harvard. 'He has a lifetime of business experience. He has intimate knowledge of financial markets and an ability to explain economic issues in clear terms,' Bush said of Paulson.
- John Lipsky, appointed First Deputy Manager of the IMF in September 2006, was vice-chairman of J.P. Morgan, an investment banking firm, and had worked at the IMF for ten years until 1984. On being approved he said it would be a homecoming to an institution he knows well.

In terms of the backgrounds and private sector affiliations of the key players making major policy changes, in terms of the knowledge and expertise that they bring to bear and, more controversially, in terms of the interests they serve, the notion of a Wall Street–Washington Alliance might more accurately be described as an investment banking–Washington institutional complex, centred on the Treasury Department, the IMF and the World Bank, but with an intellectual offshoot to the US Ivy League universities, especially Harvard

University, particularly the Economics Department and the Harvard Business School, whose MBA, doctoral and executive education programmes train much of the corporate, banking and policy elite. This institutional complex exercises a range of interconnected powers that reach back into the capital market and forward into the production of policy, with control exercised as a combination of expertise, meaning experts armed with specialized knowledge, connections with the financial, corporate and governmental worlds, and command over financial resources, especially large blocks of investment capital. Economic power over policy formation is exercised in combinations of ideas, expertise and money. The power complex is inhabited by a policy elite that moves effortlessly among the top echelons of the financial institutions, the US government, the IFIs and the business schools of a small number of elite universities.

If we re-read the neoliberal 'Washington Consensus' (see Chapter 4), adopted by the financial governance institutions in the 1980s, and dominant ever since, from a bankers' perspective, we can see that minimizing state spending, increasing competitiveness, securing property rights (especially those of foreign companies) and export-orienting economies to produce hard currency all increase the capacity of developing countries to repay principal and interest. This does not amount to some kind of cynical conspiracy by bankers and financial corporations to create puppet economic regimes, despite the evidence that meetings recur among banking, government and governance allies. And once appointed to bureaucratic positions, bankers have considerable freedom to interpret what remains, however, predominantly a banking point of view. An export-oriented, privately controlled market economy with a state committed to low fiscal deficits ('prudent fiscal policy') *is*, however, the bankers' conception of a 'sound' economy, even when rethought in terms of the common good. The bankers' honest and sincere view is that a 'sound economy' is best for everyone. The problem is that a sound economy does not sound so good to those about to be cut off from public services as a result of prudent fiscal policy, or forced to pay exorbitant prices for water, electricity and other recently privatized services.

The Washington–Wall Street Alliance, the OECD and the G7/8 governments have established, protected and reinforced a neoliberal policy regime that served to deregulate the world economy (in terms of national state intervention), freeing the way for global, and particularly US, corporations, the trading of industrial commodities without interference, and the movement of capital assets across national boundaries that have been reduced in significance. For critics, rather than a 'sound' global system, the result is a wild economy of colliding interests and imminent debt crises, initiated by financiers, but escaping the control of any particular interest or institution. Bankers emphasize financial reform in debtor countries, and they believe that real economic growth is the only way debtor countries can service debts and repay loans. They think that the financial structure and the quality of financial services play a decisive role in making real growth possible, and that, reciprocally and mutually, investment in production and in long-term development projects is crucial to a country's financial status, its creditworthiness with regard to banks and, by extrapolation, to the international financial system and its stability. The IMF and the World Bank were established in 1944 to play this dual role, of stabilizing the global financial structure and encouraging economic development. The question remains, however: what kind of development, towards what ends, and in whose interest? The answer is: neoliberal development, to make profit and pay interest, to corporations and wealthy people. In this, they have been fantastically successful – revisit Figure 1.1 to see what I mean. Fantastically successful, that is, for those already fantastically rich.

Global risk management

The 'investment community' has a wide range of information available when it gazes out on the world in search of profit. Essentially, investors are concerned with balancing two criteria: the return they can expect from an investment in a country, compared with the risks associated with that investment. There are lots of 'business climate' and 'competiveness' surveys and indices that quantify what are essentially subjective judgements on the risk/benefit ratio. Some are produced by the global governance institutions themselves. The World Bank has a private development strategy promulgated in the belief that: 'Without the dynamic force of private initiative, disciplined by competitive markets, people will stay poor. Private sector development [involves] a refocusing of the role of the state to provide room and support for entrepreneurial activity. When the private and public sectors complement each other, people will escape from poverty.' The strategy therefore 'promotes the private sector by helping to create the right investment climate – the macroeconomic conditions, the governance, and the infrastructure to encourage both domestic and foreign investment' (World Bank 2006c). The bank offers 'privatization toolkits', publishes a journal, *Public Policy for the Private Sector*, on innovations for private-sector-led and market-based solutions for development, and conducts enterprise surveys measuring business perceptions of the investment climate. The World Bank's 2005 *World Development Report* was entitled 'A Better Investment Climate for Everyone'. It argued that 'a better investment climate provides better opportunities for poor people' (World Bank 2005) because a good investment climate is critical to economic growth. How to get a better investment climate? Essentially, through reducing unjustified costs and risks faced by firms and through eliminating barriers to competition. The World Economic Forum (2006) publishes a Global Competitiveness Report each year, in collaboration with 'leading academics' and a global network of 122 'partner institutes' that monitors the competitive condition of national economies. The Global Competitiveness Report evaluates economies' potential to achieve sustained economic growth based on the Growth Competitiveness Index – 'drawn from economists' understanding of the processes of economic growth and development'. The western European countries rank high on the Global Competitiveness Index, and Latin American and African countries rank low – Venezuela is 80th and Bolivia 92nd of 95 countries ranked by the index; Angola is last.

These indices pale, however, before the services provided by Morgan Stanley, a New York-based investment banking firm. Let us look at this investment bank, perhaps the most important international investment bank, in some detail. Morgan Stanley began its 'emerging market' index series in 1987. Its main product – MSCI (Morgan Stanley Capital International Inc.) Benchmarks – is used by 22 of the largest 25 firms managing assets globally, while Barra Risk Products (a subsidiary) is used by 23 of the largest 25 firms managing assets globally. Morgan Stanley divides the world into 23 'developed markets' and 26 'emerging markets' – 10 in Asia, 7 in Latin America and 6 in eastern Europe. The designation 'emerging market' is primarily based on GDP per capita – about $4,000 in 1996 when the index was adjusted. Emerging markets have higher levels of government regulation, restrictions on repatriation of capital and greater perceived risk than developed markets. Morgan Stanley says that markets develop as economic growth accelerates, companies begin to raise capital in public markets, trading mechanisms are set in place, regulations are liberalized and investor interest grows. The MSCI Emerging Markets Index follows developments in twenty-five emerging markets but is particularly interested in what it calls the BRIC countries, Brazil, Russia, India and China, believing, in the words of Jim O'Neill, global economist at Goldman Sachs, that these may be among the dominant world economies by 2050 because they have changed their political systems to embrace global capitalism (Wilson and Purushothaman

43

2003). So the Morgan Stanley index indicates to countries, and firms within these countries, what they should do to attract investment from the biggest capital market in the world.

As well as providing information on these countries, and 2,600 companies within them, Morgan Stanley is also a major actor in the countries it surveys. Based on its long experience and global reach, including 'superior access to important leaders at the corporate and government levels', and with 54,000 employees working in 600 offices in 30 countries, Morgan Stanley offers institutional investors, from large institutional investors and 'high-net-worth' (rich) individuals to retirement plan participants investing a minimum of $500,000, an Emerging Markets Equity portfolio. As Morgan Stanley explains, their investment strategy integrates a top-down country allocation with a bottom-up stock selection approach. In terms of countries, they say, during the second half of the 1990s, many emerging markets eliminated ineffective fixed exchange rate systems, strengthened their banking sectors, increased their use of Generally Accepted Accounting Principles and improved their focus on return on investments. Morgan Stanley evaluates twenty-five to thirty of these countries and emphasizes those where macroeconomic, political and social trends are improving (fiscal policy, GDP growth, capital and trade flows, currency valuation, free market reforms, political developments) but market valuation lags behind fundamental improvement. Within these countries, as the bottom-up part, Morgan Stanley (2006a) looks at 1,200 equity securities. In addition, they perform valuation measures to determine which companies can be purchased at attractive prices and operate under sound business models. They follow 400–450 companies in their 'closely followed universe', making 1,000 company visits a year, interviewing company management on the regulatory and competitive environment – they believe management ownership of stock to be favourable. From this they select a portfolio of 150–175 companies on the basis of cash flow, sensible use of cash flow, sound business models and shareholder-friendly management. They sell securities when they judge them to be fully valued, detect fundamental deterioration at the margin, find attractively valued securities elsewhere to replace well-performing issues or when they change their overall strategic country allocation policy – that is, when they shift towards a new sector or area of the world. Emerging markets are volatile so Morgan Stanley engages in risk management that is ongoing and integrated into all levels of their investment process. In 2006 the Morgan Stanley Institutional Fund Emerging Markets Portfolio held Class A shares in the following countries: Russia 12.82

per cent, South Korea 12.31 per cent, Brazil 12.24 per cent, South Africa 11.56 per cent, Mexico 9.62 per cent, Taiwan 8.70 per cent, India 7.44 per cent, China 6.49 per cent, Poland 3.31 per cent and Turkey 2.60 per cent. Their global focus lies in telecommunications and technology, energy and commodities – in 2006 their main holdings were in financials, energy, consumer discretionary, information technology and consumer staples. Valuations are very attractive in these countries, they say, and the emerging markets are currently trading at large discounts to the rest of the world. The Emerging Markets Portfolio has given average annual returns of 10.37 per cent since inception in 1992, and 21.23 per cent in the period 2000–06, net of Morgan Stanley fees of 1.2 per cent (Morgan Stanley Institutional Fund 2006; Morgan Stanley 2006b).

What kinds of emerging market companies are involved? In June 2006 the fund's leading holdings were in: Petroleo Brasileiro SA or Petrobras, a Brazilian multinational oil and gas company partly owned by the Brazilian government (3.65 per cent); America Movil SA de Cv (America Movil), a provider of wireless communications services in many countries in Latin America (3.13 per cent); Lukoil, the largest Russian hydrocarbons (oil, natural gas) company (3.06 per cent); Wal-Mart de Mexico SA de Cv, with 780 stores and restaurants in 100 cities throughout Mexico, and 62 per cent owned by Wal-Mart Stores of the USA (2.96 per cent); and Grupo Televisa SA, the largest media company in Latin America, with four networks and 260 affiliated stations in Mexico (2.95 per cent). Generally Morgan Stanley is interested only in large corporations with an emphasis on telecommunications, utilities and banking, and in big countries, such as Brazil, Mexico and Russia (Morgan Stanley 2006a).

But let us look more closely at the companies that investment banks like Morgan Stanley buy shares in. Petrobras is a formerly government-owned Brazilian oil company headquartered in Rio de Janeiro, founded in 1953 by the Brazilian president Getúlio Vargas. America Movil was spun off from Teléfonos de Mexico (Telmex) and Telmex was a government-owned industry nationalized in 1972 and privatized in 1990, with the buyers, Carlos Slim, France Télécom and Southwestern Bell Corporation, paying over the course of the next several years, using money earned by the phone service. Lukoil is a former state-owned oil company comprised of the Langepasneftegas, Uraineftegas and Kogalymnefte gas production associations and selected refining operations, privatized in 1993. Wal-Mart de Mexico, formed in 1992 by buying into the 122-store Aurera-Bodega chain, dominates the retail economy of Mexico, accounting for 2 per cent of gross internal

45

product, and pays its non-union 'associates' an average of 13 pesos an hour (about $1.20) as compared to their non-union US associates' $9.50 (unionized supermarket workers, by comparison, make $19 an hour in the USA); Grupo Televisa SA in Mexico was founded by the Azcarraga family with strong links with the US conglomerate RCA, and was regulated by Article 42 of the Mexican constitution, which stipulates state ownership of electromagnetic waves transmitted over Mexican territory. In the Third World, share purchasing by banks, together with mergers and acquisitions by US- and European-based TNCs, has concentrated on newly privatized state-owned companies spanning water, energy, telecommunications and financial services. In many countries, acquisition of formerly public services by TNCs, especially water, has generated widespread popular resistance. What has happened is this: the 'investment community' has long pushed for the privatization of public enterprises as part of a neoliberal policy regime. Investment banking institutions have been major advocates of privatization and investment bankers have used global governance power to put neoliberal policies, such as deregulation and privatization, into effect. The change in direction of economic policy, from an essentially Keynesian to a neoliberal position, was overseen by investment bankers. All over the world state industries, once nationalized to capture the benefits of economic activity for the country's people, have been sold, often under dubious circumstances, to rich, well-connected people domestically, but eventually ending up in substantial foreign ownership. In many cases, these state industries form the nucleus of Third World TNCs. In others, foreign TNCs buy them directly. These privatized formerly public companies generate large profits. Who gets these profits? Investors. So investment banks provide expertise to governance, which pushes policies the banks favour, which generates high returns, which go to the banks' customers and the investment banks themselves. The banks make their money in two ways: selling information; and profiting from governments following it. These interests do not conflict ... they coincide. And while foreign portfolio investment is touted as good for Third World development – by the World Bank, for instance – what really occurs is the growth of a chain of TNCs that mainly benefits investors. This is development for the already-rich.

Foreign direct investment

Foreign direct investment (FDI) is defined as long-term investment by a foreign company in an enterprise resident in another national economy. The FDI relationship consists of a parent enterprise and a foreign affiliate which together form a TNC. To qualify as FDI the investment must give the parent enterprise control over its foreign affiliate – UNCTAD (2005) defines control as owning 10 per cent or more of the ordinary shares or voting power of an incorporated firm. In the post-war years the USA accounted for about three-quarters of new FDI (between 1945 and 1960). Since that time FDI has spread to become truly global. The main types of FDI are:

Greenfield investment: direct investment in new facilities or the expansion of existing facilities. Countries value this kind the most because they think greenfield investment will create new production capacity and jobs, transfer technology and know-how, and provide links with the global marketplace. This often undercuts local industry, however, while profits flow to the multinational's home economy.

Mergers and acquisitions: the primary type of FDI, occurring when existing assets are transferred from local firms to foreign firms. Acquisitions provide no long-term benefits to the local economy – owners of the local firm are paid in stock from the acquiring firm, meaning that the money from the sale does not reach the local economy.

In 2004, world FDI inflows amounted to $648 billion, of which 36 per cent went to developing countries. According to UNCTAD (ibid.) this inflow stems from intense competitive pressures that make firms explore new ways of improving their bottom line, including expanding operations in the fast-growing markets of emerging economies to boost sales, and rationalizing production activities with a view to reaping economies of scale and lowering production costs. Higher prices for commodities have led to FDI in countries rich in natural resources, such as oil and minerals. FDI outflows from all countries in 2004 were $730 billion, with firms based in developed countries (the USA, the United Kingdom and Luxembourg) accounting for most ($637 billion). East Asia is also emerging as a source of FDI, with dramatic growth in FDI flows from Hong Kong, but also increased investments by TNCs from other parts of East Asia and South-East Asia. Most of these investments are intra-regional within the economies of East and South-East Asia. Inter-regional investment from Asian economies to distant countries has also increased, however. For example, a key 'driver' of Chinese outward FDI is growing demand for natural resources. This has led to significant investments in Latin America. Indian TNCs also invested large amounts in natural resources in other regions, primarily in African countries and the Russian Federation. Asian investment in developed countries is increasing as well: for example, acquisitions of US and EU firms by Chinese and Indian TNCs – such as the acquisition by

Lenovo (China) of the personal computers division of IBM (USA). The total stock of FDI is about $9,000 billion worldwide, attributed to 70,000 TNCs and 690,000 affiliates abroad, with total annual sales by foreign affiliates amounting to almost $19,000 billion. Ranked by foreign assets, General Electric (USA) is the largest non-financial TNC worldwide, followed by Vodafone (United Kingdom) and the Ford Motor Company (USA). International investment in services, particularly financial services, is growing, especially through mergers and acquisitions. Large TNCs dominate world financial services in terms of total assets and the number of countries in which they operate. Financial TNCs from France, Germany, Japan, the United Kingdom and the USA account for 74 per cent of the total assets of the top fifty financial TNCs. Citigroup (USA) is the biggest, followed by UBS (Switzerland) and Allianz (Germany). FDI levels surpass those of other private capital flows to developing countries as well as flows of official development assistance (ODA). In 2004, FDI accounted for more than half of all financial flows to Third World countries and was considerably larger than ODA. FDI is concentrated in a handful of countries, however, while ODA is the most important source of finance in most of the poor countries (ibid.).

The pursuit of FDI as an engine of growth is a formula prescribed by mainstream economic theory, and by the global governance organizations. 'The overall benefits of FDI for developing country economies are well documented,' claims an OECD report (OECD 2002: 5). The report sums up the conventional wisdom about the promise of FDI like this:

> Given the appropriate host-country policies and a basic level of development, a preponderance of studies shows that FDI triggers technology spillovers, assists human capital formation, contributes to international trade integration, helps create a more competitive business environment and enhances enterprise development. All of these contribute to higher economic growth, which is the most potent tool for alleviating poverty in developing countries. (ibid.: 5)

In addition, the report goes on, FDI 'may help improve environmental and social conditions in the host country by, for example, transferring "cleaner" technologies and leading to more socially responsible corporate policies' (ibid.: 5). In the 1980s, the policy emphasis was on 'getting the prices right' – eliminating domestic policies, such as energy and food subsidies, that create differences between domestic and global prices. In the 1990s, the trend was 'getting the macro-policies right', especially the deregulation of financial markets. Currently,

48

the policy focus lies on fashioning the right 'enabling environment' for FDI – creating or strengthening legal, regulatory and political institutions providing transparency, property protection and financial stability to foreign investors. At the regional and global levels investment agreements try to 'make the world safe' for FDI, by expanding protections for foreign investors. These greater rights for investors come at the expense of the flexibility and diversity of national development policies, and TNCs have used new international rights, policed by the WTO and other governance institutions, to question national environmental and health regulations (Gallagher and Zarsy 2006). Countries adopt laws and regulations with a view to making their investment environments more investor-friendly – as with opening up new areas to FDI, liberalizing legal frameworks, lowering corporate income taxes, giving exemptions from import duties and providing special investment and depreciation allowances, all in a bid to attract FDI. A US company, A.T. Kearny, runs a 'confidence survey' that 'tracks the impact of likely political, economic and regulatory changes on the foreign direct investment intentions and preferences of the leaders ... of the world's largest 1000 firms' (A.T. Kearney 2004: 3). They produce an FDI Confidence Index that ranks countries in terms of attractiveness as an FDI destination: at present, China ranks highest, followed by the USA and India. For corporate CEOs the main critical risks that countries pose to FDI are government regulations (cited by 64 per cent of global investors), country financial risk (60 per cent), currency or interest rate volatility (51 per cent), political or social disturbances (46 per cent) and corporate governance issues (30 per cent), followed by a series of intellectual property theft and security issues, including activist attacks on corporate brands. CEOs think that India should reduce its bureaucracy (i.e. the FDI approval process), be politically stable and maintain its low-cost advantages to be competitive for FDI. So countries are disciplined in terms of policy formation and implementation by the requirements of foreign direct investors. Countries go along because they want the benefits that 'everyone' says flow from direct investment.

Or nearly everyone. While countries restructure their policy regimes to become more attractive to FDI, the benefits often do not amount to much. FDI happens only because TNCs expect to extract profit from a country. Foreign investment in Africa was $18 billion in 2004, and $14 billion the previous year. Much of that investment was aimed at Africa's resource-rich oil and mining industries, which often generate low-tax revenues, carry high environmental and social costs, and benefit mainly the elite – 85 per cent of Nigeria's oil revenues go to 1 per

Economic power

49

cent of the population (Watts 2006: 11). A study by UNCTAD looked at Tanzania and Ghana as examples of countries experiencing booms in foreign investment – particularly in their gold industries. Both receive only 5 per cent of the value of their gold exports (BBC 2005). Case studies followed by McKinsey and Company, a management consulting firm, concluded that policies to attract foreign business do more harm than good (Beattie 2003). An article examining much of the recent statistical and case study evidence about the impacts of FDI in generating efficiency spillovers, promoting growth and improving environmental performance in developing countries paints an ambiguous picture: FDI has been found to have positive, neutral or negative impacts on all three counts. 'The poorer the country, the more likely is the FDI impact negative' (Gallagher and Zarsy 2006). FDI powerfully affects policy formation. But the benefits accrue disproportionately to the foreign investor and the local elite, but not the mass of people in the country invested in. Never forget that underdeveloped countries send more funds back to developed countries than they receive – in 2005 this 'negative net investment' was $527 billion (United Nations Secretary-General 2006).

From global risk to global angst

What the world has now is a global bribery system. Private finance capital says to democratically elected governments: create (through policy) the right business climate for us to make profits, we will invest in your country, and maybe jobs, income and development will be created. Create the wrong business climate, and we will not come near you. Create the wrong business climate and The Market will ruin you. Ignore us and you will languish in underdevelopment for ever. This power of capitalist refusal is so established that capital is granted extraordinary rights over making policy in the first place. Economic policy is conceived, specified and enforced by capitalists, usually financiers, in consultation with their peers, with their eye always on The Market. Corporations exercise control over the world's economies through direct control over large portions of their productive, financial and other service activities. They exercise indirect control by requiring business-friendly policy environments before and during investment that is conventionally seen as vital for the development of Third World countries.

In this chapter I examined how private capital makes and influences public policy the world over. This is how 'freedom and democracy' really work. 'Freedom' means granting unrestricted access to profit by global financed capital. 'Democracy' means that democratically elected states make room for corporations. In this context, 'corporate democracy' means more power for shareholders rather than upper management – democracy is restricted to the class of investors. Everyone knows about this system. Few mention it, directly. This is because capital terrorizes all participants in The Market. When policy is announced all eyes turn to The Market's reaction.

This reaction of The Market is the most difficult question of all, in the area of international finance, and elsewhere in market economies. 'The Market' means the various capital markets centred on Wall Street, but more generally all markets where producers compete to sell, and buyers may not buy. Saying that Wall Street is the most powerful actor in setting the policies used by global governance institutions to develop countries implies a more conscious collective rationality than is the case. The central financial institutions located on Wall Street are the equity and bond markets, and these no one controls, not even the investment bankers. While financial analysts may objectively 'study the numbers' in evaluating whether to invest client money in the bonds or shares issued in foreign countries, the decision is rendered into highly subjective judgement, little more than a guess, by extreme uncertainty about the future, when the bonds will be repaid or the shares sold. George Soros, head of the Quantum Fund, 'the best performing investment fund in history', says of financial markets:

> Each market participant is faced with the task of putting a present value on a future course of events, but that course is contingent on the present values that all market participants taken together attribute to it. That is why market participants are obliged to rely on an element of judgment. The important feature of bias is that it is not purely passive: It affects the course of events that it is supposed to reflect. This active ingredient is missing from the concept of equilibrium employed by economic theory. (Soros 1998: 47)

The international financial market lies at the meeting point in global space where a world of biases and guesses collide – up goes the New York skyline into the stratosphere as a result. Yet the collision of uncertainties in the market also determines the economic fate of nations, states and billions of people in the global economy. As one commentator says: 'National governments find themselves in environments not merely of risk but of radical uncertainty … governments often cannot know whether the response of world markets to their policies will be merely to make them costly or to render them completely unworkable' (Gray 1998: 74–5). Global development, directed by IFIs, private and public, has this radical uncertainty at its heart.

y a worker worries all year about how to feed her kids when she
her job. Many a financier worries all night about the price of
shares next morning – but then, they are well compensated for the
risks they take, risk being more valued than work in bourgeois economics. This worrying is not confined to financiers. All corporations
are vulnerable to competition – even General Motors and Ford. That
is one reason why, they say, they resort to bribery – they have got to
make a buck. But corporations behave, increasingly under neoliberalism, in predatory ways even when they are making record profits
– 'in anticipation of leaner times'. They are egged on by 'investment
analysts' who themselves compete to be the most 'aggressive' advisers
in the business. The price of freedom is eternal anxiety.

THREE
Ideological power

§ The global capitalism I have been describing has to be rationalized if it is going to work, and if large numbers of people are going to work for it. Rationalization occurs under a dominant economic imaginary. And that imaginary is made by the academic discipline called 'economics'. Control over this disciplinary imaginary is a fundamental source of power. Following the arguments made about ideology, hegemony, imaginary, discourse and belief in Chapter 1, a detailed discussion of economics as ideology is central to the argument I am presenting. My claim is that economic theory is ideological in the sense of being committed to class and national interests. Economic ideas follow logics that are constructed rather than discovered – that is, made up with an interest in mind, rather than discovered innocently, latent in reality. This social construction includes the economic ideas and terminologies employed in policy-making power. The construction of economic ideas, rationalities and imaginaries is important – so we know what we are talking about, thinking about or, rather, what we are thinking with. We have to know where the ideas we think with (employ in analysis) come from. This means starting with ideas that are so accepted they are thought to be normal, natural, inevitable, if they are ever thought at all. Just as language relies on speakers following the intricate codes of language, without stopping to examine them (unless there is a problem with clarity, and then the pause is brief), so economic thought employs the codes of an economic rationality that is assumed rather than critically inspected. The ability to project ideas into the 'naturally assumed' is one main source of ideological, hegemonic power. As I said in Chapter 1, this power over the making of economic imaginaries (theory and policy) is held by institutions and experts concentrated in global mind centres. These institutional complexes manufacture the codes of economic discourse and, perhaps more importantly, ensure that the codes are so thoroughly normalized (to use Foucault's term) they are basically unquestioned, except by organized alternatives (with their own codes, etc.). These dominant codes of economic thought seem to be well thought out, mathematically elaborated, persuasively presented, often with a lot of money and talent invested in them.

The highest-quality theoretical explanations for policies are produced in academia, especially the elite universities of the English-speaking countries, particularly, since the 1940s, universities in the USA. What academics can do better than others is produce ideas as a system of knowledge that is coherent, thorough, logical, so respected it is taken to be normal. Academics produce ideas that are well thought out and phrased precisely in a manner that is theoretically correct. Academics have the time to think through ideas to iron out the illogical wrinkles. Academics present the ideas to intelligent but captive audiences while teaching. Academics create the minds of future recipients of economic policies, so that the accuracy of theory becomes a self-fulfilling prophecy. That is, the power elite make the world in the image of the economic theory they believe in and think and act through. Academics discuss variants on the accepted theory endlessly at professional conferences, pools of expertise filled with intellectual sharks waiting to bite at the first sign of deviance – these maintain the currency of the discourse, keep it up to date, lend the appearance of dynamism. Discourses of significance must be logical and coherent, tried during constant argument, and adjudicated to be true by a court of academic jurors entrusted with the power to pin the medal of truth on a statement that waits to be accepted into the domain of the dominant discourse. Truth judged in this way – as science – is accepted as superior to the mysticisms of religion, yet truth is a modern belief as well, although for myself a better belief than religion (it's a bit more believable!). Policies are backed, then, by rationalities and theories developed particularly by academics. And modern academia is embedded in the culture of the European Enlightenment.

Policy as enlightenment

In the modern world, that European space-time of intellectual dominance beginning in the seventeenth- and eighteenth-century Enlightenment, reason, logic and scientific thought are said to prevail. Reason advances knowledge; knowledge facilitates science; science serves the liberating aims of progressive societies. In enlightenment thinking ethics too can be based on the crystallized lessons of human experience, mediated or interpreted by rational inspection, rather than relying on divine revelation for persuasive and enforcing power. Human reasoning that interprets experience replaces God as moral authority. Rational interpretation by the scientist replaces divine revelation beamed down to the priest. The rational individual becomes self-guiding, possibly self-governing, rather than slave to (religious and civil) authority. The modern aspiration is that all people sharing a similar ethical rationality might agree on a system of norms to guide the operation of society. These democratic norms are the rational basis for modern policies. Self-disciplined by ethical reason, individuals might voluntarily adhere to policies made through rational democratic decision-making, rather than constantly require the discipline of laws to adhere to the requirements of policies, or fear God's wrath if they do not do as they are told. The benefits of science could thus be shared by all in a just, egalitarian, ethical and technologically advanced modern society. Even more, using a universal scientific method, 'there can be nothing so remote that we cannot reach to it, nor so recondite that we cannot discover it' (Descartes 1968: 92). Thus the sense of limitless, self-directed progress embedded in modernism. These are the beliefs that intellectually empower modern policy-making. What could possibly be wrong with such beliefs?

Modern beliefs in rational decision-making have been questioned several times since their inception, although without much effect, until recently. There has always been conservative, religious disbelief in rationalism, people in places like Alabama who prefer the Bible to *Scientific American*. But until recently these people could be dismissed as religious relics. Now they form the mass conservative support for neoconservatism, an ideology that by itself has little in the way of a widespread base. At the other extreme, and stemming from the widespread political and cultural scepticism of the 1960s, social theory in the late 1970s took a critical turn that deeply affected attitudes towards modern thinking, even issues like development that had been assumed to be both rational and good (e.g. Escobar 1995). Post-structural thinking, especially in its postmodern forms, emphasizes the other side of rational modernity, its peasant, female and colonized victims, its disciplinary institutions (schools, universities, prisons, psychiatric clinics) and, more generally, the sacrifices made through the self-exercise of rational control – the idea that modern people suffer by continually scrutinizing their behaviour through the lenses of logic and rationality. In postmodern philosophy, modern reason and even rationalized ethics are reinterpreted critically, not as source of liberation, but as a sophisticated kind of domination, a mode of Western control, acting through disciplinary institutions, includ-ing policy-setting institutions. In the post-structural view (Foucault especially), modern reason's claim to universal truth is interpreted as a claim to universal power. The West tries to control the world by controlling the way people think, imagine and plan for a 'better future'. Some postmodern theorists, Deleuze and Guattari, but also

55

Baudrillard at times, go beyond this criticism of Western control over rationality, to reject its philosophical basis in modern assumptions about the coherence of explanation or the structural character of causation. They argue instead for fragmentation, multiplicity and indeterminacy.

I do not go that far. It should be clear by now that I see the world in terms of a highly structured geography of power. I want equally structured, yet critical, alternatives that also claim rationality. I come to criticize rationality, not abandon it. Fragmentation and indeterminacy weaken the opposition to well-organized systems of corporate and financial control. And I prefer scientific 'truth' to its predecessor, religious faith – indeed, I find the retention of religion in modernity to be the source of horrific crimes – religion creates irrational hatreds, science enables bigots to kill en masse. I draw from post-structuralism the recognition that Western social-scientific thought is not neutral, universal rationality, realizable by all minds once they have been awoken by enlightenment. Instead social science in particular is but a way of thinking, a Western mode of thought that contains and continues the ideological effects of unequal power relations. As Derrida (1971: 213) said in one of his cogent moments: 'the white man takes his own mythology, Indo-European mythology, his own logos, that is, the mythos of his idiom, for the universal form of that he must still wish to call Reason'. I extend this into the position that policy is not scientifically based in the sense of being backed by undeniable, theoretical truth, but rather policy is scientifically based to claim the power and appearance of science, all this to legitimize class-biased interventions into the reconstruction of economic reality. I admire post-structural criticism without liking its nihilistic politics.

The geography of reason

Modern economic policy-making is immersed in the culture of Western rationality. Western rationality is the hegemonic global form of deep and careful thought applied to scientific, technical and policy matters. Contemporary globalization has involved the spread of Western rationality so that it now affects minds the world over, sometimes as a dominant way of thinking, sometimes as a mentality to be thought against. The growth to ideological hegemony of Western knowledge occurred in two stages that parallel broader transformations in political and economic hegemony: the era of British dominance, 1846–1940; and the era of American dominance, 1941 to the present. The connection between the two, economic and rational hegemony, is not just a matter of language; there is continuity of intellect, reason and the taken-for-granted. The globalization of Anglo-American rational culture, phrased in English, concentrates intellectual power in a few cultural-ideological centres. Where might these mind-making centres be?

The world's dominant intellectual power centres are now located in countries populated by English-speaking people. This geography can be explained through a kind of consciousness location theory based on a power-geographic interpretation of Max Weber's rationalization thesis. For Weber, modern, Western rationalism means several inter-connected capabilities: the ability to think logically on an empirical basis – theoretical rationalism; the capacity for humans to control the world through calculation – scientific-technological rationalism; the systematization of meaning patterns – metaphysical-ethical rational-ism; and a rationally organized, methodical way of life – practical rationalism (Schluchter 1979). That is, rationality is logic, technology, rationalized ethics and methodical practice. Where does the modern, rational way of life come from? Weber explained the Western rise to dominance in terms of a historical process unique to the Europeans, specifically northern, Protestant Europeans, and especially the Cal-vinists – i.e. the followers of the Protestant theologian John Calvin (1509–64). In Calvinism, Weber argued, the world was treated as a reality separate from God (i.e. god 'transcended' the world after mak-ing it), deprived of symbolic significance, magical evidence of God's wisdom, and lines of access to God's will. Instead those acting as members of the Elect – those who thought they would attain eternal grace (go to heaven) – treated the world as a set of resistant objects that tested their mastering and ordering capacities. In this – the world as a system of natural objects that could be understood objectively rather than religiously – we find the possibility of materialistic and scientific thought. The mind is liberated from mesmerization by gods, goblins and ghosts, and can think rationally rather than mystically about the real causes of natural and social events. Furthermore, the Calvinist doctrine of predestination – the belief that ascendance to heaven was predetermined at birth rather than earned by good deeds – induced an acute sense of separation from others among Protestants because of intense, existential anxiety over the individual's spiritual standing. The early modern personality, Weber says, came to be motivated by intel-lect, rather than habit or feeling, with long-term, planned direction, continuous rather than intermittent activity, and with responsibility for outcomes taken by the individual, rather than blamed on fate. Under-neath was a simple intuition: the individual proved (to its anxious, austere self) that it was a member of the Elect by acting in a god-like way, in the sense of relating to the world (including the individual itself) as God was thought to do – through mastery and distance, through rationality and control, and with long-term perspective. In terms of economic action, Calvinists considered themselves ethically bound to sustain profit over a series of operations through relentless, steady and systematic, rational activity in business. The ascetic entrepreneur strove for maximal returns on assets while abstaining from immediate enjoyment of the fruits of his labour. Hence capital accumulated through continuous investment and repression of all-too-human feelings of solidarity towards others – 'the entrepreneur is ethically authorised, indeed commanded, to act individualistically' (Poggi 1983: 73). Once successful, however, Calvinists legitimized profit-making, salved conscience and relieved alienation by giving back to the community through philanthropy. As Weber (1978: 164) said: 'the Puritan conception of life ... favoured the tendency towards a bourgeois, economically rational, way of life ... It stood by the cradle of modern "economic man".' Through a comparative study of religious cultures other than Calvinism, Weber concluded that science has reached the stage of 'authenticity' only in the West – the reference is especially to mathematics and the exact natural sciences, with their precise rational foundations. Science and technology intersect with the profit motive to produce a path of rational economic development unique to the West (ibid.: 338–9). Hence for Weber the modern rationalism of world mastery was the product of an ethical, religious and institutional development characterized by the 'disenchantment' of the world, that is ridding the world of mystical forces except, of course, that distant God (Weber 1958; Schluchter 1979).

What seems to have happened, Weber says, is that under the previous Catholicism intense religiosity and intense economic activity had been mutually incompatible – although, necessarily, the Church had to tolerate wealth, for the Pope and the bishops were rich themselves. This changed during the sixteenth century, when the wealthiest cities and regions, primarily in western Europe, turned to Protestantism. Indeed, under Protestantism, the middle class of merchants and artisans developed heroic qualities of character in defence of an asceticism that combined rationalism with entrepreneurialism (Bendix 1960: 78). Who were these new, modern people? As Christopher Hill has argued, the English Puritan tradition has long been rational, bourgeois and democratic (Hill 1958). Even more, the migrants who founded New England in the 1620s and 1630s were Calvinist Protestants of a virulent and separatist kind. Stephen Innes (1995) argues that Calvinist moral capitalism combined networks, norms and systems of trust that made commercial activity possible with an individualism highly motivated by a religiously based economic culture that fostered industrious and striving behaviour; together with a high savings and investment rate enforced through prescriptions against conspicuous consumption. Work in New England was both economic function and spiritual expression. In New England the Puritans constructed a society that was, from the beginning, democratically capitalist, in the limited sense of widespread male ownership of property, and politically democratic, in the (also limited) sense of the town meeting and the congregation's election of pastors. Protestantism, especially Calvinist sects like the Scottish Presbyterians and the New England Congregationalists, involved people reading English translations of the sacred texts for themselves and, what is more, debating their message among themselves. Reading the Bible meant being able to read (and write), while debating meant thinking for oneself – logically, again to the limited degree that religion (e.g. predestination) is rational. The two regions of the world with the highest literacy rates – Lowland Scotland and Massachusetts – corresponded with the highest densities of Calvinists. Additionally, the Calvinist practice of demonstrating membership of the Elect not only through economic success but also through philanthropy took the specific social form of founding and supporting educational and intellectual institutions. Again, New England is the archetypal region: not a town without a library usually named after a leading local capitalist, and the largest concentration of leading universities in the world (the Boston metropolitan area alone has seven). In Old and New England we find a synthesis between profit and intellect that proved to be accumulative: profit supported education; intellect furthered innovation; innovation made profit. Yet we must add another historical dimension, present from the beginning. It has to be remembered that the Puritans were invaders of a territory long occupied by Indian tribes who, after initially helping the Pilgrims survive, were essentially eliminated (Cronon 1983). Also, the Protestant merchants of Boston, Salem, Newburyport and Providence, like those of Bristol and Liverpool, accumulated wealth as members of the triangular trade among Europe, West Africa and the Caribbean, and therefore shared in the economic surpluses generated by slaving and slave labour (Frank 1979: 14–16). That is, the rationality developed in the Protestant centres of learning and culture has always been biased by an ethics that allowed the exploitation of distanced others – rationalizing ethics is a fine source of excuse. The glow of Western rationality has always hidden a dark underside.

Geography of academia

Nevertheless, the regions of Protestant dominance, symbolized by the two Cambridges (England and New England), have been the main centres in a thought system deemed to be rational during the long development of modernity. All eras, even modernism, have a sense of tradition. This sense of tradition is rooted in places where thought of the approved, valued kind has been most intense. Rational thought of the Western kind is susceptible to tradition in a particularly powerful way. For if it is the case, as Weber believed, that modern, Western rationalism facilitated European world mastery, in terms of conquest of the natural (physical) and spatial (global) worlds, then the places where rationalism was born, the places where it was developed, the geographic moments of innovation, the great minds that thought there, have significance like none before. These are the places where intellectuals learned how to conquer the universe. Hence, the rational tradition has a geography, and the places of scientific discovery exude intellectual power. This is true of the places of original rationalization, but is even more the case for the places of the nineteenth-century scientific revolution, when rationality was envisaged as technology, and the new techniques solidified European dominance in the world. Most of the early discoveries, when minds newly and partially released from the shrouds of religious mysticism launched into the unknown (or rather the mistakenly known), were made by industrial practitioners (James Watt) or upper-middle-class dilettantes (Charles Darwin). But as the nineteenth century progressed, academia became increasingly significant as the repository of past thoughts and the fountain of new knowledge. The regions of Protestant rationality, principally in Britain and the USA, housed the most famous, powerful universities in the world. Rational traditionalism, industrial progress, profit and family fortunes, the philanthropic feedback, the relative freedom of thought allowed by Protestantism, all contributed to the concentration of theoretical power in these emerging mind centres. Then in the twentieth century, the democratic belief in the right to education put the power of states tinged by social democracy behind the reinvestment of tax money into high-quality public universities open to all bright students. (I am one little result of this.) Academia, in the modern sense of institutions of research and teaching, largely freed from the constraints of religion, developed in the heartlands of modern rational capitalism, as its intellectual fervour.

Academia can be thought of as a complex of research and teaching institutions typified by, but not limited to, regional complexes of elite universities. Each university consists of a physical space, a campus endowed with a set of resources, such as libraries and laboratories, a student body marked by certain class, ethnic and regional backgrounds, a political, humanitarian and artistic tradition under constant revision, and a faculty and staff hired to re-create intellectual specializations, organized primarily as disciplines. Academia has two main products: ideas, theories, philosophies that form the intellectual basis for an informed expertise; and students imbued with the ideas, skills, styles, traditions and connections that mark them as alumni. Academia controls the content and contours of professionalism as an accepted style of intellectual practice and behaviour – we could call this the 'professional social order'. More profoundly, academic institutions and the disciplines control the flow of ideas into and out of a store of knowledge legitimized as scientific in the Western tradition of rationalism. The disciplines are ranked according to scientific status, with economics recognized as the social theory most resembling physics, and other disciplines arrayed below in a changing but relatively stable order. Scientific status lends persuasive power to statements, positions and consultative advice on policy.

Hierarchies of knowledge

Academia is structured into a hierarchy of institutions. One level of structuring, by language and country, follows the Weberian argument outlined above. Intellectual discourse requires a common language to smooth the daily connections among millions of dispersed thinkers and actors. This language is English, the common language in the realms of business, science and culture: for example, 95 per cent of the scientific articles published in major periodicals are in English (Bollag 2000). Similarly, most of the world's leading universities are located within the English-speaking countries. Of the 50 leading universities in the world, according to *The Times* (London), 21 are in the USA, 7 in the United Kingdom and 14 in former British colonies for a total of 43 in English-speaking countries. (This is based on a survey of 1,300 academics in 88 countries – Halpin 2004.) At the top in each country are a small number of leading universities that recruit and educate future members of the elite class and whose faculty and research associates produce research findings that inform policy. Whereas British universities once prevailed (and still do in that nationalist prejudice that somehow persists in believing that 'British is best'), now US universities are the most prestigious. Within the USA, which are the leading universities? The most revealing single measure is the university or college endowment, by which is meant the funds given or bequeathed usually by college alumni (previous students) and

TABLE 3.1 US college and university endowments, 2004 (over $2 billion)

Institution	Endowment ($)*
Harvard University (Cambridge, MA)	22,587,305,000
Yale University (New Haven, CT)	12,740,896,000
Princeton University (Princeton, NJ)	9,928,200,000
Leland Stanford Junior University (Stanford, CA)	9,922,041,000
Univ. of Texas System Administration (Austin, TX)	9,360,113,745
Massachusetts Institute of Technology (Cambridge, MA)	5,869,800,000
Columbia University (New York, NY)	4,493,085,000
Univ. of Michigan (Ann Arbor, MI)	4,243,352,775
Emory University (Atlanta, GA)	4,086,000,000
Washington University (St Louis, MO)	4,083,958,000
Univ. of Pennsylvania (Philadelphia, PA)	4,019,000,000
Northwestern University (Evanston, IL)	3,884,629,679
Univ. of Chicago (Chicago, IL)	3,620,728,000
Cornell University (Ithaca, NY)	3,314,228,858
William Marsh Rice University (Houston, TX)	3,302,000,000
Texas A&M University (College Station, TX)	3,240,693,652
Univ. of Notre Dame (Notre Dame, IN)	3,123,454,523
Duke University (Durham, NC)	2,832,921,999
Dartmouth College (Hanover, NH)	2,454,294,000
Univ. of Southern California (Los Angeles, CA)	2,399,960,000
Vanderbilt University (Nashville, TN)	2,264,845,000
Univ. of Texas at Austin (Austin, TX)	2,038,938,294
Univ. of California, Berkeley (Berkeley, CA)	2,037,297,000

Note: * Endowment is market value at fiscal year-end 2004.
Source: Council for Aid to Education (2005).

invested and accumulated by the university acting as a corporation. These universities are of two types: (1) private universities that are members or near-members of the Ivy League, a term coined in the 1930s denoting famous private universities on the East Coast that emphasized scholarship and sports; (2) public universities in large states with high average family incomes, especially in areas where education has traditionally been highly valued – Calvinist states. The endowment enables a university to pay professors (but not the staff of secretaries, research assistants, etc.) more than the going rate. According to the AAUP (American Association of University Professors) full professors at private universities granting doctoral degrees made an average of $131,000 a year in 2005; at the private universities shown in Table 3.1, full professors make salaries in the $140,000–$170,000 range (Harvard

$169,000, Princeton $157,000). At public universities granting doctoral degrees, full professors make an average of $102,000, but at those listed in Table 3.1 salaries are in the range of $115,000–$130,000. The highest-paid 5 per cent of professors in the elite US universities make salaries in the $180,000–$235,000 range. Professors are paid most in New England and the Middle Atlantic regions (AAUP 2005/06), the traditional heartland of US education. The elite universities spend more on libraries ($25–$100 million a year) and have the largest collections (5–15 million books, with Harvard holding 15.4 million books and Yale 11.4 millions – Association of Research Libraries 2004). They finance research and conferences, invite famous people from all over the world, have low teaching loads, and so on. When a Harvard professor speaks, the media take notice.

Economics as discipline

At these prestigious universities, economics is the leading social science. Elite universities compete to attract well-known or rising star economics faculty usually trained at other elite universities. Economics is usually the largest social science department on campus, with an average of sixty faculty members (Harvard has fifty-eight), more than twice the size of, for example, sociology departments. Faculty from these departments circulate within a system of elite institutions, as with the IFIs, the leading think tanks, economics organizations and government departments. Harvard economics professors have served on the Council of Economic Advisors; the Federal Reserve Banks of Boston and New York; as Chief Economist and Director of Research, International Monetary Fund; as Chief Economist, US Department of Labor; and as president, American Economic Association. Most economics departments have one or two members thinking from alternative perspectives to the ruling mainstream, but collective opposition in the discipline is relegated to departments like that at the University of Massachusetts, split evenly, by agreement, between radicals and conventionals. Individual economists and academic departments are usually ranked according to publications (number, prestige of journal, citations, etc.). Of the top 100 economists in the world, 88 per cent work in the USA and 10 per cent in Britain (Coupe 2002); they are trained at Harvard, the University of Chicago, MIT, Princeton and so on – the leading departments in the world (Table 3.2). US economics departments turn out about a thousand PhDs a year, more than half of which now go to graduate students from outside the country.

In addition to economics departments, academia is home to several hundred economics research institutions. The most prestigious of

Ideological power

63

these is the National Bureau of Economic Research (NBER), a private, non-profit, non-partisan research organization dedicated to study-ing the science and empirics of economics, especially the American economy. It is 'committed to undertaking and disseminating unbiased economic research among public policymakers, business professionals, and the academic community'. The NBER is located in Cambridge, Massachusetts, with branch offices in Palo Alto, California, and New York City. Founded in 1920, the NBER, with Simon Kuznets working for it, organized a system of national accounts for the US government in 1930, which marked the beginning of the official measurement of GDP and other related indices of economic activity. Owing to its work on national accounts and business cycles, the NBER provides the official start and end dates for recessions. It is the largest eco-nomics research organization in the USA. Sixteen of the thirty-one American winners of the Nobel Prize in Economics have been NBER associates, as well as three of the past Chairmen of the Council of Economic Advisors, including the current NBER president, Martin S. Feldstein. Yet the single most important intellectual influence pushing economic policy to the right has also come from Feldstein, a rightist economist who has long taught 'Ec 10', a 'decidedly anti-tax, free market-leaning introduction to economics' to thousands of students at Harvard University, many of whom have gone on to prestigious positions in the US Treasury Department (Leonhardt 2002).

US economists are organized institutionally into the American Economic Association, organized in 1885, with a membership now of about 18,000. The association publishes *The American Economic Review* (AER), the *Journal of Economic Literature* (JEL) and the *Journal of Economic Perspectives* (JEP); the AER limits the type of article published largely to conventional topics; most articles in the JEL are commissioned by the editors; the JEP is supposedly more open, but actually commissions most of the papers it publishes. 'Com-missioning' means that only ideas already approved by the editors are published in the journal – a better word is 'disciplining'. It costs an outsider (non-member of the association) $200 to submit an article to the AER. Economists have their own Nobel Prize. Whereas the prizes in Physics and Chemistry, Medicine, Literature and Peace were instituted by the will of Alfred Nobel, a Swedish chemist, industrialist and the inventor of dynamite, the prize in Economics was funded in 1968 by the Bank of Sweden. The prizes have been awarded over the last few years for contributions to game theory analysis; dynamic macroeconomics and business cycles; analysis of economic time series with time-varying volatility; integrating insights from psychological

TABLE 3.2 Ranking of economics departments by publications in the top thirty research journals, based on affiliation at time of publication, 1995–99

Rank	University	Country
1	Harvard University	USA
2	University of Chicago	USA
3	MIT	USA
4	Northwestern University	USA
5	University of Pennsylvania	USA
6	Yale University	USA
7	Princeton University	USA
8	Stanford University	USA
9	University of California, Berkeley	USA
10	New York University	USA
11	Columbia University	USA
12	University of California, San Diego	USA
13	University of Michigan	USA
14	UCLA	USA
15	Cornell University	USA
16	University of Texas, Austin	USA
17	University of Rochester	USA
18	Tilburg University	Netherlands
19	University of Wisconsin	USA
20	LSE	UK
21	University of Minnesota	USA
22	Boston University	USA
23	University of Toronto	Canada
24	University of Montreal	Canada
25	Brown University	USA

Source: Table 3 of Kalaitzidakis et al. (2003).

research into economic science; establishing laboratory experiments as a tool in empirical economic analysis, especially in the study of alternative market mechanisms; analyses of markets with asymmetric information; methods for analysing selective samples; and other conventional, mainly methodological topics. This is a relatively closed disciplinary universe.

The discourse of Keynesian economics

Modern economics dates from the work of Adam Smith (1937) and David Ricardo (1911), classical economists of the late eighteenth and early nineteenth centuries. Economics was made into a science by the marginalist revolution of the middle to late nineteenth century. Neoclassical economics is based on a theory of the economic

Ideological power

65

actor that is often termed '*Homo economicus*'. This theory assumes that when behaving economically, people are 'rational' in the sense that they act as atomistic individuals seeking to maximize utility as consumers, or profit as entrepreneurs, at the least possible cost, under conditions of perfect knowledge. This simplifying assumption, which transforms subjects into objects, enables economics to resemble physics, the leading natural science of objects. Neoclassical economics appeals to the scientific mind because it is mathematically elegant. The aim is to represent an economy in the abstract terms of a single equation – not quite Einstein's $E = MC^2$, but similar. Yet scientific elegance came at a price. To produce this elegant model, the neoclassical economists had to simplify complex subjectivities into objective modes of behaviour, and strip away the environments of economic action, so that the economic world became a sterile plain populated by clockwork 'people'.

Even within quite conventional economics, this has produced damning criticism – particularly in the area of rationality. Herbert Simon (1957), for example, says that people are partly rational, or that rationality is limited or bounded – 'boundedly rational agents experience limits in formulating and solving complex problems and in processing (receiving, storing, retrieving, transmitting) information' (Williamson 1985: 553, quoting Simon). More recently, Daniel Kahneman (2003) has stressed the role of intuitions – thoughts and preferences that come to mind quickly and without much reflection – in economic decision-making. Joseph Stiglitz originally made a reputation by arguing that asymmetric information is a key feature of the world. In most situations, the two sides of a market have vastly different information about the good or service transacted, sellers typically knowing more about what they are selling than buyers, so that adverse selection occurs. That is, low-quality products drive out high-quality products unless other actions are taken – signalling and screening – so that the economic transactions that occur are different from those that would emerge in a world of perfect information (Arnott et al. 2003). Criticisms like these, earning Kahneman and Stiglitz Nobel Prizes in Economics, begin to undermine the notion of *Homo economicus*, the rational, perfectly informed automaton occupying the central position in the whole marginal-market-competitive system of the neoclassical economic imaginary.

Neoclassical harmony had already been disturbed by John Maynard Keynes (1883–1946), a Cambridge economist and member of the Bloomsbury circle of artists and intellectuals. In the 1920s, Keynes had begun to systematically demolish the postulates of the old approach

– for example, the idea that wage earners were maximizers, or the truly nasty neoclassical notion that unemployment was voluntary. Such criticism would have been ignored were it not for the Great Depression. In explaining this, Keynes (1936) found that the creation of demand by supply (as with Say's Law) could occur at any level of employment or income, including very low levels of employment, so that full employment was but one of many economic possibilities. The particular level of employment, Keynes thought, was determined by aggregate demand for goods and services. Assuming that the government had a neutral effect, two groups influenced aggregate demand: consumers buying consumption goods; and investors buying production equipment. Consumers increased spending as their incomes rose, but this was not the key variable in explaining the overall level of employment, for consumption depended on income, which depended on something else. In the Keynesian system, real investment (spending on new factories, tools, machines and larger inventories of goods) was the crucial variable. Investment resulted from decisions made by entrepreneurs, under conditions of risk, and could be postponed. The decision to invest, Keynes said, depended on comparisons between expected profits and the prevailing interest rate. Here the crucial component was 'expectation' or, more generally, the degree of investor confidence. The cost of the capital used in investment Keynes explained in terms of speculation about future stock prices, which in turn determined interest rates, as savings moved from one fund to another. This also depended essentially on expectations about the future. When investors bought machines, providing income to machine builders (companies and employees), these spent money, further increasing national income, with the 'multiplier effect' (the degree of economic expansion induced by investment) varying with the proportion of additional income that was spent rather than saved (the marginal propensity to consume), and so on; a decrease in real investment had the reverse effects. The government could influence this process through interest rate and other monetary policies, shifting the economy from one equilibrium level to another, generally to higher employment levels. To keep aggregate demand fairly consistent and thus minimize the impact of business cycles, the government must keep the rate of investment reasonably constant. To this effect, the government should engage in *compensatory spending* to counterbalance private sector investment, minimizing its indirect effect on unemployment. The general name given to Keynesian regulation of an economy is 'demand management'.

Keynes himself doubted that merely changing interest rates would be sufficient to significantly alter business confidence and thus invest-ment. Subsequently conservative Keynesian economists have seen the manipulation of interest rates as a relatively non-bureaucratic, non-state-intrusive method, by which the central bank of a country tries to influence national income and employment – an alternative being tax reduction. Liberal Keynesian economists ('liberal' in the New Deal sense, rather than the nineteenth-century, free-trade sense) see deficit spending by governments (thus increasing demand) as a more effective measure: the 'liberal' aspect being that deficit spending can be used to improve social services. While favouring the latter course, the liberal Keynes thought that the government spending part was crucial, rather than the social investment part: burying banknotes in old mines, filling these with refuse and having private enterprise dig them up was better than nothing, if the goal was to increase employment. Keynes proved theoretically, however, what recurring depressions had long shown in practice: free markets did not spontaneously maximize human well-being. Instead, the state had to intervene through demand management, changing the aggregate level of demand in an economy through monetary and fiscal policies. Keynes also pointed to the chaotic core of market-based decision-making, the utter uncertainty that haunts the capitalist imagination, uncertainty as a self-fulfilling prophecy, uncertainty that when spread widely can cause depression. Hence the pretence of eternal optimism when economic pundits forecast the economic future.

While Keynesian economic policy was available from 1936 onwards, the Depression of the 1930s was ended by pragmatic governmental intervention (as with New Deal employment-generating programmes), spontaneous realizations ('we have nothing to fear but fear itself') and the militarization of the Western economies connected with the Second World War. In the post-war period, economic growth theory was promulgated by economists other than Keynes (who died in 1946), particularly through policies designed to maintain full employment. Full employment and a better life were promises that all political parties, Republican or Democrat, Conservative or Labour, were forced to make to millions of soldiers returning from a war that saved the West. The question 'whose society did we risk our lives for?' was too close to the surface for the previous political-economic platitudes to survive. Particularly in western Europe, political attitudes turned in a socialist direction. The British working class ejected Winston Churchill, conservative hero of the war, yet bitterly hated by the unions, to elect a Labour government – a government committed to full employment, heavily subsidized state-run social services (such as the National Health Service), educational reform (scholarships for university students) and significant income redistribution achieved by taxing the rich and paying the poor (family allowances). Also, in many countries outside the USA, the state directed what remained a basically capitalist economy, with key industrial sectors (transportation, mines, steel, chemicals) nationalized – that is, owned and run by state corporations. This (Fabian) socialist version of social democratic politics merged with leftist theoretical interpretations of Keynesianism to produce a political economics that favoured the working class – not merely because they spent income redistributed to them, but because they deserved higher incomes and free social services, for working people are the producers of value. Indeed, this view came, for a while, to be taken for granted by popular opinion in the western European countries, and in the 'working-class paradises' of Australia and New Zealand. In Britain, the Beveridge Report of 1942 resulted in a comprehensive system of social security and the National Health Service after the end of the Second World War. Its basic, motivating principle was banishing poverty, declaring: 'A revolutionary moment in the world's history is a time for revolutions, not for patching' and the 'organisation of social insurance should be treated as one part only of a comprehensive policy of social progress' (Beveridge 1942).

The USA has never been social democratic. Comparable social legislation, such as the Employment Act of 1946, was far more limited than its European equivalent. The federal government was instructed to achieve full employment, established by the Act as a right guaranteed to the American people. But there was strong opposition to the wording of the Bill, with a number of congressmen arguing that business cycles were natural in a free enterprise economy and compensatory spending should be exercised by the state only in the most extreme cases. Some also still believed that the economy would naturally drive towards full employment levels. And some were against an outright, state guarantee of employment. The final Act was not so much a mandate as a set of suggestions. When the USA took over the role of guardian of the West from Britain, the resulting political economy is best described as Military Keynesianism – that is, the maintenance of high growth rates through 'defence' spending by the state (Turgeon 1996) – rather than Social Keynesianism – that is, the maintenance of high employment rates through state planning and social progress. Nevertheless, returning to the evidence shown in Figure 1.1, Keynesianism did well for working people.

In the post-war period of Keynesian dominance, economics focused more on growth theory than in the past. In the Harrod-Domar model,

Ideological power

increasing economic growth basically involved increasing the savings rate, in some cases through the state budget, and using the resulting funds to invest in the social as well as the productive economy. Development policies based on the Harrod-Domar model were used in left-leaning countries in the 1950s – the social democracies of western Europe and many countries in the Third World, where the state led development programmes – for example, India's First Five Year Plan between 1951 and 1956 was based on the Harrod version of Keynesianism. In Latin America, 'structural economists' like Raul Prebisch concluded that the region's underdevelopment was due to its emphasis on primary exports. The solution lay in structural change: industrialization using an import substitution strategy (i.e. replacing industrial imports with domestic production, under the cover of tariff protection), relying on income from primary exports to pay for imports of capital goods, the state to programme industrialization and, paradoxically, foreign companies to help start local businesses. This approach was widely adopted in Latin America, as elsewhere in the Third World, with impressive results as industry grew rapidly. What came to be called the NICs (New Industrial Countries – Brazil, Mexico, Hong Kong, Singapore, Taiwan) collectively had growth rates of 8.4 per cent in 1964–73 and 5.3 per cent in 1973–83, with the East Asian countries sustaining growth rates in the order of 10 per cent a year often for a decade or more (OECD 1988). More importantly, as industrialization moved from the production of products like textiles to products like steel and automobiles, increasingly unionized workers were able to obtain higher wages from employers and better services from Third World states. In general, Keynesian economic theory established the legitimacy of state intervention in market economies with the aim of achieving growth rates decided on the basis of social policy. Subsequently, some degree of state intervention has become more or less accepted in mainstream economics, and in conventional politics, where parties contend on the basis of which can best run the economy, that is with economic growth, low inflation and low unemployment rates.

Something drastic happened to the core Keynesian economies between the late 1960s and the early 1980s. Gerard Dumenil and Dominique Levy (2004) call the combination of unemployment, slow technological and economic growth, increased frequency of booms and recessions, runaway inflation and monetary and financial crises a 'structural crisis'. Their key to the complex of causes of the crisis of Keynesianism is the rate of profit – essentially the ratio between annual profits and the capital employed to produce them. The rate of profit for companies in the USA and Europe declined from a height of 20–23 per cent in the early 1960s to 13 per cent in the early 1980s – from which it has risen almost continuously since, to its original level in Europe, but not in the USA. The basic cause of the decline, for Dumenil and Levy (ibid.: 32), was a slowing down of technological change. The productivity of capital (output per unit of the capital fixed in machines) dropped sharply beginning in the second half of the 1960s. This is explained more by the increased capital used than a decline in the productivity of the labour-using machines – that is, mechanization was expensive. Faced with a slowdown in technological change, employers tried to shift the burden to employees, but real wages only began to decline in 1971–72 (and this has continued more or less ever since), hence a sharp decline in the profit rate in the late 1960s. Investment and capital accumulation slowed down and unemployment rose from 3.5 per cent in 1970 to 8 per cent in 1975 and 9.5 per cent in 1982–83 in the USA and to 10 per cent in Europe in 1985. Dumenil and Levy see this as the pressure on employers to reduce direct wages, worker benefits and the social welfare system. We have to add here, to make up for a silence on the part of Dumenil and Levy, that during the 1970s inflation rose, especially in the late 1970s, when it was higher than ever before. One basic cause on 'supply-side' inflation was OPEC's imposition of huge increases in the price of oil in 1973 and subsequent years, the lending of 'petrodollars' to non-oil-producing Third World countries, and the resulting debt crisis of the early 1980s. Another basic cause of high unemployment was the arrival on the labour market of the 'baby boomers' born just after the Second World War.

The stagflation of the 1970s (economic stagnation, marked by low growth rates and high unemployment, combined with high inflation) was interpreted by many economists as meaning that there were fundamental, structural deficiencies in Keynesian economics and in Keynesian economic policy. This interpretive moment was seized on by neoliberal theorists such as Friedrich von Hayek and Milton Friedman (discussed below), who managed to persuade the broader discipline of economics, or at least a good part of it. Yet the economic crisis of the 1970s was 'solved' by Keynesian means – the biggest fiscal deficits ever, before or since, during the first Reagan administration in the USA. The money was spent on a military build-up and on the Star Wars fantasy – hence the term 'Military Keynesianism' for this and subsequent times, such as the Gulf War and the fatal invasion of Iraq. The USA uses its economic power, including its ability to finance its military machine through massive

71

Three

budget deficits, to dominate the world, to invade countries on false pretexts, to arm its proxy in the Middle East so that Israel also invades and bombs its neighbours, again almost at will – all this to spread neoliberal democracy. Meanwhile those billions of dollars could be used to feed and house the millions of people who, even at the centre of civilization, even a few blocks from the White House, are homeless and hungry – that is, to improve social democracy. The crisis of the 1970s was an interpretive event, based on real problems in the evolving global capitalist system, but only one of several directions that could have been chosen.

We move now to the economic theorists who made the fatal interpretation that has led to the neoliberal disaster.

The discourse of neoliberal economics

Neoliberalism originated in political-economic theories formed in Germany and Austria in the late nineteenth and early twentieth centuries. In Germany, a historical school of economics had long been critical of the abstract nature of marginalist economics and the notion of equilibrium. Economists like Wilhelm Roscher (1817–94) and Gustav Schmoller (1838–1917) thought that it was difficult to keep supply and demand 'balanced' in advanced capitalist economies. Crises were probable, particularly when caused by lack of demand (underconsumption by underpaid workers). Other German economists influenced by the historical school stressed the instabilities in capitalist development coming from uneven growth in the various sectors of an economy (for example, steel, shipbuilding, railways growing unevenly). The German historical school was empirical rather than abstract, looked at the very long term, and tended to be far more critical of capitalism than neoclassical Anglo-American economics. A bitter debate between Schmoller and Menger in the 1880s split German-speaking economics into antagonistic camps for decades – Schmoller thought that classical and neoclassical economics erred in finding universal laws, preferred induction to deduction, and found naïve the notion that people were motivated entirely by self-interest. By comparison, the Austrian School of economics, led by Menger's students Friedrich von Wieser (1851–1926) and Eugen von Bohm-Bawerk (1851–1914), was abstract and anti-historical in method and more politically conventional than the German historical school. Perhaps the most brilliant of the second generation of Austrian economists was Ludwig von Mises. Von Mises can be considered the founder of neoliberalism.

Von Mises was able to position his technical ability to make

72

innovative contributions to monetary and banking theory (his *Theory of Money and Credit*, 1953) within a broader social philosophy that idealized classical (nineteenth-century) liberalism. Responding to the rise of socialist ideas, like the Marxists, to the development of socialist parties in western Europe and eventually to the Soviet revolution in Russia, von Mises believed that socialist ideology was a menace to Western civilization, and that classical liberalism alone could uphold freedom (von Mises 1983: 204). Society, for von Mises, originates not in some social contract but in the character of the individual – 'egoism is the basic law of society' (von Mises 1932: 402). All social phenomena are spontaneous, unplanned outcomes of choices made by rational individuals. The individual encounters social necessities, however, as when the division of labour increases productivity and makes social cooperation more profitable than self-sufficiency. Humans obey the fundamental laws of social cooperation because they are in the person's rightly understood self-interest – obedience to law allows maximum individual freedom, and the pursuit of rightly understood self-interest also assures the highest attainable degree of general welfare. 'The point of departure of all liberalism lies in the thesis of the harmony of rightly understood interests of individuals' (von Mises 1983: 182). For von Mises, the consumer interest counts above all other interests, and all interests are harmonized by market forces, establishing what von Mises called 'consumer sovereignty'. A state may be necessary, but liberalism teaches that its power must be minimized and, especially, laissez-faire should be left unhampered to work its miracles of development. This sociology is the foundation for von Mises's economic theory of laissez-faire or the free market economy. Harmony, not conflict, exists between consumers and entrepreneurs, between entrepreneurs, managers and employees, and so on. This philosophy, together with theories about the market process, money, interest rate and cycles, justifies von Mises's conception of freedom and his advocacy of laissez-faire. Laissez-faire prevails because it is scientifically demonstrated to be the best policy (Gonce 2003).

Von Mises (1922) argued that socialism could not work in an advanced industrial economy. The basic problem, according to von Mises, is that economic calculation is impossible in a socialist community. Where there is no market, there is no price system, and where there is no price system, there can be no economic calculation. Exchange relations in productive goods can be established only on the basis of private property in the means of production. The problem of economic calculation, he said, is the fundamental problem of

73

socialism. Theorists could write and talk about socialism for decades without touching this problem. For von Mises, this demonstrated the devastating effects of the Marxian prohibition on scientific scrutiny of the working of a socialist economy. To prove that economic calculation would be impossible in the socialist community is to prove also that socialism is impracticable. Everything brought forward in favour of socialism in thousands of writings and speeches, all the blood that had been spilt by the supporters of socialism, could not make it workable. The masses might ardently long for it, innumerable revolutions and wars might be fought for it, but it would never be realized. Every attempt to carry it out would lead to chaos that would quickly dissolve the society based upon the division of labour into small autarkic groups. And if socialism cannot work, neither can specific acts of government intervention in the market – what von Mises called 'interventionism'. (This line of reasoning was criticized in the 1930s by the Polish Marxist economist Oskar Lange and others – see Roberts 1971.)

These ideas were elaborated further by Friedrich von Hayek, a student of von Mises. Von Hayek argued that people have little knowledge of the world beyond their immediate surroundings. This is the crucial ingredient that makes the price system work. Prices are not merely 'rates of exchange between goods', but are also 'a mechanism for communicating information' (von Hayek 1945). Von Hayek saw the free price system not as a conscious invention (that is, intentionally designed by humans) but as a spontaneous order. In a complex, uncertain environment, economic agents are not able to predict the consequences of their actions, and only the price system can coordinate the whole. The efficient use of resources, von Hayek claimed, can only be maintained by the price mechanism operating in free markets. The price mechanism synchronizes local and personal knowledges, allowing society's members to achieve diverse, complicated ends through spontaneous self-organization. Price signals are the only possible way of letting economic decision-makers communicate tacit knowledge or dispersed knowledge to each other, in order to solve the economic calculation problem. For von Hayek the 'fatal conceit' of the socialists was that they believed this complex system could be designed by a planning system that gets the prices right. Von Hayek argued that in centrally planned economies an individual or a select group of individuals must determine the distribution of resources, but that these planners will never have enough information to carry out this allocation reliably. An economy can never be designed by social planning, but emerges spontaneously from a complex network of interactions among agents with limited knowledges. Von Hayek attributed the birth of civilization to private property. In von Hayek's view, the central role of the state should be restricted to maintaining the rule of law, with as little intervention as possible. The apparatus of the state should be used solely to secure the peace necessary for the functioning of a market coordinating free individuals. Von Hayek saw himself as a liberal in the English Whig tradition – the Whigs being a party in England in the seventeenth century, advocating popular rights, parliamentary power over the Crown and toleration to dissenters. Classical liberalism or 'Manchester School liberalism' supports the individual rights of property and freedom of contract. It advocates laissez-faire capitalism, meaning the removal of legal barriers to trade and cessation of government-imposed subsidy and monopoly. Economic liberals want little or no government regulation of the market. Economic liberalism holds that the value of goods and services should be set by the unfettered choices of individuals – that is, market forces. Some would also allow market forces to act even in areas conventionally monopolized by governments, such as the provision of security, and courts. Economic liberalism accepts the economic inequality that arises from unequal bargaining positions as being the natural result of competition, so long as no coercion is used. Von Hayek (1984: 365) thought that liberalism of this classical kind 'derives from the discovery of a self-generating or spontaneous order in social affairs … an order which made it possible to utilize the knowledge and skill of all members of society to a much greater extent than would be possible in any order created by central direction, and the consequent desire to make as full use of these powerful spontaneous ordering forces as possible'.

In *The Road to Serfdom*, von Hayek (1994) argued that both fascists and socialists believed that economic life should be 'consciously directed' and that economic planning should be substituted for the competitive system. But to achieve their ends, planners had to create power of a magnitude never before known. Democracy was an obstacle to this suppression of freedom. Therefore, planning and democracy were antithetical. Von Hayek thought that concentrating power so it can be used in planning not merely transforms but heightens power. By uniting in the hands of a single body power formerly exercised independently by many, power is created in amounts infinitely greater than any that existed before – indeed, is so far reaching as almost to be different in kind. No one in competitive society can exercise even a fraction of the power possessed by a socialist planning board. Competition is the only system that can minimize the power exercised by one person over another. The power of a millionaire employer over the individual is less than that possessed by the smallest bureaucrat wielding the coercive power of the state, deciding how people are allowed to live and work. Indeed, a poorly paid unskilled workman in the USA, for von Hayek, was more free to shape his life than many an employer in Germany, or a much better-paid engineer or manager in the Soviet Union. He thought that his generation had forgotten that the system of private property is the most important guarantor of freedom. It is only because the control of the means of production is divided among many people, acting independently, that we as individuals can decide what to do with ourselves. In the hands of private individuals, what is called economic power can be an instrument of coercion, yet it is never control over the whole life of a person. But when economic power is centralized as an instrument of political power it creates a degree of dependence scarcely distinguishable from slavery. Thus, for von Hayek, in a country where the sole employer is the state, opposition means death by slow starvation.

Thus, what was promised as the Road to Freedom (socialist planning) was in fact the High Road to Servitude. Democracy embarking on a course of planning, with the goal described in vague term as 'the general welfare' through central planning, was like people committing themselves to taking a journey together without agreeing where they wanted to go. Drawing up an economic plan in this fashion was even less possible than, for instance, successfully planning a military campaign by democratic procedure. As in strategy, it would become inevitable to have to delegate the task to experts. And even if, by this expedient, a democracy should succeed in planning every sector of economic activity, it would still have to face the problem of integrating these separate plans into a unitary whole. There would be a stronger and stronger demand that some board or single individual should be given power to act on the people's behalf. The cry for an economic dictator is a characteristic stage in the movement towards planning. Thus the legislative body would be reduced to choosing the persons to wield practically absolute power. The whole system would tend towards that kind of dictatorship in which the head of the government is in position by popular vote, but where he has all the powers at his command to make certain that the vote will go in the direction he desires. Thus, for von Hayek, planning leads to dictatorship because dictatorship is the most effective instrument of coercion. There is no justification for the widespread belief that, so long as power is conferred by democratic procedure, it cannot be arbitrary. It is not the source of power which prevents it from being arbitrary; to be free from dictatorial qualities, the power must also be limited. A true 'dictatorship of the proletariat', even if democratic in form, if it undertook centrally to direct the economic system, would probably destroy personal freedom as completely as any autocracy has ever done. Hence, the realization of the socialist programme means the destruction of freedom. Democratic socialism, the great utopia of the last few generations, was simply not achievable. And further collectivism means the end of truth. To make a totalitarian system function efficiently, it is not enough that everybody should be forced to work for the ends selected by those in control; it is essential that the people should come to regard these ends as their own. This is brought about by propaganda and by complete control of all sources of information. Hence, von Hayek concluded, the guiding principle in any attempt to create a world of free men must be this: a policy of freedom for the individual is the only truly progressive policy.

Von Hayek was a professor at the London School of Economics (1931–50), the University of Chicago (1950–61) and Freiburg University in West Germany until his death in 1992. He was mentor to the Mont Pelerin Society, begun in 1947 at a hotel in Switzerland, attended annually by the leading lights of neoliberalism, and dedicated to the 'exchange of ideas about the nature of a free society and ... the ways and means of strengthening its intellectual support' (Leube 1984: xxiii). But all this went relatively unnoticed until the Royal Swedish Academy of Sciences, or rather the Bank of Sweden, awarded the 1974 Nobel Prize for Economic Science to Gunnar Myrdal and Friedrich von Hayek 'for their pioneering work in the theory of money and economic fluctuations and for their penetrating analysis of the interdependence of economic, social and institutional phenomena'. Von Hayek became more important in the late 1970s and early 1980s, with the rise of conservative governments in the USA and the UK. Margaret Thatcher, Conservative Party Prime Minister of the UK from 1979 to 1990, was a disciple of von Hayek. Soon after Thatcher became leader of the Conservative Party in 1974, she interrupted a staff member's presentation on a middle way between left and right, reached into her briefcase and took out a book, Friedrich von Hayek's *The Constitution of Liberty*. 'This is what we believe,' she said. Soon after, she met von Hayek at the Institute of Economic Afairs, a free market think tank in London. Asked for his opinion of her, von Hayek said: 'She's so beautiful' (Yergin and Stanislaw 1999: 107–8). After winning the 1979 election, Thatcher appointed Keith Joseph, director of the Hayekian Centre for Policy Studies, as Secretary of State for Industry with the mission of redirecting economic strategy, and she elevated Ralph Harris, director of the Institute of Economic Affairs, to the House of Lords in recognition of the role he had played in rebuilding Conservative Party philosophy. Ronald Reagan too read von Hayek and took advice from Hayekian economic advisers. Even so, a colleague of von Hayek's at the University of Chicago, Milton Friedman, was more important as an influence on Reagan, and on the remaking of economic policy in the 1980s.

Friedman is the leading theorist of the monetarist school of economic thought. He finds a close link between inflation and the money supply. Inflation, he says, can be controlled by limiting the amount of money in the national economy, a function performed in the USA by the Federal Reserve Bank. Friedman rejects fiscal policy as a tool of demand management, and thinks that the government's role in guiding the economy should be limited. This is set in a historical vision that 'the two ideas of human freedom and economic freedom working together came to their greatest fruition in the United States' (Friedman and Friedman 1979: 309). While Americans are imbued with freedom as part of the very fabric of their being, they have strayed from this principle, forgetting that the greatest threat comes from the concentration of power in the hands of government, he says. Friedman argues that the Great Depression, or 'Great Contraction', had been caused by a financial shock whose duration and seriousness were magnified by a subsequent contraction in the money supply caused by misguided policies pursued by the directors of the Federal Reserve Bank. Rather than being a failure of the free enterprise system, the Depression represented a tragic failure of government(!). Friedman argues that governments should not intervene in currency markets, an idea that became the basis of freely floating exchange rates. Following Friedman's (1958) lead that 'millions of able, active and vigorous people exist in every underdeveloped country' and 'require only a favorable environment to transform the face of their countries', neoliberal policies aimed at creating 'more competitive markets with brave, more innovative entrepreneurs' took over a previously liberal, interventionist development economics in the 'counter-revolution' of the 1970s and early 1980s (Straussman 1993; Toye 1987). Friedman lectured in Chile during the military dictatorship of Augusto Pinochet, when thousands of leftists were being murdered by the state. Professors from the Chicago School of Economics were advisers to the Chilean government and Chicago graduates, known as 'the Chicago boys', served in Chilean ministries. Even so, Friedman was awarded the Nobel Prize in 1976 'for his achievements in the fields of consumption analysis, monetary history and theory and for his demonstration of the complexity of stabilization policy'. (Altogether five members of the Chicago school have been awarded the Nobel Prize in Economics.) He was a member of Reagan's Economic Policy Advisory Board in 1981. After retiring, Friedman went to the Hoover Institute at Stanford University, a think tank closely allied with the Reagan administration.

The ideas propagated by von Mises, von Hayek, Friedman and others in the Chicago school have become central notions in mainstream economics. As Palley (2005: 20) points out, the two central principles of neoliberal economics – that 'factors of production' (labour and capital) get paid what they are worth and that free markets will not let factors go to waste – have been 'extraordinarily influential' since 1980. This influence passed through Friedman's monetarism, prevalent during the 1980s, and the 'new classical economics' associated with Robert Lucas, also of the Chicago school, and a Nobel Prize winner. New classical economics restresses the neoclassical assumption that all economic agents are rational (utility-maximizing) and have rational expectations. Unemployment is the result of government intervention in this perfect, self-adjusting realm. Hence the state should refrain from intervening (Lapavitsas 2005). So mainstream economics 'takes competitive markets as the norm' and sees value-driven state interventions like the introduction of labour standards 'as a distortion which will lead to misallocation and inefficiencies' (Tabb 2004: 335–6). Mainstream economics worships the market as ultimate arbiter of the trajectory of economic development.

As chief economist of the World Bank, and former faculty member at Harvard University, Laurence Summers once asked what was the most important thing that could be learned from an economics course. He said that he tried to leave his students with the view that the invisible hand is more powerful than the hidden hand of the state – things happen well without direction, controls and plans. 'That's the consensus among economists. That's the Hayek legacy. As for Milton Friedman, he was the devil figure in my youth. Only with time have I come to have … increasingly ungrudging respect' (Yergin and Stanislaw 1999: 151).

Critique of neoliberalism

It has been difficult to restrain my criticism while outlining this discourse. Let me now comment on the neoliberal school of social and economic thought. Neoliberalism is founded on an assumption about the inherent nature of human beings, seen by von Mises and von Hayek as egotistic and self-interested, and by Friedman as imbued with freedom. This assumption is elaborated into the further view that social phenomena are spontaneous, unplanned outcomes of choices made by rational, self-interested individuals. Markets can harmonize these choices. And markets and free price systems are not conscious inventions but arise spontaneously. The question is: does this vision have any basis at all in historical reality? Take markets, for instance. Karl Polanyi (1944) argues to the contrary that there was nothing natural or spontaneous about 'free markets' – 'The road to the free market was paved with continuous political manipulation, whether the state was involved in removing old restrictive regulations ... or building new political administrative bodies.' Markets were social and institutional constructions, and require rules and regulations to function effectively. The assumption of egotism made in neoliberal thought is pure make-believe. Was the person purely egotistical in feudal society, with its communal social orders and guild allegiances, or in the state societies of India and China, with their long traditions of social obligation and respect for order and position? We are dealing here with a fabrication, a utopian vision, a fantastic dream about an imagined past. The idea is that these natural qualities of the human being and these spontaneous events of history culminated in nineteenth-century, laissez-faire liberal society, when the economy ran itself via self-regulating markets. But as Polanyi says: 'There was nothing natural about laissez-faire; free markets could never have come into being merely by allowing things to take their course. ... Laissez-faire itself was enforced by the state.' As to the notion that markets are populated by autonomous, self-interested actors, economic sociology has argued conversely that actors in markets develop durable, moral relationships of trust, with a sense of fairness and responsibility, while abstaining from opportunism (Granovetter 1985). But this notion of free individuals meeting freely in markets is not only factually incorrect, it misunderstands the market relation. There is a dense and somewhat obscure passage in Marx's (1973: 243–5) *Grundrisse* criticizing the supposed elevation of competitive selfishness into a higher order of the common interest: Marx thinks instead that the common interest 'proceeds as it were behind the back of these self-reflected particular interests, behind the back of one individual's interest in opposition to that of another'. More than this, the 'common interest' decided in this selfish way becomes an alienated force controlling individuals rather than being controlled by them, so that they are forced by competition to do things they know to be socially and environmentally destructive. The idea that markets 'harmonize' social relations, as with relations between employers and employees, is contradicted by a century and more of struggle and strikes – this is not a history of harmony, it is a record of violence. (Only a member of the elite, who never worked in a factory or office, was never subject to the arbitrary whim of a boss to take away the livelihood of the worker and her family, could say that employers have less power than the lowest civil servant.) Perhaps the strongest claim, made by the two vons, Mises and Hayek, is that the price system synchronizes individual knowledges into a higher, competitive economic order – produces development in effect. But prices act as signals only for a limited part of the content of commodities, labour content and capital investment. Prices do not represent these very well because markets hide more than they reveal. And prices do not represent social and environmental costs and long-term consequences at all. Market systems are environmentally destructive and socially irresponsible as a result. More than this, market systems are environmental disasters! As to prices as signals, the democratic state can signal a higher order of rationality by deliberately increasing prices by adding sales taxes – for example, cigarettes are highly taxed (and should be taxed more) to signal through the price/tax mechanism that smoking kills people. And people smoke because the 'rationality' of the market is produced by advertising. The economic calculation problem may have some purchase on state systems, like that of the former Soviet Union, but social democracies use combinations of markets and planning, with planning employed to achieve socially agreed upon goals – in this sense planning is democratic, markets are irrational and dictatorial. I could go on … and on again. But the thought recurring as I read this ego-philosophy is: whose interests does it serve? Who are these free individuals, and what does freedom mean in this ideological system? Clearly the neoliberals are not talking about workers in factories, nor women in families, nor peasants on plantations. They mean, by the free individual, the entrepreneur, the capitalist, the boss. And they mean, by freedom, the opportunity to make money, which buys everything (except happiness). These theorists are against the state because it may limit the freedom to make more money, and it might redistribute existing wealth. These guys disguise their support for rich people to become even richer using the lofty terms of freedom and democracy. These people are disgusting.

Economics as tragedy

Economics has been a specialized field of modern knowledge since the mid-nineteenth century. More than other kinds of social knowledge, economics claims the status of 'science', particularly in terms of its logical rigour and mathematical sophistication. More than any other species of academic practitioner, economists are experts treated with respect because they are thought to be the ultimate professionals, giving guarded advice, using specialized terms that refer to a knowledge taken to be scientific. Economics has its own philosophical basis, its own typical kinds of practice, and especially its own language fully understandable only by the cognoscenti, so that pronouncements have to be translated into simple terms for the 'ignoranti' (to coin a term) every night by experts on the news. Yet economic ideas are formed within an intellectual cocoon, whose conditions of entry are so severe, in terms of scholastic preparation, linguistic competence, mathematical ability, professional attitude and publication record, that merely attaining entrance commits the member to the aims and rules of the club. Specialization and intellectual isolation result in a highly formulated discipline, with rigorous rules of academic and practical conduct – for example, very careful forms of expression using a closely defined set of terms – within a protected theoretical environment. Academic economics has a well-organized institutional framework with elite departments interlinked with other powerful institutions, as with government and governance. This is a relatively closed knowledge system in terms of the production of ideas. Criticism is relegated to the institutional periphery – it's not that economists are deaf to criticism, it's more that they do not know that criticism is happening. And yet economics controls through policy the lives of billions of people. This is tragedy.

Economics is not an interest-neutral science of society. Economics is a liberal ideology devoted to the bourgeoisie. Modern economic theory, the pride of social science, rests on an empirical base (i.e. a set of generalized facts about the world) that is precarious in the extreme. Indeed, I argue that economics is a fiction, a story made up virtually out of thin air, but a story made up to serve an interest. Economics results from a particular class- and nation-biased reaction to the rise of modern market systems. Yet this ideology has been universalized, eternalized, naturalized and normalized as a scientifically true discourse valid for all people, all situations and all times – contemporary mainstream economics is said to be not only the best of social sciences, but the best set of theories imaginable for guiding the most important human activity of all, the material production of existence. We speak here of that line of economic thought stemming from the classical tradition of Adam Smith and David Ricardo, scientized by nineteenth-century neoclassical (marginalist) economics, modified by twentieth-century Keynesian economics, and resuscitated in the neoliberal economics of the late twentieth and early twenty-first centuries. Political economy comes from the British liberal enlightenment, a movement that favoured the new class of manufacturers and small property owners in their 200-year class struggle against the monarchy, against the mercantilist state and against the aristocracy. Its original conception of the good society – small, hard-working (Protestant) male property owners competing in markets who elected a government with limited powers of regulation – was corrupted from the beginning in Locke's extension of property rights to include the product of the labour of other workers and means of production beyond those any working owner individual could employ. Within the context of this prejudiced enlightenment thought, Adam Smith, David Ricardo and the classical economists constructed the theoretical framework of a specialized disciplinary knowledge. At this stage all the early political economists openly championed the industrial bourgeoisie and its right to profit, the efficiency generated by self-regulating markets, the concentration of industrial production through the division of labour in the most progressive nation-state in the world (Britain), but also the expansion of the market system to the entire world, again under British domination. All of this they simply made up, out of their prejudiced social imaginary – people were innately self-interested, market competition produced efficiency, and so on. With neoclassical, marginalist economics we find mathematical fantasy, behaviours made up, unrealistic assumptions, equilibriums that never happen. Between 1870 and 1900 capitalism actually lurched from one crisis to another. Economics dreamed of equilibrium. So when the Great Depression of the 1930s arose out of nowhere economists had nothing to contribute, nothing to say, except nonsense.

Except Keynes, a brilliant maverick, willing to recognize that equilibrium theory disguised a fundamentally flawed, hopelessly unstable capitalist economy. Even so, it took the socialist upheaval of the post-war years to turn Keynesian theory into a policy instrument beneficial to the working class. Pragmatic, Keynesian social democracy produced thirty years of high growth rates and the redistribution of income to poor people. And for a while, economics pretended conviction – 'we are all Keynesians now'. Yet capitalism remained prone to crises that even Keynesian policy could not remedy. And economics was still founded on neoclassical, mathematical fantasy. Hence the real crisis of capitalism in the 1970s was interpreted as the failure of Keynesian policy. States came under the control of right-wing ideologues. A neoliberal policy regime reversed the social justice of the Keynesian interlude. Liberal economics turned easily towards neoliberal economics. Economics reverted to its historic role of making money for already rich people. Economics is tragic politically – it serves the hegemonic interests of the entrepreneur, the rich people. Economics is a tragedy of intellect. Its combination of theoretical simplicity with methodological sophistication is fatal to disciplinary self-criticism and external critique. Economics is tragedy for poor people yearning for something far different from the world of intellect. Economics needs to change – funda*mentally*.

FOUR
Political power

§ Policy is produced and enforced by political institutions in centres of power. These centres are immediately composed of legislative institutions, as with President, Senate and House of Representatives in the USA, or Parliament in the UK, and vast bureaucracies administering the departments of government – State Department, Treasury and so on. Yet this only begins to describe merely the obvious components of the state apparatus. The legislatures and government bureaucracies of modern states are surrounded by thousands of specialized private institutions inhabited by the crème de la crème of the policy elite. 'Lawmakers' do not craft policy documents. They do not think through the complex logics of policy prescriptions. Experts in lobbying firms and think tanks do the work of conceiving and writing the documents that give direction and coherence to policy formulations. Hence the notion of 'the state', 'the government' or even 'political institutions' has to be expanded to include these private bureaucracies. Describing this broad set of political institutions might amount merely to a spatial-institutional cataloguing of neutral expertise if we were dealing with a democratically determined political hegemony. After all, the political supposedly lies within the realm of democracy, people vote for the party that controls the state, and the democratic state controls governance institutions. It might appear, therefore, that policy is democratically determined and expertise serves merely as facilitator. Essentially, people would get the policies they vote for. If only this were the case! The trouble is, however, that democracy is corrupted by economic power and expertise is biased in the manner described in Chapter 3. Expertise reinforces political-economic power. And finally, for the last thirty years, the entire complex of political institutions has proposed, supported, modified and enforced a neoliberal economic policy regime that is antithetical to the interests of the majority of working people. How this happened, and what complex of institutions carried it out, is the topic of this chapter.

The great U-turn

Let me begin by saying something obvious. The USA never came near to socialism. The influence of the socialist parties of the early twentieth century on the Democratic Party was limited or non-existent. The post-war period did, however, see an extension of the New Deal into various government programmes to increase public welfare, while the 'Great Society' and the 'War on Poverty' of the 1960s vastly enlarged what had been a meagre system of anti-poverty programmes. By 1970 American liberal democracy had a distinctly social democratic-Keynesian tinge to it. Even US President Nixon – and he was no liberal – assumed that the state should intervene to regulate the economy and to provide for social welfare. As we have seen, this system of state-regulated capitalism delivered high rates of economic growth along with rising real incomes for working-class people. The Eastern Establishment, made up from the elite universities, the financial institutions and the old, rich families that take a liberal Republican stance, more or less, reluctantly accepted the Keynesian compromise between capital and labour. But that compromise meant that the share of national income going to the rich declined – the highest-income 0.1 per cent of the US population (the super-rich) had received 6–9 per cent of national income before the Second World War and this fell to 2 per cent for most of the 1950s, 1960s and early to middle 1970s. Then, within a decade, the share of the top one-tenth of 1 per cent rose to 6 per cent in 1988. What happened to bring about this great U-turn?

Recall that governments, economies, social systems and cultures in the Western political democracies faced massive and continuous protests in the 1960s and early 1970s. If anything, the anti-war movement in the USA, previously a bastion of repressed social stability (in the McCarthy years of the cold war), represented the leading edge of global discontent. (I was on the March on the Pentagon, when the government had to be protected by thousands of troops with fixed bayonets.) Students and workers all over the world looked to Berkeley for the latest in rebellious culture. And it was exactly the sons and daughters of rich and upper-middle-class parents who formed the vanguard of protest at the huge anti-war demonstrations. Something had to be done to restore ruling-class power.

In 1971, Lewis F. Powell, a corporate lawyer, member of the boards of directors of eleven corporations and about to be appointed to the US Supreme Court, wrote a memo to his friend Eugene Sydnor, Jr, director of the US Chamber of Commerce. A few sentences from the memo convey its essential message:

No thoughtful person can question that the American economic system is under broad attack ... The most disquieting voices joining the chorus of criticism come from perfectly respectable elements of society ... One of the bewildering paradoxes of our time is the extent to which the enterprise system tolerates, if not participates in, its own destruction ... The overriding first need is for businessmen to recognize that the ultimate issue may be survival – survival of what we call the free enterprise system, and all that this means for the strength and prosperity of America and the freedom of our people ... It is time for American business – which has demonstrated the greatest capacity in all history to produce and to influence consumer decisions – to apply their great talents vigorously to the preservation of the system itself. (Powell 2006)

With that, Powell outlined a set of strategies for a counter-revolution led by business; it should use political power aggressively and with determination – without embarrassment and without the reluctance that has been so characteristic of American business. With an activist-minded Supreme Court, the future Justice concluded, the judiciary might be the most important instrument for social, economic and political change. So much for judicial impartiality. Usually, patricians are careful not to leave paper trails like this. The Powell memo was leaked to Jack Anderson, a liberal syndicated columnist, and became widely known. Powell's memo is best seen as symptomatic of one faction of elite thinking at the time. We can surmise many other such declarations of renewed ruling-class conscience. As a result, corporations began to spend $900 million a year on political action. They called for class warfare, for business to recapture and reorient the Republican Party (and later, with Clinton, the Democratic Party as well), for alliance with the Christian Right, for the disciplining of students and labour. 'During the 1970s, the political wing of the nation's corporate sector staged one of the most remarkable campaigns in the pursuit of power in recent history, so that by the early 1980s corporations had a level of influence not seen since the boom days of the 1920s' (Edsall 1985: 107; Harvey 2005).

What *is* the connection between economic power – the power of corporations, banks and wealthy people – and political power – the power wielded by the President, Congress, the cabinet and senior government officials over economic policy? In *The Global Class War* Jeff Faux (2006) argues that the US state, the most powerful on earth, is an integral part of capitalist class power. The 'governing class' in Washington, Faux points out, is overwhelmingly made up of corporate executives and corporate lawyers – he gives many examples from recent Republican and Democratic administrations. Beyond providing virtually every cabinet officer and senior official, corporations also finance political campaigns, provide well-paying jobs for defeated candidates and retired civil servants, give grants to think tanks and fellowships to journalists, pay lobbyists and influential insiders, and so on. Corporate influence, Faux says, is so pervasive in the federal and state governments that it is invisible (in the sense of being taken for granted – see Chapter 1), while the process of government is overwhelmed by the influence of money (e.g. $4.5 billion spent by the top 100 lobbyists between 1998 and 2004). The last instance of a law passing despite significant business opposition was the Occupational Health and Safety Act of 1975. The rich, Faux continues, wield influence through access to politicians purchased through lobbying and campaign contributions. And the class of rich people – members of the boards of directors of major corporations and political and cultural celebrities – is actually quite small, perhaps 50,000 people in the USA, and lesser numbers elsewhere. Breaking into that class is getting more difficult. The share of income it receives is getting larger. Their ownership of wealth is becoming more concentrated (the wealthiest 1 per cent of households own 33 per cent of all corporate shares). Faux wonders why such concentrations of power and wealth are tolerated in democracies. Toleration, he concludes, depends on convincing people that they have the opportunity to lead a satisfactory life.

The Counter-Establishment

Sydney Blumenthal, in *The Rise of the Counter-Establishment* (1986), tells a similar story, but with a different emphasis. 'When government created a bureaucracy of regulators and planners,' he says, 'business created its own cadre to cope with them,' and he lists 12,000 Washington lawyers representing business before regulatory agencies and federal courts, 9,000 lobbyists, 42,000 trade association personnel, and so on, making up a 'standing army' of 69,000 (in the early 1980s) that influences the legislative process. By the 1970s, Blumenthal says, business had become profoundly disillusioned with the post-Second World War Keynesian consensus, believing that federal regulatory agencies hampered productivity, that government expenditures produced inflation, and taxes inhibited investment. Business saw Washington as controlled by the liberal (New Deal) establishment. And business felt isolated, exposed and subject to mounting criticism – poll after poll in the early 1970s showed businessmen to be held in as low repute as politicians. Instead business wanted the state to serve its (business) interests. To make government work in their favour, they had to increase their investment in politics. Blumenthal calls the result the Counter-Establishment. This was an alliance of conservative intellectuals who thought in terms of the political economy as a whole; and corporate managers newly converted to the importance of ideas and newly encouraged to be more conservative and socially conscious. By the middle 1980s, he says, there were dozens of Counter-Establishment think tanks, foundations and institutes devoted to almost every public policy area. Some, like the Hoover Institute and the American Enterprise Association (AEA), had been founded earlier, and were revitalized. The American Enterprise Institute (AEI), successor to the AEA, had been little more than a letterhead (with only two resident scholars in 1969), but by 1985 had a staff of 176, with 90 adjunct scholars and an annual budget of $12.6 million raised from corporations. Others were more recent. The Heritage Foundation was begun in 1973, had a staff of 105, a budget of $10.5 million from new Sun Belt money, the Coors family, and thousands of small donations from conservative individuals mobilized through direct mailings. Blumenthal stresses the active role of American frontier Sun Belt entrepreneurs in the construction of this counter-revolution – self-made businesspeople, who saw the corporation as the projection of the individual, who preached economic, free market egoism – 'free enterprise, individualism, survival of the fittest – these are their dogmas' (Blumenthal 1986: 57). Wealthy Sun Belt entrepreneurs felt excluded by the Eastern Establishment. They saw crisis in the establishment as an opportunity to redeem the American dream of individual opportunity. The Counter-Establishment was a way of systematizing their power in a new political system.

Blumenthal stresses the importance of William Simon, a full partner at Salomon Brothers investment bank, named by Nixon as energy tsar in 1973, who later served as Treasury Secretary. In his book *A Time for Truth*, Simon described what he called the liberal 'New Despotism' as a morbid assault on ability and justice, driven by an ideology of equality, propagated by the political intelligentsia of the social democracies – an intelligentsia 'as stubborn and ruthless a ruling elite as any in history' (Simon 1979: 232). The instrument of redemption, for Simon, was the investment of multimillions from business in a 'counterintelligentsia' that would assail the fortress of liberalism. Simon's role was to accumulate money for this, from the John M. Olin Foundation, of which he became president, and other conservative and neoconservative business sources like the Institute for Educational Affairs, which Simon founded with the neoconservative Irving Kristol.

As governor of California in the 1960s, and as Republican presidential candidate in 1980, Ronald Reagan was directly supported by Sun Belt entrepreneurs. Blumenthal (1986: 33) describes the Reagan administration as 'a vast web of ideological patronage'. Whereas previous Republican administrations had been staffed by businessmen and party professionals, now hundreds of officials with links to the Counter-Establishment were appointed to key jobs. The immediate circle around Reagan had a strong commitment to Counter-Establishment think tanks – thirty-four from the AEI for instance. More than half the senior appointments to the first Reagan administration were from (right-wing) think tanks (Abelson 2002: 133). They immediately set about informing him of supply-side economics – an update of Say's law that supply creates its own demand – including the hilarious Laffer curve, in which a tax cut, by increasing business incentive, would produce greater production, raise government revenues and pay for itself. Even so, the Reagan years saw the biggest fiscal deficits in US history: Reagan, the anti-Keynesian, anti-state ideologue, solved the stagflation of the 1970s through Military Keynesian policies. Alongside the election of Reagan, Margaret Thatcher became Prime Minister in Britain in 1979, and Helmut Kohl was elected Chancellor of West Germany in 1982. Together these right-wing politicians launched an all-out attack on social democracy.

Thus, the period from the middle 1970s to the late 1980s witnessed a secular shift in political-economic opinion in all the capitals of the West. Business reacted to a Keynesian welfare state that they thought had gone too far: income had flowed down to the poorest people, instead of up to them; and the state had tolerated, even mollycoddled, student and worker protesters. There were plenty of places, such as the Trilateral Commission or the Business Roundtable, where these disturbing tendencies could be discussed. And Blumenthal is probably right in arguing that new Sun Belt entrepreneurs – what might be called the Western Establishment – were the leading faction within the capitalist class pushing the new doctrine. But the extent of elite reaction, and its commonality of themes, indicates a broad consensus occurring through simultaneous realizations by thousands of increasingly like-minded patriotic, conservative people. Then too capitalism was changing. Production was reorienting towards high-technology methods and products. Globalization increased the intensity of competition. Finance capital was on the ascendancy – no longer outdated notions of investments made for life in trusted, established companies, but more investments made for a few days, maybe a few minutes, in activities that once had been the purview of disreputable gamblers. While the reaction of the renewed elite took several forms, many were amazingly similar to Powell's agenda. In particular, a leading institutional role was played by a new, ideologically more activist, set of right-wing think tanks. The Heritage Foundation produced an 1,000-page blueprint for change called *Mandate for Leadership: Policy Management in a Conservative Administration*, and Reagan, as President, gave a copy to all members of his cabinet with instructions to read it; the Foundation claimed that 60 per cent of its proposals were adopted by the Reagan administration (ibid.: 135). The late 1970s to early 1980s counter-revolution made rightist commitment not only acceptable, but even necessary for policy formation – it took a right-wing intellect to formulate a right-wing policy. The counter-revolution positioned hundreds of think tanks at the centre of policy formation. Think tanks have remained there ever since.

Think tanks

Think tanks are non-profit research institutes that employ expertise to provide advice and ideas on issues of policy. The name 'think tank' has been around only since the 1950s, but the Brookings Institution, founded in 1916, was nevertheless probably the first. Until 1970, there were only a few think tanks, mostly focused on offering non-partisan policy and military advice to the US government. After 1970, the number of think tanks increased rapidly, so that there are now about three hundred significant think tanks, and thousands of others with lesser significance, in the USA, mainly located in Washington. Of the think tanks with clear ideological allegiance, two-thirds are conservative, and one-third are liberal (Rich 2004: 20). FAIR (Fairness in Accuracy and Media) conducts an annual survey of think tank citations in the mainstream US news media. FAIR finds a consistent preference for citing conservative think tanks over progressive ones. The 2006 survey of think tank citations – based on 27,229 citations in major newspapers and TV and radio transcripts that appear in the Nexis database – found that 40 per cent of citations in 2005 were of conservative or centre-right groups, 47 per cent were of centrist groups and 13 per cent were of centre-left or progressive groups. The centrist Brookings Institution was the most widely cited think tank, and the second-most quoted think tank was the conservative Heritage Foundation. The leading left-leaning think tank, the centre-left Urban Institute, received less than a third of Heritage's total and approximately one-fifth of Brookings's citations (Dolny 2006). We have to remember that the news media are big businesses, are controlled by even bigger ones (Disney, General Electric ...), and carry economic news ... in their 'business section'!

Political power

Some of the most important think tanks influencing economic policy include, from the political right to the political left:

The Heritage Foundation Founded in 1973, the Heritage Foundation formulates and promotes conservative public policies based on the principles of free enterprise, limited government, individual freedom, traditional American values and a strong national defence. The Heritage Foundation has an annual budget of $36 million. It has, since 1995, published an annual Index of Economic Freedom that offers 'the international community' a 'user-friendly index of economic freedom' as a tool for policy-makers and investors. The index rates countries according to their 'degree of economic freedom', by which is meant low levels of government intervention in the economy, few restrictions on foreign investment, little bank regulation and little government control over wages and prices – in 2006 Hong Kong, Singapore and Ireland were most economically free; Venezuela ranked 152nd (Heritage Foundation 2006).

American Enterprise Institute for Public Policy Research AEI's purposes are to defend the principles and improve the institutions of American freedom and democratic capitalism – limited government, private enterprise, individual liberty and responsibility, vigilant and effective defence and foreign policies, political accountability and open debate. Some 175 people work at AEI's headquarters in Washington, DC, and in addition about a hundred adjunct scholars and fellows, mainly at US research universities, conduct research for AEI and participate in its conferences. AEI is financed by donations from corporations, foundations and individuals and by investment earnings from an internal endowment. Its revenues are about $25 million a year. AEI publishes essays and research reports such as *Economic Outlook*, *Development Policy Outlook* and *Latin American Outlook* (American Enterprise Institution 2006).

The Brookings Institution The Brookings Institution is devoted to 'independent research and innovative policy solutions'. In the 1930s the Brookings Institute was an important source of the Keynesian-type thinking that formed part of Roosevelt's New Deal. Brookings scholars try to provide high-quality research, policy recommendations and analysis on a full range of public policy issues to policy-makers and the media. The Brookings Institution took in $35 million in donations in 2005. It claims political neutrality – it wants to 'inform the public debate, not advance a political agenda'. Even so, since the middle 1990s the Brookings Institution has collaborated with AEI in an AEI–Brookings Joint Center for Regulatory Studies (Brookings Institution 2006).

The Institute for International Economics (IIE) The IIE is a research institution devoted to the study of international economic policy. It offers 'objective analysis and concrete solutions to key international economic problems' to government officials and legislators, business and labour leaders, management and staff at international organizations, university-based scholars and their students, other research institutions and non-governmental organizations, the media and the public at large. In 2001, the institute helped create the Center for Global Development to address poverty and development issues in low-income countries. The institute's annual budget is about $8 million (Institute for International Economics 2006).

Institute for Policy Studies (IPS) The IPS says that: 'For more than four decades, IPS has transformed ideas into action for peace, justice, and the environment. The Institute has strengthened and linked social movements through articulation of root principles and fundamental rights, research and analysis on current events and issues, and connections to policymakers, academics, and activists at all levels.' The IPS mission is to 'strengthen social movements' and 'empower people to build healthy and democratic societies in communities, the US, and the world ... IPS public scholars pursue their work with a common set of 10 core values and principles: peace, justice, environmental sustainability, participatory democracy, human rights, freedom, dignity, diversity, community, and international law'. IPS somehow operates on an annual budget of $2.5 million. At any point in time, the IPS is involved in a series of projects. The IPS Global project is focused on Alternative Visions: promoting alternatives to globalization, with emphasis on issues of trade, outsourcing and the reshaping of global governance institutions (Institute for Policy Studies 2006).

In terms of their ability to influence policy, think tanks have several advantages over academic experts in universities. They hire whom they want, allowing the build-up of teams of researchers sharing a similar political orientation. They publish books themselves without going through academic refereeing processes. And they are usually located in Washington, and other capital cities, close to government and the media. Think tanks are funded primarily by corporations and foundations. They supply experts to testify to Congress, write articles for the op-ed pages of newspapers, and appear as TV commentators. Think tanks accumulate expertise from academics, from former government officials and from the research of their own resident scholars, who often serve in government and governance institutions. The policy elite circulates within a universe composed of think tanks, investment banks, governance institutions, academia and the government bureaucracies – especially, in the case of the economic policy elite, the Treasury Department.

But before we can discuss the role of government bureaucracy in the political construction of policy I need to mention something else, a matter of some significance – merely the corrupt nature of Western democracy.

Freedom and democracy

Let us begin a deconstruction of Western democracy by talking about free elections. The main thing about 'free elections' is that they are not free. Elections are expensive. In Fordist countries, where demand and taste are produced by advertising, political opinion too is made by media persuasion. Political candidates are marketed in essentially the same way as cocoa-puffs. And as with cereal, the emphasis is on appearance – it's all image, with little content – with the real policy stance hidden behind a Technicolored façade. These images cost a lot to produce and even more to distribute – especially because the image of the politician as a nice guy with a nice family striding forward with confidence has to compete with images of all those other commodities that are nice tasting and look even better. Since the 1976 election (when $67 million was spent by presidential candidates) politicians have spent a lot to get elected. Candidates in the US presidential election in 2004 spent a combined total of $881 million, congressional candidates spent a further $498 million, and senatorial candidates $245 million, with the election having a total cost of $4,000 million. About one-tenth of 1 per cent of the US adult population (231,000 people) donates over $2,000 each to political campaigns, and these donations make up 75 per cent of the total contributions; 26,000 people donate 36 per cent of total contributions. This money comes overwhelmingly (74 per cent) from business sources rather than labour (3 per cent). A congressional candidate has to raise $1 million for each election, and a senatorial candidate $7 million. In the past, the Republican Party raised twice as much as the Democratic Party, but this has changed, and now both parties raise similar amounts – from the same rich businesspeople (Center for Responsive Politics 2006a). A candidate must get large amounts of money from a group of 100,000–150,000 rich people to be able to run a campaign. Candidates who do not appeal to this group of rich people, or are not wealthy themselves, never have a chance. They raise a few million dollars at most, they do not appear on television, they are not seen in media debates, and the electorate never hears of them. Rich people choose political candidates.

Once in office, politicians are kept in line by lobbying. In addition to campaign contributions to elected officials and candidates, companies, labour unions and other organizations spend $2.2 billion each year to lobby Congress and federal agencies. Some special interests retain lobbying firms, many located along Washington's K Street, known for its think tanks, lobbyists and advocacy groups; others have lobbyists working in-house. The pharmaceutical industry spends $636 million a year, electric power $385 million, mortgage banks $250 million, commercial banks $218 million, securities and investment firms $209 million, insurance companies $332 million and business associations $125 million. In terms of class, finance, insurance and real estate spend almost ten times as much as labour on lobbying. Altogether the financial sector spends $500 million a year on campaign contributions and lobbying. And 130 former members of Congress are lobbyists (Center for Responsive Politics 2006b). The number of registered lobbyists in Washington has doubled since 2000 to 34,750, while the amount that lobbyists charge their clients has also doubled. Lobbying employs nearly half the politicians and congressional aides who return to the private sector when they leave Congress, and salaries have risen to about $300,000 a year for the best-connected congressional aides who 'move downtown' from Capitol Hill or the administration. New corporate clients pay $20,000 to $25,000 a month in retainer's fees to lobbying firms (Birnbaum 2005). And politicians get richer while in office. One study has found that during the boom years of 1993–98 a majority of US senators were trading stocks, and beating the market by 12 percentage points a year on average. By comparison, corporate insiders beat the market by 5 per cent, and typical households underperformed relative to the market by 1.4 per cent. This cannot be random or simply the result of good financial advice. These people are using their inside information to get richer.

So it is perfectly clear that enormous sums of money are spent during elections, through campaign contributions, and, subsequent to elections, on lobbying those elected, as 'normal' components of US-style democracy. Why is this money invested in the democratic process? The phrase used in polite, political discourse to describe what is bought by campaign contributions and lobbying is 'access'

95

– that is, elected representatives who rely on money for their position respond positively to big donors by listening to what they have to say about policy. Money buys access and access is used to influence policy-making. This, however, is merely the polite version – told by people within the loop. We, the people outside the charmed circle of commentary that big money dominates, do not have to be polite (although I am employed by a university that tries its best to get donations to the college endowment ... from rich people). What does big money buy? Beyond access and influence, money buys control. That is, campaign contributions in the hundreds of millions, and lobbying that costs billions a year, ensure control over the democratic, political process. By whom? By the class of people and the economic activities that *can* contribute money in the millions. That means rich people, the 0.1 per cent of rich people who donate 75 per cent of campaign contributions, and the corporations that provide 90 per cent of the lobbying funds. It would be unrealistic to assume that money is spent to ensure that politics serves the interests of the poor – giving to the poor is left to philanthropy. It is more realistic to say that big money goes into the political process to ensure that candidates stand, politicians are chosen, the government operates, and policies are formulated, in the interests of the rich. The interests of the rich are: protecting the right to make and keep money and the right to make lots more in the future. Recall from Chapter 1 the following phrase: within the richest 1 per cent of the US population, the super-rich – that one-thousandth of the population (145,000 people) making an average of $3 million a year – doubled its share of total national income between 1980 and 2002 while the share earned by the bottom 90 per cent of people fell. The democratic process has been bought, successfully, to ensure that the existing class structure not only continues, but becomes even more dominated by the super-rich. Money is spent to use government, governance and the political process to deepen and broaden, through policy, the arena within which money can be made. For example, in the period 1945–80, during the Keynesian policy regime, the federal tax rate for the highest income bracket varied between 70 and 90 per cent. The rate dropped precipitously in the 1980s, with the advent of neoliberalism, to less than 30 per cent in 1990, and has remained there ever since. And now President G. W. Bush wants to lower it again. Money is used to propagate, protect and enforce the policy regime that has been proven to generate more money for the rich, less for the majority and very little for the poor. Money is used to buy adherence to policies that extend the range of moneymaking to the entire world. The policy regime that results is called neoliberalism.

So we have a self-reinforcing circle in which money buys control of government and governance and these extend the ability of big money to make more. Is this any way to run democracy?

A couple of times a year, the US news media report on the corruption of particular politicians 'caught with their hands in the till', so to speak. For example, in 2005 a Texas grand jury indicted House Majority Leader Tom DeLay (R-TX) on a charge of criminally conspiring with two political associates to inject illegal corporate contributions into the 2002 state elections that helped the Republican Party reorder the congressional map in Texas and cement its control of the House in Washington. The indictment forced DeLay, one of the Republican Party's most powerful leaders and fund-raisers, to resign. DeLay had co-led the 'K Street Project' – a project of the Republican Party, begun in 1995, to pressure lobbying firms in Washington to hire only Republicans in top positions and to reward them with access to influential officials. But the point is not that individuals like DeLay are corrupt. The entire political system is corrupt. In politics all money corrupts, and a lot of money corrupts absolutely.

In Chapter 1 I discussed two theories of class control over the state: in essence, capital threatens the state through investment strikes, and capital and the state are the same elite people – hence the US Senate is called 'millionaires' row'. We can now add a third connection: capital simply buys the state. Democracy is supposed to mean one person, one vote. But in corrupt democracy it is one million dollars, one vote. This is not democracy. It is plutocracy – rule by the rich in the guise of democracy. And it is self-reinforcing plutocracy in the sense that 'campaign reform' can be carried out only by Congress, and the existing members of Congress depend on continuing campaign contributions from wealthy people to get elected – and when they leave Congress, they also become lobbyists. So when presidents speak of spreading democracy, from its home in the USA, to the rest of the world, they are speaking about spreading control by rich, American businesspeople to the entire globe. This diffusion of democracy includes the spread of a policy regime based on freedom of enterprise – particularly US-led enterprise. This regime wants to create the right business climate for enterprise to make profit, and for the profits to be freely repatriated to New York, London and other centres of global capital accumulation. Politicians support it because they believe in 'free enterprise'. They also support profit-making and wealth accumulation from the world's people because they get their cut of the money to pay for their part of the media extravaganza, the spectacle called 'elections'. And the media restrict their criticism to lambasting particularly corrupt individual politicians because most of the money spent on elections is spent on advertising carried by … the media. That is, the media themselves depend on political corruption to make money. Again, the global policy regime that comes from, and pays for, this entire corrupt system is called neoliberalism. Remember this as we go through the main institutions that construct policy. All these institutions are controlled, in the end, by presidents, senators, congressmen, prime ministers, MPs and others who come from this nasty, immoral political process.

Government bureaucracy – the Fed

The US Federal Reserve Bank system was created by Congress in 1914. The Federal Reserve Act provided for a Federal Reserve Board with five (now seven) governors appointed by the President and confirmed by the Senate, located in Washington, and twelve regional Federal Reserve Banks owned by member banks in their districts, and supervised by boards of nine directors, six of whom were to be chosen by the member banks, and three appointed by the Fed in Washington (Wells 2004). The President designates, and the Senate confirms, two members of the board to be chairman and vice-chairman, for four-year terms. The primary responsibility of the board members is the formulation of monetary policy. The seven board members constitute a majority of the twelve-member Federal Open Market Committee (FOMC), the group making key decisions affecting the cost and availability of money and credit in the US economy. The board sets reserve requirements and shares the responsibility with the Reserve Banks for discount rate policy. These two functions plus open market operations constitute the monetary policy tools of the Federal Reserve system. Members of the board routinely confer with officials of other governmental agencies, representatives of banking industry groups, officials of the central banks of other countries, members of Congress and academics. They meet frequently with Treasury officials and the President's Council of Economic Advisors, evaluating the economic climate and discussing objectives for the economy. Governors also discuss the international monetary system with central bankers of other countries and are in close contact with the heads of US agencies that make foreign loans and conduct foreign financial transactions. The primary responsibility of the central bank is, however, to influence the flow of money and credit in the US national economy. It does this by controlling the purchases and sales of government securities in the open market, actions that in turn affect the availability of money and credit in the economy. The boards of directors of the Federal Reserve Banks also initiate changes in the discount rate, the rate of interest on loans made by Reserve Banks to depository institutions at the 'discount window' of the central bank. All depository institutions subject to reserve requirements set by the Federal Reserve – including commercial banks, mutual savings banks, savings and loan associations and credit unions – have access to the discount window. Additionally, the Federal Reserve system, through the Reserve Banks, performs services for the US Treasury and other government, quasi-government and international agencies. Each year, billions of dollars are deposited in and withdrawn by various government agencies from operating accounts in the US Treasury held by the Federal Reserve Banks.

Government bureaucracy – the Treasury

The US Treasury Department, administered by the Secretary of the Treasury, appointed by the President, is the most influential agent in the making of global economic policy. The Treasury advises the President and Congress on fiscal policy. This is carried out by departments operating under the Secretary of the Treasury's supervision, including offices dealing with Domestic Finance, Economic Policy and International Affairs. The Treasury's Office of International Affairs says that it 'protects and supports economic prosperity at home by encouraging financial stability and sound economic policies abroad'. The office surveys and analyses in depth global economic and financial developments and 'engages with financial market participants, foreign governments, international financial institutions, and in multilateral fora to develop and promote good policies'. The office is headed by an Under-Secretary and an Assistant Secretary of International Affairs, with Deputy Assistant Secretaries for the various regions of the world, and for trade and investment policy, international finance and debt, international monetary and financial policy and technical assistance. The Office of Development Policy works with governments and development institutions, particularly the multilateral development banks, the IMF, and advises on international and regional organizations such as the G7/G8, APEC and the Summit of the Americas. Essentially it is the Treasury and the Office of International Affairs which forms any US administration's global economic policy regime. (I have interviewed a former official at the Treasury Department, who served as US alternate executive director to the World Bank and as principal Deputy Assistant Secretary for International Affairs. He told me that his vote at the World Bank was controlled by the Treasury. On non-controversial issues, he was allowed to follow the already agreed policy position, and vote without consulting the Treasury. On controversial or supremely important issues, he phoned the Treasury for instructions on how to vote.)

Who makes the significant decisions on global economic policy at the Treasury? There are no formal studies of the US Treasury Department. Robert Rubin, Secretary of the Treasury 1995–99, has, however, written a lengthy account of his time there (Rubin 2003). Reading his account of US decisions on the financial crisis in Mexico in 1995 (the 'peso crisis'), the following scenario emerges. The Secretary of the Treasury is appointed by, and reports to, the US President – in Rubin's case, this was William Clinton. The Secretary receives expert reports from the upper echelons of Treasury experts, specifically in this case from the Deputy Secretary, at that time Laurence Summers. At times of crisis, an inner group of officials meets frequently: in this crisis the group consisted of Rubin, Summers and Alan Greenspan, Chairman of the Board of Governors of the Federal Reserve of the United States, and 'a conservative free-marketeer and an economist grounded in both macro policy and an acute empirical understanding of the American economy' (ibid.: 8). For important decisions, where large sums of money are involved, key members of Congress, such as the leaders of both parties and the chair of the Senate Banking Committee, are phoned and called on personally (by Summers), and in some cases senior officials, such as Rubin, Greenspan and the Secretary of State, appear before the Senate and House Banking Committees. The Secretary assembles a group mainly of Treasury officials at the assistant and under-secretary levels, with one (Dan Zelikow, Deputy Assistant Secretary for International Affairs at the US Treasury Department) acting as 'head of the Mexico task force'. The group also meets with the top officials at the National Security Council. The group consults regularly with the managing director of the IMF, at that time Michel Camdessus, and the deputy director of the IMF, Stanley Fischer, formerly chair of the Economics Department at MIT. Rubin was also in constant touch with his counterpart at the finance ministry in Mexico, Guillermo Ortiz, Secretary of Finance, and a graduate (in economics) of Stanford University. Rubin had no time to consult with the Group of 7 (G7) countries, much to their annoyance, in making policy of global significance. At the height of the crisis, the finance minister of Mexico came to Washington to negotiate with the IMF and the US Treasury Department. Summers and the Assistant Secretary for International Affairs also travelled secretly on a US Air Force plane to talk with the President of Mexico, Ernesto Zedillo, an economist with a doctorate from Yale University, about 'our economists'... proposals to reform aspects of Mexico's economic policy and reestablish confidence' (ibid.: 27). The result was an agreement signed in the Cash Room of the US Treasury involving US currency swaps and loan guarantees worth $20 billion; an IMF stand-by credit agreement of US $17.7 billion; a Bank for International Settlements $10 billion line of credit; and a Bank of Canada offer of US $1 billion. The US assistance was provided via the Treasury's Exchange Stabilization Fund, without the approval of Congress. A similar procedure was used in the South Korean financial crisis of 1997, where the US position (reached by top Treasury and Federal Reserve officials) was to bring about a 'structural reform' of a system involving Korean state officials in bank lending ('crony capitalism') that would 'bring back market confidence' (ibid.: 233). In this case, the US State Department was involved in decisions affecting a country bordering on North Korea.

Based on Rubin's account, the following individual actors were involved in economic policy decisions centred on, but not confined to, the US Treasury Department:

- Robert Rubin, Secretary of the Treasury, formerly director of the National Economic Council, and before that co-senior partner at Goldman Sachs, an investment banking company. Rubin was educated at Harvard University in economics and law. His position on economic policy, sometimes called 'Rubinomics', is based on forceful deficit reduction, free global markets and investments in education training and the environment.
- Alan C. Greenspan, Chairman of the Board of Governors of the US Federal Reserve Bank, with degrees in Economics from New York University. Greenspan worked as an economic analyst at the Conference Board, a business- and industry-oriented think tank in New York City, and then was chairman and president of Townsend-Greenspan & Co., Inc., an economic consulting firm in New York City, and from 1974 to 1977 chairman of the Council of Economic Advisors. Greenspan was long associated with the extreme right-wing writer Ayn Rand and was a proponent, with her, of an exaggeratedly laissez-faire capitalism.
- Laurence Summers, Deputy Secretary to Rubin, formerly Under-Secretary of the Treasury for International Affairs and Chief Econ-omist for the World Bank. Summers is the son of two economists at the University of Pennsylvania and is a nephew of two Nobel laureates in economics: Paul Samuelson and Kenneth Arrow. He has an economics degree from MIT, and a PhD from Harvard

University, and taught at MIT and Harvard. Summers is a zealous proponent of free trade and globalization. Between 1999 and 2001 he served as Secretary of the Treasury, and from 2001 to 2006 as president of Harvard University.

- Jeffrey R. Shafer, Assistant Secretary and subsequently Under-Secretary for International Affairs of the US Treasury, responsible for international economic and financial issues, focusing on strengthening economic growth and financial stability in both developed and developing countries, fostering financial market development and liberalization, and strengthening the IMF and multilateral development banks. Previously he held a series of high-level positions at the Organization for Economic Cooperation and Development (OECD), and prior to that served with the Federal Reserve Bank of New York, the Federal Reserve Board and the Council of Economic Advisors. He has a BA in Economics from Princeton University and an MPhil. and PhD degrees in Economics from Yale University. He later became vice-chairman of Citigroup's Public Sector Client Group working with governments in Asia, Latin America and Europe on financial stabilization, liability management, debt issuance and privatization.

- David A. Lipton, Assistant Secretary and later Under-Secretary for International Affairs of the Treasury. He was an economist at the International Monetary Fund from 1981 to 1989, and worked for the United Nations Development Programme and the World Institute for Development Economics Research. He has a BA in Economics from Wesleyan University and both an MA and a PhD in Economics from Harvard University. While Deputy Assistant Secretary for Eastern Europe and the former Soviet Union, he designed and implemented a policy of US leadership in support of comprehensive, market-oriented reform in transitional economies and worked to involve the G7 and IFIs in that process.

- Timothy F. Geithner was a long-term Treasury official, who served as Under-Secretary for International Affairs from 1998 to 2001. He later became director of the Policy Development and Review Department in the IMF, with a central role in the design and implementation of Fund policies and in the review of its financial programmes and assessments of member economies, and then president and CEO of the Federal Reserve Bank of New York. Before joining the Treasury, he worked for Kissinger Associates, Inc. He has a degree from Dartmouth College in Government and Asian Studies and a master's in International Economics and East Asian Studies from the Johns Hopkins School for Advanced

International Studies. Geithner serves as chairman of the G10's Committee on Payment and Settlement Systems of the Bank for International Settlements. He is a member of the Council on Foreign Relations and the Group of Thirty, a member of the board of directors of the Center for Global Development in Washington, DC, a member of the board of trustees of the RAND Corporation and a trustee of the Economic Club of New York.

- Sylvia M. Mathews, chief of staff to Secretary of the Treasury Robert E. Rubin and formerly deputy director of the Office of Management and Budget, assistant to the president, deputy chief of staff to the president. Mathews is a graduate of Harvard University and is a Rhodes Scholar. Later she became President, Global Development Program of the Bill and Melinda Gates Foundation.

- Dan Zelikow, Deputy Assistant Secretary for International Affairs at the US Treasury Department. Before managing the US financial support programme for Mexico in 1995 as head of the Mexico Task Force, he directed the Treasury's overseas technical cooperation, involving finance ministries and central banks. He later became a managing director of J.P. Morgan, an investment banking company, with responsibility for multilateral financial institutions, export credit agencies and key emerging-markets clients. He also coordinates J.P. Morgan's activities to facilitate Iraq's financial reconstruction and helped to found the Trade Bank of Iraq.

- Edwin M. Truman, director of the Division of International Finance of the Board of Governors of the Federal Reserve System from 1977 to 1998. He was Assistant Secretary for International Affairs of the US Treasury from December 1998 to January 2001, and has been senior fellow since 2001 in the Institute for International Economics, a Washington think tank. His areas of speciality are international monetary economics, international debt problems, economic development and European economic integration.

- Laura D'Andrea Tyson, chair of the President's Council of Economic Advisors from 1993 to 1995 and chair of the National Economic Council from 1995 to 1996. From 1998 to 2001, she was dean of the Haas School of Business at the University of California, Berkeley. She has been a member of the Council on Foreign Relations since 1987, and is a director on several corporate boards. She is currently dean of the London Business School. Tyson has a degree in economics from Smith College and a PhD in Economics from the Massachusetts Institute of Technology, and has been on the faculty of the Economics Department at Princeton University and a professor of economics and business administration at the University of California, Berkeley.

- Michael Froman, chief of staff of the Department of the Treasury and Treasury Secretary Robert E. Rubin's adviser on international and domestic economic policy, financial regulation, enforcement, tax, budget, management and communications issues. Previously, Froman was Treasury Deputy Assistant Secretary for Eurasia and the Middle East, from January 1993 to December 1995, and director for International Economic Affairs on the National Economic Council and the National Security Council at the White House, where he worked on a wide range of international trade and foreign investment policies. He is now president and chief executive officer of CitiInsurance, the international insurance operation of Citigroup, and fellow at the Council on Foreign Relations. Froman received a bachelor's degree in Public and International Affairs from Princeton University, a doctorate in International Relations from Oxford University and a law degree from Harvard Law School.

- Caroline Atkinson, Senior Adviser to the Secretary and Senior Deputy Assistant Secretary for International Affairs, US Treasury Department, 1997–2001. She had previously been Special Adviser for Financial Stability at the Bank of England (1994–96); Assistant Director, International Monetary Fund (1983–94); and economics and finance reporter for the *Washington Post*. Later she became a senior director of Stonebridge International (an international advisory firm to global business) and Deputy Director for the Western Hemisphere at the IMF.

What can we learn from the biographies of these key actors, the policy elite that constructs global economic policy? In terms of academic background, institutional career path and political-economic allegiances, these key actors share several similar traits and have similar career paths: training in economics, business administration and law at elite, private US universities, especially Harvard and MIT, followed sometimes by brief stints as a professor; several years' experience in the US Treasury Department, as economist and assistant or under-secretary, or in the Federal Reserve Bank; brief sojourns at an IFI, especially the IMF, or national and international banks; periods at think tanks, policy institutes and private consulting companies; and, most importantly, years spent in the private banking world centred on Wall Street, with the investment banks being of paramount importance. Economic policy is constructed in Washington by a policy elite of a few thousand experts that circulates freely between the public and private spheres, especially among investment banks, think tanks, government bureaucracies, the IFIs and elite academia – the Pentagon of political-economic power. Within this pentagon, liberals, neoliberals and conservatives get along with each other, sharing key assumptions about private ownership, free markets, competition, 'sound policy' (fiscal responsibility, monetary stability), the need for market confidence (i.e. support of the financial markets) and the necessity for international investment and free trade. Policy intervention is made under the explicit assumption that the key to economic growth is investor confidence. The policy elite is made up of clever, educated, experienced people, usually from middle- to upper-middle-class backgrounds, who are dedicated to their work in the strong belief that they are serving global humanity through the advice they give to the US government and the international regulatory system. These are people with a global social conscience exercised through philanthropy, but also through their commitment to global capitalism and economic growth as the eventual solution to problems of poverty and disease. This policy elite influences policies constructed at the IFIs in two ways: they represent US economic power and its expert knowledge; and they are the experts running the IFIs – they are all the same people.

The IFIs

The idea of establishing international financial institutions to regulate global development came as a response to growing economic problems in the inter-war years. An international bank to aid post-First World War reconstruction was first proposed at a conference in Brussels in 1920. Another proposal, to restore the gold standard, stabilized via central bank cooperation, but managed by an international convention, was discussed in Genoa in 1922. In the middle 1920s, the League of Nations helped arrange loans to stabilize the economies of several European countries. Discussion of a Bank for International Settlements (BIS) took place in 1930. Since then, regular meetings have been held in Basle, Switzerland, among central bank governors and experts from other financial agencies. The BIS conducts its own research in financial and monetary economics and collects, compiles and disseminates economic and financial statistics, supports the IMF and the World Bank, performs traditional banking functions for national central banks (e.g. gold and foreign exchange transactions), as well as trustee and agency functions. The main international financial institutions, however, were formed by governments through the 1944 Bretton Woods agreement.

The IMF, headquartered in Washington, DC, essentially serves as a short-term lender to countries in distress mainly over exchange rate depreciations and external debt. The IMF insists on 'conditionalities' to guide a country's future development before it grants a loan. This is one main form of disciplining extended through policy discourse from Washington to the capital cities of the countries of the world (Figure 1.2). The USA has 17 per cent of the voting shares in the IMF. By comparison, the collective votes of the Fund's forty-seven sub-Saharan African member countries currently amount to 5 per cent, shared among three executive directors representing the continent. In 2006 a proposed quota adjustment could reduce Africa's collective share of the vote to 2.1 per cent. A country's quota determines its financial membership commitment to the IMF, which in turn determines its voting power within the institution as well as its access to IMF financing. The main institution set up to govern development at Bretton Woods was the IBRD or World Bank, also headquartered in Washington. Of the bank, one writer says: 'its real importance lies in its influence over the developing world's policies ... In many poor countries, World Bank economists drive government strategy ... Other big aid donors ... can be influential, too. But the Bank is almost always in the lead, partly because a multilateral institution is best placed to coordinate rival flag-waving programs, but mostly because the Bank's analytical machine has more intellectual juice in it' (Mallaby 2004: 3). For the first decade of its existence, the IBRD made loans for the post-war reconstruction of Europe. As it turned towards the richer Third World countries in the 1950s, the World Bank concentrated on project loans for infrastructural development. In the late 1960s and 1970s, the World Bank added a basic needs programme aimed at poverty alleviation. In 1979 the bank began to stress programme loans to induce 'reforms' in recipient, mainly middle-income, countries – by 'reform' was meant structural adjustment lending to promote export orientation and trade liberalization. In this, the World Bank followed the lead of its senior partner, the IMF, under a division of labour that allocated 'stabilization programmes' (short-term adjustment lending) to the IMF and longer-term 'structural adjustment lending' aimed at correcting deeper 'structural' problems to the World Bank. Under this new orientation, poverty took a back seat to new driving forces of macroeconomic policy, stabilization and balance of payments adjustments, all understood within a neoliberal doctrine stressing strict limits to governmental intervention and the virtues of flexible, self-adjusting, free markets. Stabilization and structural adjustment are the main forms of disciplining by policy discoure emanating from the IFIs in Washington (Figure 1.2). Some commentators find the World Bank shifting at the end of the 1980s and in the early 1990s to a revised neoliberal model stressing market-friendly state intervention and good governance (political pluralism, accountability and the rule of law) with a renewed emphasis on social issues like poverty and education and a dedication to debt reduction. Both the IMF and the World Bank now say that they are committed to global development through debt relief for poor Third World countries and to poverty eradication. Again, this is a subtle, gentle, 'generous' form of discipline carried by policy discourse to Third World countries. At any time the economies of 120 nation-states, and the livelihoods of 2.5 billion people, might be under their direct supervision, even their yearly inspection, within what used to be called, and is still best termed, 'structural adjustment', but is now more charitably termed 'poverty alleviation' or 'Millennium Development Goals'.

We have to understand this policy turn in the context of mounting criticism. Third World social movements have increasingly called for debts to the First World to be eradicated. Moral outrage in the developed countries tended to focus on the issue of debt relief for poor countries. Conventional, and even conservative, opinion had, by the late 1980s, reached the conclusion that debt levels were unsustainable, and that some kind of organized relief was necessary. While the debt crises of the 1980s mainly concerned middle-income Third World countries, such as Mexico, Brazil and Argentina, in the 1990s the main emphasis of IMF/World Bank debt management shifted towards the lowest-income Third World countries. Loans to these very poor countries had been made mainly from official sources, with government-to-government loans, export credits, official development assistance and loans from the IMF, World Bank and regional development banks (Birdsall and Williamson 2002: 13–21). The Highly Indebted Poor Countries (HIPC) initiative was started in 1996 after widespread and increasingly well-informed criticism of the Bretton Woods institutions, led by Jubilee 2000, a faith-based coalition that believed that the 2,000th anniversary of the birth of Christ was an opportune time for a 'jubilee' in the form of a forgiving of debts. The HIPC programme combines debt reduction with 'policy reform' aimed at raising growth rates and reducing poverty in the world's poorest countries. The HIPC initiative was intended to manage, and even 'resolve' in the IMF's optimistic language, the debt problems of the most heavily indebted poor countries (originally forty-one countries, mostly in Africa) with a total debt of about $200 billion. In these countries debt service obligations consumed large parts of

107

the countries' export earnings. Half of the 615 million people in the current HIPC countries live on less than $1 a day. The HIPC initiative, in the IMF's (2000) words, 'seeks a permanent solution to these countries' debt problems by combining substantial debt reduction with policy reforms to raise long-term growth and reduce poverty'. By adopting policies judged 'sound by the international community', debt relief to the eventual extent of $60 billion would be granted. As a mere seven countries qualified for assistance in the first three years of the facility's operation, the HIPC initiative was 'enhanced' in 1999 to provide interim debt relief, between the decision and completion points that immediately reduced debt service costs. The enhanced facility joined debt relief more obviously with poverty reduction. To qualify for assistance under the HIPC initiative, or to get concessional loans from the IMF or the World Bank, countries have to prepare poverty reduction strategies with the participation of members of civil society. As the World Bank explains: 'A country reaches the completion point once it has implemented the reforms agreed to at the decision point and it has also satisfactorily implemented a Poverty Reduction Strategy and maintained sound macroeconomic policies.' At that point, the country is granted irrevocable debt relief. The Poverty Reduction Strategy Papers (PRSPs) are then endorsed by the boards of the IMF and the World Bank as the basis for the institutions' concessional loans and for relief under the enhanced HIPC initiative. Donors, including the IMF and the World Bank, provide advice and expertise. Twenty-nine countries are receiving debt relief under the HIPC initiative. Of these, eighteen have passed through to the 'completion' point and are receiving irrevocable debt relief. Eleven have reached their 'decision' points and are receiving interim debt relief. In 2006 the World Bank agreed to provide $37 billion in debt relief over forty years to completion-point HIPCs as part of their participation in the Multilateral Debt Relief Initiative (MDRI). This is based on an agreement signed in 2005 at a G8 summit in Gleneagles, Scotland, whereby G8 leaders pledged to cancel the debt of the world's most indebted countries, most of which are located in Africa. Nevertheless, developing-country debt (including middle-income countries) continued to rise from $500 billion in 1980 to $1 trillion in 1985 and around $2 trillion in 2000. What the IMF calls the forty-one 'HIPC countries' (i.e. the lowest-income countries) had an increase in total indebtedness from $60 billion in 1980 to $105 billion in 1985, $190 billion in 1990 and $205 billion in 2000 (IMF 2000).

The World Bank and the IMF operate primarily as bankers to the central banks of nation-states. They cooperate on a daily basis with finance ministries, with central banks and with the big private banks. These private banks have power over development policy formation because they control access to capital accumulations through financial markets. Any conception of the regulation of global development by quasi-public financial institutions has to take the broader connection with the banking world into account. This alliance of powerful institutions in the USA operates within a broader context of international institutions, such as the Organization for Economic Cooperation and Development (OECD), representing thirty industrial countries, and through organized, intergovernmental meetings. Since 1975, the heads of state or government of the major industrial countries have met annually to deal with major economic and political issues facing the global capitalist system. The most important meeting was the International Conference on Financing for Development, held from 18 to 22 March 2002 in Monterrey, Mexico, which led to the Monterrey Consensus on financing development. At first France, the United States, Britain, Germany, Japan and Italy were referred to as the Group of Six (G6) countries, and then with Canada in 1976 the Group of Seven, or G7, and in 1998, with the full participation of Russia, the Group of Eight, or G8. The G7/8 summit deals with macroeconomic management, international trade and relations with developing countries – including debt forgiveness. In addition, the G7/8 holds a series of ministerial meetings among finance ministers, foreign ministers and environmental ministers, among others. Since 1999 the G7/8 has also sometimes met with other 'emerging market' countries, such as Argentina, Australia, Brazil, China, India, Mexico, Russia, Saudi Arabia, South Africa, South Korea and Turkey, referred to as the G20 within the framework of the Bretton Woods institutional system. Even so, a leading issue remains why a small number of countries and finance institutions should control development in a world that considers itself to be democratic.

The Washington Consensus

As economic policies do not arise from those about to be developed, the question has to be: where do the policies practised by the IFIs come from, and whose interests do they serve?

One account widely referred to in answering such questions has been advanced by John Williamson, senior fellow at the (Washington) Institute for International Economics, who has served in positions in the World Bank and the IMF and as visiting professor at MIT and Princeton universities, as well as consultant to the UK Treasury. In 1989 Williamson (1990, 1997) coined the term 'Washington

FIGURE 4.1 The pentagon of policy power: Washington Consensus

Consensus' to refer to the policy reforms imposed when debtor countries in Latin America were called on to 'set their houses in order'
and 'submit to strong conditionality' – what Latin America needed
according to Washington. By 'Washington' Williamson meant the
political Washington of the US Congress and senior members of
the administration, and the technocratic Washington of the IFIs, the
economic agencies of the US government, the Federal Reserve Board
and the think tanks, such as the one at which he works. By 'policy'
he meant policy instruments rather than more general objectives of
policy or the eventual outcomes of policy. In terms of the institutional
formation of recent neoliberal economic policy, the term Washington
Consensus can be used to refer to some of the interest groups we
outlined earlier: the political interests that brought right-wing 'progressive reform' ideals to Washington in the middle 1970s and early
1980s, for instance; or the bureaucratic-technical interests whose
professional training in neoclassical economics proved amenable to
Hayekian and Friedmanesque persuasion. My version of the institutions producing the Washington Consensus is shown in Figure
4.1. Interestingly Williamson downplays the academic component
of policy formation, what we have called the Cambridge (Harvard)
connection, and forgets almost entirely the economic interests, well

represented in Washington, but headquartered elsewhere. The World Bank and the IMF operate primarily as bankers to the central banks of nation-states. Banks have power over policy formation because they control access to capital accumulations. And capital accumulations are institutionally controlled by commercial and investment banks. These banks are headquartered outside Washington in commercial cities like New York, Boston, London, Zurich and Tokyo.

The set of 'policy instruments' derived from the Washington Consensus, and applied to borrowing countries by the World Bank and the IMF, was said by Williamson to include:

1 Fiscal discipline: large and sustained fiscal deficits by central and provincial governments are a main source of macroeconomic dislocation in the forms of inflation, balance of payments deficits and capital flight. These deficits result from lack of political courage in matching public expenditures to the resources available. An operational budget deficit in excess of 1–2 per cent of GNP is evidence of policy failure.

2 Reducing public expenditures: when government expenditures have to be reduced the view is that spending on defence, public administration and subsidies, particularly for state enterprises, should be cut, rather than primary education, primary healthcare and public infrastructure investment.

3 Tax reform: the tax base should be broadened, tax administration improved and marginal tax rates should be cut to improve incentives.

4 Interest rates: financial deregulation should make interest rates market-determined rather than state-determined, and real interest rates should be positive to discourage capital flight and increase savings.

5 Competitive exchange rates: exchange rates should be sufficiently competitive to nurture rapid growth in non-traditional exports but should not be inflationary – the conviction behind this is that economies should be outward-oriented.

6 Trade liberalization: quantitative restrictions on imports should be eliminated, followed by tariff reductions, until levels of 10–20 per cent are reached – the free trade ideal, however, can be temporarily contradicted by the need for protecting infant industries.

7 Encouraging foreign direct investment: foreign investment brings needed capital, skills and know-how and can be encouraged through debt–equity swaps – exchanging debt held by foreign creditors for equity in local firms, such as privatized state enterprises.

Barriers impeding the entry of foreign firms should be abolished. Foreign and domestic companies should be allowed to compete on equal terms.

8 Privatization: state enterprises should be privatized. Private industry is more efficient.

9 Deregulation: all enterprises should be subject to the discipline of competition – this means deregulating economic activity in the sense of reducing state controls over private enterprise.

10 Securing property rights: making secure and well-defined property rights available to all at reasonable cost.

In brief, said Williamson (1990: 18), the economic position on which Washington concurred in setting policy for the rest of the world, but did not necessarily follow itself, could be summarized as 'prudent macroeconomic policies, outward orientation, and free market capitalism'. He thought this represented a 'sea change' in attitudes in Washington. But he believed that this list of policies making up the Washington Consensus stemmed from classical mainstream economic theory – by 'mainstream theory' Williamson meant neoclassical economics with some Keynesianism. From my perspective, the Washington Consensus is mainstream economics greatly influenced by neoliberalism, particularly in its anti-state attitudes – deregulation, privatization, etc.

The most important factor in achieving market reforms, for Williamson, was not the hard conditionality imposed by the IFIs, but a change in the 'intellectual climate' for economic growth and the provision of useful 'concrete advice' (Williamson 1994: 595). In brief, a not-so-silent revolution in economic opinion had to occur with professional economists as the main political agents. Regardless, most Latin American countries began to use policies consistent with the Washington Consensus, such as 'opening up their foreign trade, cutting budget deficits, and selling off state assets, including many utilities' (Kuczynski 2003: 25). After a brief surge in foreign investment (as privatized companies were bought up) and a rise in the stock markets, Latin America went into crisis. Williamson (2003: 2) said that Latin Americans were entitled to feel disappointed because it had been widely expected that reforms, such as those proposed by the Washington Consensus, 'would get the region back on a growth path that would allow living standards to start catching up with those in industrial countries'. This regional economic crisis, seen by many as resulting from the Washington Consensus, led to a scramble for position on the part of institutions that had pushed the Washington agenda. Let us follow the institutional production of a revised discourse, a 'post-Washington Consensus', using the cases of the main think tank involved, the Institute for International Economics, and the IFIs.

After the Washington Consensus

Recall that the IIE claims to be a non-partisan research institution providing timely, objective analysis and concrete solutions to key international economic problems. Yet the Washington Consensus was widely interpreted as a policy project based on free market reforms that were informed by neoliberalism, and neoliberalism is seen as a right-wing ideology cooked up in the USA and forced on the world by Washington-based institutions. Williamson disagreed with this, saying: 'Audiences the world over seem to believe that this signifies a set of neoliberal policies that have been imposed on hapless countries by the Washington-based international financial institutions and have led them to crisis and misery. There are people who cannot utter the term without foaming at the mouth.' He claimed that critics do not disagree with the policy agenda laid out by the Washington Consensus as much as they disagree with its supposed neoliberalism. 'I of course never intended my term to imply policies like capital account liberalization ... monetarism, supply-side economics, or a minimal state (getting the state out of welfare provision and income redistribution), which I think of as the quintessentially neoliberal ideas.' (Williamson's own personal position is 'classically liberal' in the tradition of Locke, Smith and Mill.) Williamson (ibid.: 325) thought that the notion of a Washington Consensus 'was a godsend to all those unreconstructed opponents of reform who yearned for socialism or import substituting industrialization or a state in which they could play a leading role', in the sense that it implied Washington imposing neoliberal agendas on the world. He also claimed that he was merely reporting on the Consensus, not advocating it. So the IIE economics distanced itself from the Consensus particularly, and neoliberalism especially.

The question then became: what went wrong and what could be done? Williamson (ibid.: 2) and the Latin American economists he works with 'do not take the view that the liberalizing reforms of the past decade and a half, or globalization, can be held responsible for the region's travails in recent years'. Argentina, he says, was regarded as the poster child for the Washington Consensus, but went into crisis. But this was because of an overvalued peso and fiscal laxity. More generally, too many 'emerging markets' encouraged money to flood in and overvalue their currencies. Then too the 'first generation' of

Washington Consensus reforms were not completed, especially labour market reform (something implied by the Washington Consensus but not directly mentioned). And finally the objective informing the reforms – accelerating economic growth – had been narrow – it should have been growth plus equity (i.e. modest redistribution of income from the rich to the poor). In concert with leading conventional economists from the Washington think tanks, and from universities and research institutions in Latin America (most of whom had been ministers of economy in Latin American governments during the 1980s and 1990s), Williamson proposed a new 'reform agenda'. This was composed of the following elements: 'crisis proofing' – actions to curb the economic volatility of the region; completing the first generation of Washington Consensus reforms, especially labour market reform – making labour markets more flexible; and a se-ries of 'second generation' reforms, such as institutional reform of the judiciary, the powerful teachers' unions, the civil service and the financial sector – Williamson (ibid.: 13) adds, however, that none of these economic institutions compares in importance with reforming 'political institutions that can allow a Hugo Chavez to capture control of the state and ravage an economy'; and a new agenda of limited income redistribution through the tax system, giving poor people access to assets through education, titling programmes to provide property rights to the poor, land reform that recognizes the property rights of large landowners, and microcredit. Williamson believes that the way forward is to complete, correct and complement the Washington Consensus reforms ('reform the reforms') rather than reversing them.

I will now comment briefly on these positions. First, neoliberalism is a term referring to the renewal in the late twentieth century of the liberal reform policy agenda of the nineteenth century, with its belief in free trade and markets, and its antipathy for state regula-tion and state enterprise. The Washington Consensus represented a 'sea change' in economic attitudes towards this new liberal posi-tion. Second, Washington Consensus policies were widely adopted in Latin America and have to be held accountable for the economic disasters and the ruining of livelihoods that followed. Furthermore, the notion that 'first-generation reforms' that had disastrous effects need completing and extending invites further disaster. Such a posi-tion could only be taken by ideologues who believe in neoliberalism regardless of empirical evidence. Third, the second generation of reforms advocated by Williamson show an increased concern for poverty, income redistribution and social programmes – mitigating the disaster that the Consensus policies caused. Notice that concern is accompanied by attacks on organized labour, unions, teachers and pensioners. My own position is that the Washington Consensus reflects the interests of the institutions described in Figure 4.1 as the 'pentagon of economic policy power'. The IFIs and the investment banks in particular want fiscal discipline and lower public expenditures to ensure loan repayment … to the banks, private and public. Encouraging foreign investment as a route to development in the context of secure (private) property rights is the line pushed by mainstream economics, conventional think tanks and investment banks like Morgan Stanley, particularly when state industries are being privatized. Cutting marginal tax rates means lowering taxes for the richest income brackets, the 'investors', and is a position taken by the banks and by multinational corporations, and an economic ideology that lionizes the entrepreneur. Trade liberalization comes from Ricardian economics, and is the mainstay of economic policy vigorously supported by US state administrations, through the Treasury, since the 1970s (NAFTA, FTAA, GATT, WTO), enthusiastically adopted by the IFIs and advocated by think tanks across the political spectrum. Privatization and deregulation are based on the neoliberal attack on the Keynesian and developmental states in the eternal faith that private enterprise is always better than state intervention … especially when it rewards foreign investors. These are not politically neutral, science-based policy proposals. They come from a 'mainstream' economics infested with right-wing, pro-rich neoliberal ideologies. They are part of the immoral attitude that 'development' can only come to the poor people of the world *through* increasing the power and profit of the already rich people of the world. That's what I think.

The Washington Consensus reappraised

Let us now look at reappraisals of the Washington Consensus by the IFIs. Here I will follow an account written by Dani Rodrik, Professor of International Political Economy at the Kennedy School of Government at Harvard University. Of Turkish origin, Rodrik occupies a strategic position at the liberal and critical end of the conventional policy spectrum. Rodrik says that the Washington Consensus policies, codified by Williamson, inspired a wave of reforms in Latin America and sub-Saharan Africa that fundamentally transformed the policy landscape in these developing areas. With the fall of the Berlin Wall and the collapse of the Soviet Union, former socialist countries similarly made a 'bold leap' towards markets. Indeed, such was the enthusiasm for reform that Williamson's original list came to look tame and innocuous by comparison. The reform agenda eventually came to be perceived, at least by its critics, as an overtly ideological effort to impose 'neoliberalism' and 'market fundamentalism' on developing nations. Yet one thing that is generally agreed on about the consequences of these reforms is that things have not quite worked out the way they were intended, says Rodrik. Indeed, he thinks, it is fair to say that nobody really believes in the Washington Consensus any more. The question now is not whether the Washington Consensus is dead or alive; it is what will replace it. Practitioners of the Washington Consensus have come to think that the standard policy reforms cannot produce lasting effects if the background institutional conditions are poor. The upshot is that the original Washington Consensus has been augmented by so-called 'second generation' reforms that are heavily institutional in nature. One possible rendition of these reforms, as summarized by Rodrik, is shown in Table 4.1.

In brief, the Washington Consensus with 'institutional reform'. Rodrik counters that institutions are deeply embedded in society, and if growth indeed requires major institutional transformation – in the areas of rule of law, property rights protection, governance, and so on – how can we not be pessimistic about the prospects for growth in poor countries, when institutional changes typically happen rarely, as the result of major political upheavals?

Rodrik (ibid.) has his own way of thinking about growth strategies. Step 1, diagnostic analysis, figures out where the most significant constraints on economic growth are in a given setting. In a low-income economy, economic activity must be constrained by at least one of two factors: either the cost of finance must be too high, or the private return to investment must be low. Step 2 is creative and imaginative policy design to target the identified constraints appropriately. The key is to focus on the market failures and distortions associated with the constraint identified in the previous step. The principle of policy targeting offers a simple message: target the policy response as closely as possible on the source of the distortion. Step 3 involves institutionalizing the process of diagnosis and policy response to ensure that the economy remains dynamic and growth does not fizzle out. The nature of the binding constraint will necessarily change over time. What is needed to sustain growth? Two types of institutional reform seem to become critical over time. First, maintaining productive dynamism. Natural resource discoveries, garment exports from maquilas, or a free trade agreement may spur growth for a limited amount of time. Policy needs to ensure that this momentum is maintained with ongoing diversification into new areas of tradable

TABLE 4.1 The augmented Washington Consensus

TABLE 4.1 The augmented Washington Consensus

Original Washington Consensus

1. Fiscal discipline
2. Reorientation of public expenditures
3. Tax reform
4. Financial liberalization
5. Unified and competitive exchange rates
6. Trade liberalization
7. Openness to foreign direct investment
8. Privatization
9. Deregulation
10. Secure property rights

'Augmented' Washington Consensus – the previous ten items, plus:

11. Corporate governance
12. Anti-corruption
13. Flexible labour markets
14. WTO agreements
15. Financial codes and standards
16. 'Prudent' capital-account opening
17. Non-intermediate exchange rate regimes
18. Independent central banks/inflation targeting
19. Social safety nets
20. Targeted poverty reduction

Source: Rodrik (2006: 25).

commodities. Otherwise, growth simply fizzles out. Second is the strengthening of domestic institutions of conflict management. The most frequent cause of the collapse in growth is an inability to deal with the consequences of external shocks – i.e. terms of trade declines or reversals in capital flows. Endowing the economy with resilience against shocks requires strengthening the rule of law, solidifying (or putting in place) democratic institutions, establishing participatory mechanisms, and erecting social safety nets. When such institutions are in place, the macroeconomic and other adjustments needed to deal with adverse shocks can be undertaken relatively smoothly. What is required to sustain growth should not be confused with what is required to initiate it. Such is Rodrik's alternative proposal.

Let me comment on this. First, it is clear that Washington Consensus policies were widely put in place, and just as broadly failed – in their own terms of producing economic growth. Indeed, countries with high, sustained growth rates in the 1990s and early 2000s, such as China and India, were exactly those *not* using Washington Consensus

Political power

policies. Second, realizing this, the IFIs (or significant components of them) divided, with the World Bank becoming increasingly insecure and uncertain, while the IMF remained steadfast, and indeed thinks that reform did not go far enough! Third, the 'augmented Washington Consensus', reflecting lessons supposedly learned from the failure of the first generation of reforms, is in fact a grab-bag of miscellaneous policies conceived under various political-economic positions within conventional circles, some from the right (flexible labour markets means attacking unions) and some from a kind of renewed liberal concern (social safety nets and targeted poverty reduction) that to my mind reflects a guilty conscience about the misery inflicted on the world by neoliberal policies – it might be called 'liberal neo-liberalism'. Fourth, the liberal, critical wing of neoliberalism, well represented by Rodrik, stays well within policy convention. Policy is aimed at producing economic growth. And in low-income economies, economic activity is constrained by the high cost of finance or the low private return to investment. Basically just invest more. No hint of social transformation here! Immersion as expert in conventional policy circles, even as liberal critic, means accepting the discipline of the hegemonic discourse. It may be boring. It may be corrupt. But it pays well.

Benevolent consensus

The prevailing notions of 'new reform agenda', 'job-based social contract' and 'augmented Washington Consensus' as frontiers in hegemonic policy discourse are far too limited. Something else, a new policy formation, with a reshuffled institutional framework, arises phoenix-like from the ashes of the Washington Consensus. The key terms in the new liberal neoliberalism are poverty elimination, debt relief and Millennium Development Goals (MDGs); the key institutional actors include a broader range of rich countries than just the USA meeting as the Group of 7 or 8 (G7/G8), the United Nations as a body and as specific development agencies (UNDP especially), and one key individual ... Jeffrey D. Sachs, author of the 'shock therapy' model of neoliberal intervention in eastern Europe (Gowan 1995), director of the Earth Institute, Quetelet Professor of Sustainable Development and Professor of Health Policy and Management at Columbia University, and also director of the UN Millennium Project and Special Adviser to United Nations Secretary-General Kofi Annan on the Millennium Development Goals. Sachs spent twenty years at Harvard University, where he received his BA, MA and PhD degrees, ending up as director of the Center for International Development,

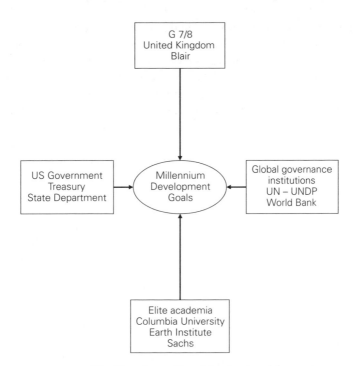

FIGURE 4.2 The liberal–neoliberal institutional formation

Harvard. Figure 4.2 summarizes this new liberal–neoliberal institutional formation.

The best entry to the new discourse is Sachs's book, *The End of Poverty: Economic Possibilities for Our Time*, published in 2005. This book appeared at a time when the great issues of global poverty, debt and development reappeared as spectres troubling global consciousness. The year 2005, it seemed, marked the onset of an era when the West would finally forgive the debts owed by the world's poorest countries, under mass, popular pressure, organized as Live 8 rock concerts by singers Bono and Bob Geldof. Bono says in his foreword to the book that 'my professor' Jeffrey Sachs has written a handbook on 'how we could be the first generation to outlaw the kind of extreme, stupid poverty that sees a child die of hunger in a world of plenty'. And *Time* magazine, which carried a long excerpt from the book in its 14 March 2005 issue, says that Sachs constructs a new way of looking at the world's billion poorest people. This was an important book reflecting and furthering the changing discourse on global development. It was the next great step for humankind, made after the supposed demise of the Washington Consensus. Maybe.

Political power

The prelude to the book's main argument unfolds as a series of vignettes cataloguing Sachs's experiences as invited visitor in a number of countries undergoing economic difficulties. As he passes through the villages of rural Malawi he finds only poverty and death in a country at the bottom of the human condition. Then in the garment factories of Bangladesh he glimpses a chance to hope – Western protesters, he says, should support increased numbers of sweatshop jobs in the Third World because they represent the first stage in rising from extreme poverty. The information technology centre of Chennai is prototypical of a new India, already several steps up. And in Beijing, Chinese economic growth is speeding ahead, full throttle. His conclusion? Economic development is a ladder with the higher rungs representing steps up the path to economic well-being. A billion people still live like Malawians – too ill or hungry to even lift a foot to the first rung. Our generation's 'challenge' is to help the poorest of the poor escape the misery of extreme poverty so they can begin their ascent to full humanity.

Sachs then presents a quick history of economic development conceived in Rostow's sense as take-off, transformation and spread from European centres – so that now, 5 billion people live in countries that have at least reached that first vital rung. Why, then, have other countries failed to achieve economic growth? Sachs discusses several categories of problems that cause economies to stagnate or decline. These include factors like governance failure and lack of innovation, but Sachs tends to rely on a kind of environmental determinism – many poor countries are poor because they are landlocked and situated in high mountain ranges (like Switzerland?), trapped in arid conditions with low agricultural productivity (like Saudi Arabia?), with tropical climates (like Singapore?) that favour killer diseases (as did once the north of England's hills and dales?). Sachs dismisses the notion that 'geography single-handedly and irrevocably determines the economic outcomes of nations', yet here, as elsewhere, at crucial points in his argument, he takes essentially an environmental determinist stance. He then spins a series of tales of his work on monetary stabilization, privatization and market reform in Bolivia, Poland, Russia, China, India and Africa. This experience led to Sachs becoming Special Adviser to Kofi Annan, Secretary-General of the UN, charged with laying out an 'operational plan' whereby the UN, participating governments and civil society could fulfil the eight MDGs that centre on the eradication of extreme poverty and hunger.

Sachs's main argument runs as follows. Briefly, 'the key to ending extreme poverty is to enable the poorest of the poor to get their foot on the ladder of development'. The extreme poor, Sachs argues, lack six major kinds of capital: enough human capital, as health, nutrition and skills, to be economically productive; business capital, as machinery and transport, to increase productivity; infrastructure, which forms critical inputs into business productivity; natural capital, which provides the environmental services needed by human society; public institutional capital, which underpins peaceful and prosperous division of labour; and knowledge capital, which raises productivity and promotes physical and natural capital. Breaking the poverty trap involves donor-based investments that raise the level of capital per person, producing a capital stock high enough that the economy is sufficiently productive to meet basic needs. Without outside donor funds the necessary investments simply cannot be financed. Ending global poverty by 2025 requires a global compact between rich and poor countries, as with the UN Millennium Project, whereby the rich countries follow through on their previous pledge (made long ago in a similar spasm of optimism) to provide 0.7 per cent of GNP as aid. Indeed, the bottom line is about $135–$195 billion a year in assistance, significantly less than the 0.7 per cent figure. As Sachs (2005: 299) says: 'The point is that the Millennium Development Goals can be financed within the bounds of the official development assistance that the donor countries have already promised.' This essentially means that the USA, presently contributing 0.15 per cent of GNP as development assistance, would have to contribute half the necessary increase, followed by Japan, Germany, France, Italy and Britain. Putting it differently, the three tax cuts made by the Bush administration, giving $50 billion a year in extra money to the already rich, provide more than enough for the USA to pay its share if spent instead as foreign assistance. Hence, our generation, heir to two and a half centuries of economic progress, can realistically envision a world without extreme poverty. But why should 'we' (the people of the rich countries of the world) do it?

This is a question that has occurred before. Earlier in this particular text by Sachs, and even now in its culminating chapters, the 'why' is usually answered in terms of the 'why not'. That is, why should we not end poverty when it costs a mere half of a per cent of GNP to do so? But this answer creates moral difficulties for Sachs, and others, for it suggests a heartless world that could have saved billions of dying babies long ago and not even noticed the cost. So why now? The answer comes suddenly: because 'hard evidence has established strong linkages between extreme poverty abroad and the threats to national security' (ibid.: 331). An economy stuck in the poverty trap often leads to state failure and failed states are seedbeds for violence, terrorism, drug trafficking and disease. If the USA and western Europe want to spend less time responding to failed states in the post-9/11 era, they will have to reduce the number of failed economies. It has been done before, with the Marshall Plan, meant to ensure Europe's economic stability and strategic security in the post-war era. At the Rio Summit on Sustainable Development and with the Monterrey Consensus, the developed countries committed to doing so again. The richest of the rich should therefore 'comfortably' come through with their contribution as a 'profound and meaningful demonstration of our generation's unique moment to secure global well-being' (ibid.: 346). Sachs is for an enlightened globalization, in the tradition of Thomas Jefferson, Adam Smith, Immanuel Kant and Marie-Jean-Antoine Condorcet, which would direct criticism at the rich governments of the world, which would encourage the anti-globalization movement to change to a more pro-corporate position, which would encourage trade by removing barriers and agricultural subsidies, and would press the USA to end its 'reveries of empire'.

Let me now criticize the Sachs argument. This book by the most prominent development economist in the world comes from a maverick-liberal neoliberalism that represents *the* leading critical edge within the hegemonic policy discourse. It resonates with the experiences of power, is full of accounts of meetings with ministers, heads of departments, presidents, prime ministers and director generals – laid out, on the whole, in a non-pretentious, non-boasting style. And for an economist, Sachs is well read, again within a seriously limited literature. What, therefore, can I say, in face of an urgent, moral appeal, by a very powerful person, connected with mighty institutions? Trashing the book might place me on the side of the Karl Roves and Dick Cheneys of this world, and who would want to be included with moral nasties like them? Assuming that UN declarations and global compacts among rich-country commitments make some difference, as with debt relief, I am supportive. And arguments like this, providing a rationale for what otherwise might dissipate as futile gestures in the general direction of empty promises, are useful indeed. But there are a couple of small points of disagreement, mentioned with trepidation in the face of such power, concerning the argument presented in Sachs's book, which have to be made. The first is economic in principle and the second is ethical in nature.

As to my first disagreement, I doubt that foreign assistance can ever 'end poverty'. This is not because not enough aid will be delivered, as indeed will prove to be the case, consuming 95 per cent of the subsequent hand-wringing debate and allowing an easy, moralizing excuse for poverty not being eliminated by 2025 ('if only we had given more'). Instead my scepticism about the Sachs argument, the MDG initiative and liberal neoliberalism in general concerns the ability of charity-based theories even to begin to understand the causes of world poverty and thus suggest policies that might indeed facilitate the end of poverty. Sachs's Fifth Avenue approach – appealing to the rich to help the poor – comes with a price label attached. Immediately, that price is a necessary lack of criticism about the sources of wealth in the presently prevailing global, corporate capitalism – Sachs's argument that poverty results not from income transfer, from poor to rich, but entirely from differential national rates of economic growth, is historically shallow. Associated with this is a lack of criticism of the presently hegemonic policy regime, the neoliberalism that has done so well for the super-rich and quietly famous, so that Sachs (ibid.: 73) blithely asserts that the rich countries have only to enable countries to get to the first rung in the ladder and then 'the tremendous dynamism of self-sustaining growth can take hold'. In the longer term, the price includes accepting a largely conventional economic historical geography, replete with take-offs, ladders of development and successful transformations, as supposedly bits of India and China represent. As a result of this blindness, in the present global context, increasing the health and education level of Third World workers through donor investments, as Sachs suggests, is likely to produce a healthier and more educated but unemployed workforce – the health part is admirable, the unemployed part not. Under all existing aid and debt relief schemes, to get their money, poor countries have to agree to open their markets to foreign competition, privatize public enterprises, withdraw the state from service provision, reduce state budget deficits, redirect their economies in an export orientation, flexibilize their labour markets, and so on down the Washington Consensus list drawn up in the belief that markets and free competition can guide any economy into the magic realm of growth, up the ladder of development in Sachs's terms, if only workers are made more employable. But opening markets, as Sachs suggests, means losing protected jobs – that is, creating unemployment in the name of 'efficiency' in countries where skilled and educated labour is already underused. Privatization, which he has advocated all over the world, as an agent of the Washington Consensus, means introducing the profit motive into, for example, water or electricity supply, and cutting off anyone who cannot or will not pay the higher rates – a lot of people have been shot for protesting against this little number, especially in

Bolivia, where Sachs has worked. Reducing swollen state deficits in the name of fiscal responsibility may sound fine until it is remembered that desperate people rely for their lives on state-supported food subsidies and free healthcare. As for exporting more, the problem is 'export what?' China monopolizes cheap labour manufacturing and the prices of coffee, cocoa and cotton are volatile and declining in the long run, so that already productive small farmers break their backs working for less than nothing. (Note that China, or a small part of it, represents a rung on the ladder for Sachs, but is a plank across that so-called ladder to countries that cannot match China's limitless supplies of labour available at 25 cents an hour.) At the same time local food production is undercut by focusing on export crops and removing tariff protections, producing a dangerous mass vulnerability to episodes of starvation. Labour market flexibility means attacking the unions, paying lower wages and eliminating what few laws might exist to protect workers. And finally, even the desired outcome, economic growth, does not necessarily reduce poverty, especially when growth follows the neoliberal design. Instead it produces a replica of the situation prevailing in its US homeland – wage stagnation for the majority, and even more wealth for those few who already have so much that they don't know what to do with it. In other words, to earn 'aid', supplicant countries have to restructure their economies neoliberally ('maintain sound macroeconomic policies') so that they reward foreign investment. All this has to be ignored, or merely sniped at (quibbles with the IMF), when appeals are made to the rich to open their pockets … generously.

As for my second disagreement, I find the ethical argument presented by Sachs … abhorrent. After reading an argument on the supposed benefits of foreign aid, all the time assuming that the aim is to make people healthier for their own sakes, we are told that the rich countries should invest in poor countries for the sake of their own security, to prevent failed states, to prevent the poor from becoming terrorists! We should invest in them … because we fear them? Give me a break. Ethics do not spring ready made from conscience alone, but rely on interpretations of the human experience that, in late modernism, take the form of theories. In the case of this book, the cruel pragmatism that passes for moral reasoning is detached from the rest of the argument, as an afterthought rather than a moving gesture. This is not just because, having written a book on ending poverty, the author was confronted with the practical question: why should a Republican administration that has just illegally invaded a Third World country support investing in the Third World poor? It is because the largely conventional economic reasoning of the book itself produces an ethical vacuum from which emerges, by random choice, depending on the circumstances, an ethics of simple morality ('we should just do good things'), or moral utilitarianism ('it will not cost much') or, at worst, the moral pragmatism of fear ('do it to save ourselves'). By 'conventional reasoning' in this last sentence I mean Sachs's environmental determinism and his Rostovian modernization theory. In terms of the first, we encounter in this book an honorary geographer who has not read any geography, so does not know the critiques of an environmental determinism that, in blaming nature, leaves little but pity as the basis for morality. In terms of the second, we encounter over and over again while perusing these many pages, and wondering about their author, a development economist who missed everything that happened to development theory between 1965 and 1995, in terms of dependency, world systems, feminism, post-developmentalism, critical modernism, and who therefore sees poverty simply, naïvely and optimistically as mere lack of sufficient modernization. Most seriously the two deficient ideologies combine to disguise the real culprit behind global poverty – the Western imperialist expansion that ruined the civilizations already existing in these 'environmentally deprived' lands – and, thereby, miss too the only viable reason for aid – as reparation for damages done in the past, and continuing into the present. The will to assist the Third World has to come from a sense of global justice, from the critical understanding that the wealth of a few caused the poverty of the many.

Millennium

The turn of the millennium saw neoliberal policy discourse turn liberally towards debt relief. Looking behind debt relief, we can see a tension between kind-hearted benevolence – the people of the developed world vowing to help the poorest people of the world by forgiving their debts – and cool-headed control – the will to manage the Third World and to make it into a mimic of the West. You would hardly know it from the news reports appearing at the time. But this 'writing off $40 billion owed to international agencies' mainly amounted to a refinancing of the IMF and the World Bank's HIPC initiative discussed earlier. As I have said, the HIPC countries have to demonstrate, to the economists at the IMF and the World Bank, that they have adopted, and are carrying out, policies judged 'sound' by the 'international community'. That 'community' is represented by the IFIs, and behind these the Secretary of the US Treasury Department and the British Chancellor of the Exchequer. At their meeting in early June 2005, the finance ministers of the G7 countries agreed to provide additional financial resources, ensuring that the financing capacity of the World Bank, the IMF and the African Development Bank was not reduced by the HIPC initiative. This will eventually lead to 100 per cent debt cancellation of the outstanding obligations of eighteen of the poorest countries in the world. The agreement was formalized at the G7 summit meeting in Gleneagles, Scotland, later in 2005. There was a lot of criticism of the fact that only a small part of poor-country debt would be forgiven and that relief would be long in coming. But whatever its problems of timing and coverage, this commitment to ending the international debt of the poorest countries does show signs of being motivated by a genuine benevolence. It does contribute to achieving the UN Millennium Development Goal of halving world poverty by 2015.

But look beneath the headlines, down the list of conclusions from the June G8 meeting, not too far, only to point 2. This reads as follows:

> We reaffirm our view that in order to make progress on social and economic development, it is essential that developing countries put in place the policies for economic growth, sustainable development and poverty reduction: sound, accountable and transparent institutions and policies; macroeconomic stability; the increased fiscal transparency essential to tackle corruption, boost private sector development, and attract investment; a credible legal framework; and the elimination of impediments to private investment, both domestic and foreign. (G8 2005)

The aspect of point 2 seized on by just about all the media was 'good government practices', such as transparency, anti-corruption and credible legal frameworks. The other aspect of point 2, macroeconomic stability, private sector development and removing impediments to private investment, domestic and foreign, together with bits on free trade and open markets in later points, went almost unmentioned. Here we find the G8 countries, or rather their treasury departments, in collusion with the IFIs, telling poor countries how they must run their economies if they want to receive debt relief. Just as the 'deserving poor' are made to do the repentance shuffle to earn a charitable handout, or the homeless pretend instant arm-waving Christian conversion to get a bed for the night, now we find the rich countries telling the poor countries of the world how they must 'reform' to get their debt relief.

But it is exactly this IFI insistence on Washington Consensus policies which have brought thousands of demonstrators on to the streets in protest whenever the World Bank and the IMF have met over the last few years. Why? Well, first it's the imperialism of economic policy, the undemocratic notion that a few thousand Western experts steeped in neoclassical/neoliberal economics know what policy regime works best for a world of others. In the original HIPC proposal, civil society organizations were supposed to be consulted in preparing a country's 'poverty-reduction and growth strategy'. But that turned out to be a front for business as usual – structural adjustment or, rather, structural transformation designed in Washington, DC. Now we find less and less reference even to 'country ownership' – the IFI euphemism for brief consultation with the local finance ministry, home to economists also trained in American and British universities. Instead it's prescription by the experts with inspections every six months. The G7 version of structural adjustment is particularly nasty because it disguises an imperialism of expertise in the wondrous garb of world humanity's most generous impulse, the elimination of global poverty.

Hope and charity

Along with debt relief and the MDGs, the early 2000s saw a renewed initiative from private philanthropy to solve the world's problems of hunger, disease and poverty. The outstanding case is the Bill and Melinda Gates Foundation, the largest charity the world has ever known, founded by Bill Gates, CEO of Microsoft, a global software corporation with 61,000 employees, sales receipts of $44 billion a year, and net receipts of $12.6 billion. Microsoft's position is based on MS-DOS, the dominant operating system for the personal computers of the 1980s, and various generations of the Windows operating system since. This has made Gates the richest person on earth. The aim of the foundation is to 'help reduce inequities in the United States and around the world ... to increase opportunity and equity for those most in need'. The foundation, based in Seattle, Washington State, where Microsoft is headquartered, has an endowment of $30 billion. On 25 June 2006, Warren Buffett, an American stock investor and major shareholder in Berkshire Hathaway, a holding company owning several insurance and manufacturing companies, and the world's second-richest person, pledged the foundation 10 million Berkshire Hathaway Class B shares (worth a further $31 billion) through annual contributions. Since 1994, the Gates Foundation has donated funds to the following areas: global health $6.5 billion; education $2.7 billion; special projects $0.7 billion; Pacific Northwest $0.6 billion; global aries $0.3 billion – for a total of $10.8 billion. Thus far the main ⌐ocus of the foundation's giving has been Aids prevention in the Third World, the eradication of poliomyelitis, vaccination and similar causes – one contribution of $800 million a year by the Gates Foundation is similar in amount to the annual budget of the UN World Health Organization. After a review of its operations, in 2006 the foundation began a global development programme 'focused on some 550 million households in the world that survive on less than $2 a day' and 'concerned with making financial and agricultural advances, and water and sanitation improvements for the poor. In Malawi, the foundation has underwritten the purchase of thumbprint readers used in establishing savings accounts for the rural poor' (Strom 2006). Those thumbprint readers will do a lot to eliminate poverty!

We need to look again at the ethical basis of moral gestures like debt relief. Feeling sorry for the poor black children portrayed in all those video clips might be a start. But it smacks of benevolent racism. And this kind of shallow sorrow is too short lived to sustain a long-term development process that includes genuine aid. An ethics that matches the enormity of global poverty has to come instead from a critical understanding of world history. It has to be derived from the fundamental realization that European expansion destroyed the civilizations of the pre-capitalist world. In the case of Africa, an ethic of sorrow has to come from letting the historical facts sink in – the record of European slaving, the taking of African resources by the most savage of means, the construction of colonial boundaries so that post-colonial states were bound to fail. Look at the map of Namibia; that Caprivi Strip was drawn to give Germany access to the Zambezi river! It is time that we Europeans apologize for what we have done to the peoples of the world. This apology can take the financial form of unconditional debt relief as reparation for what was done, and repayment of what was (and is still) taken – as the Jubilee South organizations have called for. The will to debt relief has to come from a sense of global justice. It has to come from anti-imperialist sentiment, not from a kindly reimposition of economic imperialism.

So what is the liberal neoliberal hegemony fashioned for the new millennium? At first I called it a Madonna neoliberalism, with a sweet, benevolent smile. The more I think about this humanitarian ruse, the more it seems like the Washington Consensus wearing a sly grin.

FIVE
Sub-hegemony – South Africa

§ After a century of struggle marked by the ultimate sacrifice of thousands of brave lives, South Africa's black majority was liberated from apartheid in 1994. Popular elections have subsequently demonstrated overwhelming support for the African National Congress (ANC), an alliance of black nationalists, socialist unions and radical social movements that stands for fundamental social, economic and political change. Time after time, the leadership of the ANC responded to the demands of its most militant supporters by promising that South Africa's abundant wealth would, finally, be devoted to the welfare of the black majority. Yet despite political gains in the post-apartheid period, the economic resolve of a newly liberated people has been frustrated by internal structural limitations surviving from the past and, even more, by severe limitations on what any state can do for its people in a global era driven by neoliberalism. At root, the dilemma facing South Africa's people is lack of social control over the direction taken by the national economy. More specifically the problem here, as elsewhere, is the lack of a developmental programme that achieves economic growth *through* the redistribution of incomes and the satisfaction of needs. The tensions between a people persuaded that their time has finally come and an economic structure which, even following liberation, can satisfy but a fragment of long-pent-up demands leads to a crisis of national conscience, which was only partly resolved by the well-publicized South African Truth and Reconciliation Commission. Conscience has to have beneficial material consequences for reconciliation to be believed.

As I outlined earlier, events like these can be understood through a theory of power, hegemony and discourse. Power is produced in dominant centres, such as Washington, and disseminated through discourse – neoliberal discourses of development following the Washington Consensus. By contrast, I see ANC development discourse traditionally founded on principles of socialist democracy cultivated during the epic political struggle against apartheid. In this chapter, I explain the drastic reorientation of ANC development policy, from growth through redistribution and meeting basic needs, to redistribution through growth achieved by neoliberal export-orientation, as a process of colonization: internal discursive processes were articulated with, and disciplined by, external discursive, political and financial pressures. The result is sub-hegemony. The economic policy employed in a country like South Africa comes from the articulation between dominant discourse from the centre and regional discourses originating in the periphery. Articulation takes the form of two-way interactions during which, nevertheless, disciplinary or regulatory effects pass more frequently from the universal and dominant to the regional and dominated than the other way around. There seem to be several dimensions to this disciplining effect: the imposition of theoretical legitimacy, in terms of linking formalized systems of ideas with a recognized interpretation of a dominant, regional experience, set down in a hegemonic textual tradition, and widely accepted as proven and universally applicable; the establishment of a more directly realistic legitimacy, in terms of a prevailing sense of technical viability as adjudicated by expert opinion that likewise is widely recognized; several kinds of financial legitimacy, in terms of the labelling of economic ideas as 'mature and responsible' in a social accounting process carried out usually by institutions controlling global accumulations of wealth; and popular processes of transmitting conviction from experts to people through cultural media that directly create broad, even international, patterns of consent.

In the present instance, therefore, 'colonization' refers to the imposition of elite interpretations of the experience of the West over the experiences of the peoples of the peripheries through the disciplinary media of hegemonic discourses. Colonization occurs through a series of 'articulations' among: central, hegemonic discourses; translated regional sub-hegemonic versions; and emergent alternatives, based in residual cultures, and translated into counter-hegemonic discourse by dissident intellectuals. In this geography of hegemony, the crucial moment is not the succession of competing hegemonic and counter-hegemonic discourses situated in time, nor even the array of spatially linked centres of persuasion, as much as the disciplining that occurs when one discursive tradition confronts another (see also Narsiah 2006).

Discourse of resistance

Conventional analysts claim that the ANC produced 'no substantial economic policies until 1990' (Nattrass 1994: 344). Yet a grassroots network of organizations and individuals centred on the ANC produced a series of statements on social and economic transformation that can be read as the political basis of a coherent policy discourse. The crucial founding event, the Congress of the People of 1955, adopted a Freedom Charter that subsequently became strategically important as a statement of radical opposition to the apartheid government. The actual words of the charter were written by a committee made up mainly of members of the Congress of Democrats, a white liberal-left alliance of some seven hundred activists associated with the ANC (van der Westhuizen 1994). But the document was based on lists of grievances submitted by hundreds of meetings convened all over the country, often under extremely difficult circumstances. It is an elegantly and beautifully phrased counter-hegemonic document written by intellectuals working on behalf of oppressed peoples. A preamble states the principles on which the charter rests:

> We, the People of South Africa, declare for all our country and the world to know:
> That South Africa belongs to all who live in it, black and white, and that no government can justly claim authority unless it is based on the will of the people;
> That our people have been robbed of their birthright to land, liberty and peace by a government founded on injustice and inequality;
> That our country will never be prosperous or free until all our people live in brotherhood, enjoying equal rights and opportunities;
> That only a democratic state, based on the will of the people can secure to all their birthright without distinction of colour, race, sex or belief;
> And therefore, we the people of South Africa, black and white, together – equals, countrymen and brothers – adopt this FREEDOM CHARTER. And we pledge ourselves to strive together, sparing nothing of our strength and courage, until the democratic changes here set out have been won.

Sections 4 and 5, dealing with economic rights and land reform, are particularly important for social transformation. Here the main passages read:

> The national wealth of our country, the heritage of all South Africans, shall be restored to the people;
> The mineral wealth beneath the soil, the banks and monopoly industry shall be transferred to the ownership of the people as a whole;
> All other industries and trade shall be controlled to assist the well being of the people;

Restriction of land ownership on a racial basis shall be ended, and all the land re-divided amongst those who work it, to banish famine and land hunger;

The state shall help the peasants with implements, seed, tractors and dams to save the soil and assist the tillers. (Freedom Charter in Esterhuyse 1990)

The Freedom Charter combined nationalist principles with Western democratic ideals and European socialist policies in a radical economic statement exactly about development, social control over resources and human liberation (cf. Crush 1995: xi). As a signatory of the charter, the ANC was seen (accurately) as a black nationalist organization with a radical, socialist politics.

From the 1955 meeting came the Congress Alliance composed of the ANC, the South African Indian Congress, the Coloured People's Organization, the Congress of Democrats, the South African Congress of Trade Unions, and the underground South African Communist Party (SACP). Soon after the congress, 20,000 supporters of a newly formed Federation of South African Women delivered a petition to an empty prime minister's office in Pretoria, the national capital. The South African state responded by arresting 156 leading Congress members on charges of high treason and detaining 2,000 women who refused to carry passes. In the late 1950s, a newly formed Pan African Congress (PAC), with a more black-nationalist orientation than the multiracial ANC, tried to obstruct the legal system by provoking mass arrests. Tens of thousands were taken into custody. A series of governmental measures, beginning with the Suppression of Communism Act of 1950, reinforced the repressive power of the state. The ANC was banned in 1960. Together with the PAC, the ANC in exile advocated overthrowing the apartheid government through guerrilla action and armed struggle. Hundreds of attacks were made on government buildings, before the army and police arrested and jailed leading members of all resistance organizations, including Nelson Mandela and Walter Sisulu of the ANC, who were sentenced to life imprisonment on Robbens Island (Magubane 1979). Thabo Mbeki, now prime minister, wrote in 1978 on false remedies for historical injustices: 'black capitalism instead of being the antithesis is rather confirmation of parasitism with no redeeming features whatsoever, without any extenuating circumstances to excuse its existence' (Mbeki 1985: 48).

In the 1970s, black workers organized into militant unions led strikes that shut down whole industries and entire cities. In 1976 demonstrations by thousands of Sowetan schoolchildren against the teaching of lessons in Afrikaans initiated a further year of black township turmoil. During this time, alternative visions for a future South African society were formed by dozens of social movements contending for power with the apartheid state and, sometimes, with the ANC. For instance, the Black Consciousness Movement, led by Steve Biko, Mamphela Ramphele and other activists in the black South African Students Organization (SASO), emphasized community-based, autonomous development led by cooperative decision-making, ideas that emerged from a reading of African history stimulated by the movement for black power in the United States (Manzo 1995; Biko 1996). The response by the state to this upsurge in radical activity was the killing of 575 people, 134 of them under the age of eighteen, including the murder in custody of Biko. In turn this provoked further escalation of armed resistance by the ANC and the PAC. The United Democratic Front (UDF), formed in 1983 by an alliance of unions, community groups and women's and youth organizations, called for abolition of the African homelands, set up by the apartheid government, and for a democratic South Africa. In the mid-1980s widespread actions by student and township organizations (the 'civics'), led by the UDF, made the country ungovernable. The ruling National Party detained thousands of activists under the state's emergency powers, but was forced to begin a programme of reform, without conceding white supremacy. The late 1980s saw military occupation of the black townships with widespread urban terrorism in white areas. Under a state of emergency between 1986 and 1989 some thirty thousand people were detained, with many dying in police custody. In 1987 and 1988 industrial strikes brought the economy to a standstill. At the same time, the South African armed forces were mauled by Cuban troops after an incursion into southern Angola. The country was subjected to intense foreign pressures, including a disinvestment campaign, widespread picketing of South African embassies and consulates, and the refusal of Chase Manhattan and other banks to roll over South Africa's short-term loans (Friedman 1993).

During this time of turmoil, the ANC and the UDF continued to use the Freedom Charter as basis for their claims for social and political justice. There is a considerable documentary history recording debates within the ANC on the political-economic principles of the Freedom Charter. In their 'Constitutional Guidelines' ANC officials interpreted the Freedom Charter as a guide for making a just and democratic society that would sweep away the legacy of colonial conquest and white domination (ANC 1987). The guidelines argued that 90 per cent of the land and instruments of production were held by the white ruling class. Ending poverty would mean 'a rapid and irreversible re-distribution of wealth and opening up of facilities to all'. Under the heading of 'Economy' the guidelines said that 'The state shall ensure that the entire country serves the interests and well being of the entire population,' and 'the private sector of the economy shall be obliged to cooperate with the state in realising the objectives of the Freedom Charter in promoting social well being' so that 'the economy shall be a mixed one, with a public sector, a private sector and a small-scale family sector' (ibid.). As the guidelines indicated, the ANC remained a radical, modernist organization based on socialistic principles.

After several years of informal meetings between liberal South African businesspeople and the ANC, Nelson Mandela (in 1988) invited the government to negotiate a political settlement as an alternative to civil war. When P. W. Botha was replaced as president by the more pragmatic F. W. de Klerk, the ban on the ANC was lifted, in February 1990, and the organization's leaders released from confinement, with Mandela made deputy president of the ANC. The government began to negotiate an end to exclusive white rule. The ANC's national executive committee endorsed an all-party conference under the aegis of the Convention for a Democratic South Africa (CODESA), which began to meet in the closing days of 1991. A negotiated settlement was finally reached at the World Trade Centre in Kempton Park in 1994. Elections held with black participation resulted in overwhelming victories for the ANC in 1994 and 1999.

Discourse of development

South Africa's decade of liberation, between the mid-1980s and the mid-1990s, saw intense discussion about the future course of economy and society (e.g. Sunter 1987; Bond 1991; Schrire 1992; Patel 1993). Formal discourses began to emerge, written by 'experts' on development: economic policy groups composed of radical and liberal academics advising the Congress of South African Trade Unions (COSATU) and the ANC bureaucracy; and increasingly people from business, conventional academia, the World Bank and the IMF producing counter-proposals. On the radical side, the previously dominant liberal interpretation of South African history had been replaced during the 1970s by Marxian analyses that followed leading European tendencies – Althusser and Poulantzas, Stuart Hall and cultural theory, regulation theory, and so on (Desai and Bohmke 1997). The mid-1980s saw a more formal radical research, often from neo-Marxist perspectives, on the impact of international sanctions on the South African economy, and the solution of internal social issues like housing and health. A series of conferences on the future of the South African economy, held outside the country in the late 1980s, was attended by ANC, SACP, union members and many prominent, exiled leftist academics. Inside South Africa, in the late 1980s and early 1990s, a number of research networks formed around macroeconomic policy issues. Two of the leading organizations were:

1 The Economic Trends Group (ET), formed in 1986 at the sugges-
   tion of COSATU, composed of leftist, union-oriented academics in
   Johannesburg, the University of Natal and Cape Town University.
   An important meeting was held in Harare, Zimbabwe, in 1991
   among COSATU, ET and the ANC's newly formed Department
   of Economic Planning which drew up a Draft Resolution on
   Economic Policy for circulation and discussion within the ANC
   organization. The ANC committed itself to promoting economic
   growth through redistribution, including satisfying basic needs
   and empowering the disadvantaged (Kentridge 1993). This was
   to be achieved by a mixed economy led by a developmental state
   (ANC 1991). The ANC national conference, held in May 1992,
   reaffirmed support for the 'basic needs' approach inherent in this
   document (ANC 1992). The proposal was heavily criticized by
   conventional economists, business organizations and the South
   African media, as inflationary (Marais 1998: 149–51). Later, a
   somewhat reconstituted ET research group, with help from the
   Institute for Development Studies at Sussex University, and with
   Canadian financing, conducted a detailed study of the South African economy under the auspices of the Industrial Strategy Project
   (ISP), which culminated in *Manufacturing Performance in South
   Africa* (Joffe et al. 1995). In the words of one (critical) observer,
   'The ISP's policy recommendations represent a distinct shift away
   from a national, demand-side, developmental approach to a more
   global, supply-side strategy for economic reconstruction' (Padayachee 1998: 437).
2 The Macro-Economic Research Group (MERG), founded in 1991
   on the recommendation of a mission from the Canadian International Development and Research Centre, centred on leftist
   academics in the University of the Witwatersrand Economics
   Department, with a wide network of contacts in the South African
   educational system, and initially well connected with ANC members within the country, such as Trevor Manuel, later to become

Minister of Finance, and Maria Ramos, later Director General of Finance. This proposed a post-Keynesian policy framework advocating a state-led social and physical infrastructural investment programe to be followed by sustained growth with increasing private investment (MERG 1993).

In the 1994 election, the ANC stood on ground specified by its Reconstruction and Development Programme (RDP), a popular policy document written by intellectuals from ET and MERG, together with representatives of various social movements and NGOs, and finalized by a series of workshops in a relatively open and democratic process (see Smith 1999). Six principles framed ANC policies: (1) an integrated and sustainable programme; (2) a people-driven process; (3) peace and security for all; (4) nation-building; (5) the linking of reconstruction and development; (6) the democratization of South Africa. Of these the key to economic policy was principle number 5. The South African economy, in deep structural crisis, was considered in need of fundamental restructuring. RDP economic policy was based on the principles of democracy, participation and development. In contrast to the view that economic growth and development/redistribution were contradictory processes, the RDP document claimed to 'break decisively' by integrating the two (ANC 1994: 6–7). Specifically this meant a 5 per cent economic growth rate and the annual creation of 300,000–500,000 non-agricultural jobs. The industrial strategy needed to accomplish these goals involved increasing national investment, especially in manufacturing, job creation and the meeting of basic needs. Stable policies, it was thought, would also create a climate conducive to foreign investment – the RDP mentioned, but did not stress, integration into the world economy in a manner that increased the potential to export manufactured goods. The RDP document warned foreign investors that they would have to abide by the country's laws and standards, particularly with respect to labour, and the government would ensure that knowledge and technical capacity were transferred to allow greater participation by workers in decision-making. Most of the proposals were written into a government White Paper on reconstruction and development in November 1994, entering into the official policy of the ANC-dominated government of national unity.

The White Paper differed from the RDP document in placing greater emphasis on 'financial and monetary discipline', the 'establishment of an economic environment conducive to economic growth' and 'trade and industry policies designed to foster a greater outward orientation' (Government of the Republic of South Africa 1994: 21). These can be read as signs that a reorientation of official policy had already begun with the move in decision-making from outside the country to Johannesburg, and then Pretoria, and with the inclusion of businesspeople on the redrafting team. Even so, in the first free elections held in a liberated South Africa, the ANC publicly committed itself to reconstruction and sustainable development that 'addresses the needs of our people without compromising the interests of future generations', improving the quality of life through a process of empowerment which gave the poor control over their lives, and increasing the poor's ability 'to mobilise sufficient development resources including from the democratic government where necessary' (ibid.: 15). Where vigorously applied, the RDP has worked well for poor people. In the five years following adoption of the RDP, 3 million people were provided with safe drinking water from taps within 200 metres of their houses as part of a plan by the Ministry of Water Affairs and Forestry to supply 21 million people with basic water services; the record on housing construction, by comparison, has been far less promising. The portent for the future seemed clear – there was going to be a democratic, redistributive, even socialistic, new society in South Africa.

Disciplining the ANC

It now appears, however, that the leadership of the ANC had secretly shifted allegiance away from the RDP and towards neoliberal policies well before the 1994 elections. In the period 1990–94, during which the ANC moved from illegal to legal opposition and partial incorporation into the South African state centralized in Pretoria, statements made by ANC leaders came under intense, critical attention by business spokespersons, academics, official commentators and the established media. The result was a disciplining of the ANC's radical positions as a consequence of which 'a more nuanced view won the day ... When Mandela's support of nationalisation earned a cool response inside South Africa and in the Western Media, a number of more qualified statements on nationalisation followed' (van der Burg 1990: 117). ANC leaders (Joe Slovo, Walter Sisulu, Thabo Mbeki) now found nationalization not necessarily fundamental to ANC policy: indeed, the former communist Mbeki added that nationalization had never been part of it. The ANC began to speak of policy alternatives, such as anti-trust legislation and government-appointed directors on the boards of major companies (Ceruti 1996). Asked why the ANC changed its position on nationalization, in an interview held

137

in 1995, Minister of Finance Trevor Manuel said that the collapse of the Soviet Union broke the romantic illusions of many leftists in the ANC (Habib and Padayachee 2000). The nationalization question, however, was only the most obvious aspect of a series of changes in ANC policies (Rantete 1994). Disciplinary pressure on the ANC came from two main sources: business organizations and the media within the country; and the World Bank and the IMF from outside.

Progressive business organizations, centred on the South African Chambers of Industries and Commerce and the Afrikaans Trade Institute, had long sought moderate policies from the apartheid state. Operating through the Urban Foundation liberal businesspeople lobbied for changes in housing policy, the recognition of informal housing and reform of the Pass Laws. Together with progressive clerics from some Afrikaner churches, members of the Urban Institute later formed the Consultative Business Movement (CBM – now called the National Business Initiative or NBI) to support negotiated change and pragmatic rather than 'ideological' economic policies. The CBM played a facilitative role in key negotiations, including those at Kempton Park, which brought about compromise between the ANC and the apartheid state.

When unbanning the ANC in 1990, Nationalist president F. W. de Klerk asked business leaders to articulate what the new South Africa might look like. In response, businesspeople, academics and development consultants produced a plethora of research documents on the future of the South African economy. Sanlam, an insurance conglomerate, laid out a Platform for Investment scenario castigating the ANC's 'macroeconomic populism' and calling instead for macroeconomic stringency, limited social restructuring, an outward-oriented economy and a facilitating state; the South African Chamber of Business produced *Economic Options for South Africa*, a document recognizing the need for economic reforms, but insisting that promoting optimal conditions for free enterprise to flourish was the best way of reducing poverty; the Mont Fleur scenario drew ANC and union executives into a 'social democratic' exercise that still managed to exclude redistributive state spending (Marais 1998: 150–51).

But for slick liberal sophistication, the report *South Africa: Prospects for Successful Transition* is particularly notable. The chairmen of NEDCOR, a holding group, whose main asset is Nedbank, one of South Africa's largest financial institutions, and Old Mutual, the country's biggest life insurance company, initiated a scenario exercise 'to gain greater understanding of the future business environment and ... to make the results known' (Tucker and Scott 1992: xv). A twenty-three-member team, made up largely of academic and bank economists, was assembled to run this heavily financed project. The authors of the final report, Bob Tucker, later general manager of Standard Bank of South Africa, and Bruce Scott, of the Harvard (Massachusetts) Business School, said that the scenario team performed a 'carefully researched comparative analysis' of alternative futures for South Africa based on 'liberal notions of restructuring and reform'. Forty directors and senior executives of Nedcor and Old Mutual were asked to sketch two scenarios for the transitional period 1990–95, one 'favourable' (democratic government, a bill of rights, pragmatic economic policy), the other 'unfavourable' (black government, African socialism, economic decline). Successful transition was conceptualized as stable democracy based on an equally stable social fabric, with rising incomes reasonably distributed. But as incomes had been falling, the authors of the report projected a 'change of gears' scenario based on assumptions of restructuring the economy to a higher growth path, social investment to 'stabilize the social fabric', and a change in the political process towards liberal democracy. This was described as 'controlled revolution' or 'sweeping change with social stability'. They believed that the gears of society had to be changed *before* the transition to black rule so that a new democratically elected government would inherit a 'successfully performing economy' (ibid.: 8). To achieve this they advocated redistribution *through* growth and change from an inward-looking resource orientation to an outward-looking manufacturing focus for the economy. The report emphasized stability, resisting populist pressures, a shared vision of the future, and achieving consensus. What was billed as a short-term 'scenario exercise' in the guise of 'articulating what the new South Africa might look like' became a device for implanting long-term, conventional yet liberal, business-oriented ideas about growth and development into elite and popular consciousness.

As important as the message carried by the 'scenario exercises' were the accompanying dissemination techniques:

> Their language was that of melodrama, laden with populist flip-
> pances and cartoon-like metaphors. Lavishly promoted (in the form
> of books, videos, multimedia presentations, newspaper supplements)
> their impact was ensured by a bewildering assortment of seminars,
> conferences, workshops, briefings, international 'fact-finding'
> trips and high-profile visits by carefully chosen foreign 'experts'
> – financed by business and foreign development agencies. ANC

leaders were feted with private 'orientation' sessions and confabs at exclusive game resorts. The ideological barrage was incessant, and amplified by the corporate-owned media which gleefully attacked any signs of heterodoxy and dissonance in ANC thinking. (Marais 1998: 150)

Neoliberal notions of 'redistribution through growth' in concert with an 'outward focus for the economy' began to appear with increasing frequency in discussions of development policy. In the late 1980s, the Afrikaner National Party had shifted from its previous import substitution strategy to a more export-oriented programme, codified in the Normative Economic Model (NEM) of 1993, essentially following IMF prescriptions. While first opposed by the ANC, a change in emphasis soon began towards a position more compatible with NEM and the IMF.

When Nelson Mandela was released from prison:

... [he] still believed in a classless society, while 'painfully aware' of the opposite trend. He looked for ways to reduce inequality. In September 1991 he told businessmen that only nationalization could redress the imbalances, though he would welcome an alternative. The confusing signals reflected arguments within the ANC which were more extreme than those that had raged through the socialist parties of Europe; for South Africa had long been an extreme case, both of inequality and of dependence on international capital. (Sampson 1999: 428)

Mandela believed that he was faced by the problem of building a non-racial and non-sexist society in a country whose economy was dependent on foreign investment capital. In the early 1990s his thinking shifted towards the investment part of this dilemma. The immediate occasion of Mandela's change of mind was the World Economic Forum, held at Davos, Switzerland, in February 1992. Sampson recounts the occasion for Mandela's change of heart:

He was lionized by the world's bankers and industrialists at lunches and dinners. He argued with them that other industrial countries, including Britain, Germany, and Japan, had needed nationalized industries to restore their economies after world wars. 'We are going through a traumatic experience of war against the people,' he explained, 'and therefore we need nationalization.' He was finally turned by three sympathetic delegates from the left. The Dutch Minister of Industry was sisterly and understanding, but smashed his argument. 'Look, that's what we understood then,' she explained, 'but now the economies of the world are interdepend-ent. The process of globalization is taking root. No economy can develop separately from the economies of other countries.' Leaders from two Asian socialist countries – China and Vietnam – told him how they had accepted private enterprise, particularly after the Soviet Union collapsed. 'They changed my views altogether,' recalled Mandela. 'I came home to say, "Chaps, we have to choose. We either keep nationalization and get no investment, or we modify our own attitude and get investment."' (ibid.: 429)

Also, in the early 1990s South Africa came under increased scrutiny from the World Bank and the IMF. (While teaching for a semester in Johannesburg I interviewed a person present at one of the meetings between ANC and World Bank economists. He told me that each time the ANC outlined a proposal, the economists 'opened their laptops, made a forecast of its negative effect on the economy, and blew us away'.) The World Bank assiduously courted ANC leftists as part of a 'trust-building' campaign. The bank's position was that poverty could be alleviated and jobs created through private sector expansion in labour-intensive industries (World Bank 1994, 1996; Fallon and de Silva 1994; Jonsson and Subramanian 2000). As prelude to a 1993 $850 million loan, the IMF published a report on the South African economy stressing an outward-looking macroeconomic strategy with growth trickling down to the poor through private sector employ-ment growth and increased government revenue (IMF 1992). A secret 'letter of intent' signed with the IMF in 1993, and agreed to by the ANC, committed the South African government to 'responsible management' of the economy, interpreted as cutting state deficits, controlling inflation, imposing wage restraint, adopting outward orientation and, most importantly, recognizing the superiority of market forces over state regulatory interventions, and other neoliberal positions (Padayachee 1994). According to one left critic, Patrick Bond (1997), the ANC government not only followed IMF policies, but liberalized the economy faster and further than expected. Massive international pressures lay behind this shift: 'ANC leaders including Trevor Manuel and Tito Mboweni visited the International Monetary Fund in Washington; tycoons from the Brenthurst Group – first set up by Mandela and business friends – met with the ANC to discuss economic problems; while the British and American Ambassadors kept inquiring about MERG's plans' (Sampson 1999: 466).

With these preparations, things changed rapidly when the ANC assumed leadership of the Government of National Unity after the

141

1994 elections. An independent governmental department supervising implementation of the RDP was soon closed, with its duties assumed by the office of Deputy President Thabo Mbeki. In 1995 and 1996 the battle of the scenarios intensified. The South Africa Federation coordinated a report on behalf of the business community advocating a neoliberal economic policy. By comparison, the 1.8-million-member COSATU's 'Keynesian' alternative, set out in *Social Equity and Job Creation* (COSATU 1996), advocated 'an expansion of the social wage through mass state housing financed through public borrowing, a national health programme, all-embracing social security and public job creation, as well as an enlarged public sector' (*Southern Africa Report*, November 1997). The SACP called for worker empowerment and public sector spending. Yet the question had already been settled.

Getting in GEAR

The ANC's response was dramatically revealed by the next development report, entitled *Growth, Employment and Redistribution* (GEAR), prepared by the Department of Finance, with Trevor Manuel as minister, and a team of academics, representatives of the Development Bank of Southern Africa, the South African Reserve Bank and the World Bank (Government of the Republic of South Africa 1996). GEAR reiterated the RDP's link between economic growth and the redistribution of incomes, as a concession to the left. But it argued that much higher economic growth rates were necessary to achieve social objectives. Sustained growth on this higher plane (6 per cent and 400,000 new jobs a year) required transformation towards an outward-oriented economy centred on a 'competitive platform for a powerful expansion by the tradable goods sector' within a 'stable environment for confidence' with a 'profitable surge in private investment' and 'flexibility within the collective bargaining system' (Government of the Republic of South Africa 1996: 2). A series of policies was recommended to promote an outward-oriented industrial economy integrated into the global environment and responsive to market pressures. The state's budget deficit was to be cut from 5.4 to 3.0 per cent of GDP by 2000, while trade was to be liberalized. The GEAR report called for a national social agreement to create a competitive environment for investment and economic growth, for example through wage moderation. All this was to 'break current constraints and catapult the economy to the higher levels of growth, development and employment needed to provide a better life for all South Africans' (ibid.: 2). In March 1997 Minister of Finance Trevor

Manuel delivered the first budget prepared by an ANC minister, which consolidated the ANC's support for these neoliberal policies. With this ANC economic policy was made compatible with liberal-business opinion within the country (redistribution *through* growth), and with the neoliberal structural adjustment policies outlined earlier by the World Bank and the IMF. Indeed, all three positions became virtually synonymous, except that the ANC has been particularly vigorous in pursuing privatization, deregulation and an 'internationally competitive' business climate.

South Africa's unions objected that the GEAR report was adopted to please big business rather than the working class. Critical discussion focused on three areas: (1) the proposal for cutting government expenditures as a proportion of GDP in the context of massive needs that could only be met by state intervention; (2) the government's commitment to 'flexible labour markets', widely interpreted as a euphemism for the suppression of unions; (3) the idea of privatization of parastatals (industries run by government-controlled corporations) to reduce state debt, again interpreted as an attack on the government's power to control the economy in the interests of poor people. The unions called the GEAR a self-imposed structural adjustment policy. They argued that GEAR policies reimposed social and economic conditions like those experienced under apartheid. The reply from the ANC, as illustrated by an article by Andrew Donaldson (1997), chief director of financial planning in the South African Department of Finance, was that GEAR policies of macroeconomic constraint, especially reductions in public spending, remained compatible with the RDP goals of targeting the remaining public expenditures towards the poor. Greeting such replies with scepticism, the unions threatened mass actions against GEAR, withdrawing support from the ANC and starting a more leftist party in company with the SACP. In the interests of political harmony, COSATU and the SACP ended up working for the ANC in the 1999 electoral campaign, agreeing to mute their objections to the GEAR macroeconomic policy during the campaign. As president since Mandela's retirement in June 1999, Thabo Mbeki reaffirmed the government's commitment, albeit in ambiguous language ('GEAR in the broad framework of the RDP') and with vague references to an 'African Renaissance' (for background see Smith 1999). The Ministry of Trade and Industry, under Alec Erwin (formerly an official in COSATU), signalled its commitment to GEAR by designating ten Spatial Development Initiatives (SDIs) as unregulated platforms for export-led growth. Under the Igoli 2002 plan, city services in Johannesburg are to be privatized, a measure that has aroused intense opposition led by SAMWU, the militant union of municipal workers. Even the University of the Witwatersrand is being privatized, to the disgust of faculty, students and staff. Nevertheless, the ANC remains committed to the GEAR strategy. GEAR has the backing of the elite fraction of the ANC in control of state macroeconomic policy, although it is fiercely opposed by the unions represented by COSATU (Bond 2000).

South Africa passes now into its period of greatest economic trial. The extreme, persisting racial inequalities result in a high level of social violence, exemplified by the widespread battering of women, frequent assassinations of political and union leaders, and a staggeringly high crime rate – the murder rate in Johannesburg is twice that of New York City at its worst (in 1990) and six or seven times the present New York murder rate. At the same time the country is experiencing an Aids pandemic, with 20 per cent of the population HIV-positive in a country where reproductive information faces severe problems in terms of availability and customary sexual resistance, government expenditures and health facilities are limited, and for years the prime minister doubted that the HIV virus was the causal agent. Half the people of South Africa live in rural areas, 70 per cent under conditions of dire poverty. Social transformation must entail massive redistribution of people from semi-deserts, in which millions were dumped when their lands were taken during apartheid, into habitable areas, where the vague possibility of a job exists. This process cannot begin until land is restored to its previous occupants, or redistributed to people in need – rebuilding the society without land restoration etches the inequalities of the past into the landscape of the future. The Lands Claims Commission, established by the new state in 1995, was flooded by 63,000 claims, mainly for land restitution. Only 3 per cent of the disputed land had been redistributed five years later.

Sub-hegemony

If GEAR-type policies were working, all this might be of mere doctrinal interest, significant only to us leftist academics who, like priests, are permitted to take positions purely on the basis of faith because our incomes are secure. Yet there is scant evidence that GEAR is working, even in its own terms of producing the growth that might, eventually, somehow, allow income redistribution: South Africa's unemployment rate is about 30 per cent and the economy needs to grow at a rate of 5–6 per cent a year to change this significantly. Sixty-one per cent of Africans and 38 per cent of mixed-race 'coloureds' are poor, compared with 5 per cent of Indians and 1 per cent of whites. At least 22 million people in South Africa – well over half the population – live in poverty. On average, they survive on R144 (US $24.00) per person per month. And 11.8 million of the poorest 23.8 million South Africans 'lived in households that received no social assistance in the same year [2002] ... that the [government-appointed] Committee of Inquiry into a Comprehensive System of Social Security for South Africa (Taylor Committee) recommended the introduction of a basic income grant (BIG), i.e. a grant of R100 [US $16.70] per person per month for every South African citizen, regardless of age or income level' (Centre for Civil Society 2005). The ANC and the South African Treasury Department's response was that a BIG was unaffordable, would deter foreign investors and impede economic growth.

This basically follows the position taken by the IMF, which reports every year on the South African economy in its country report. (Article IV consultations with IMF member countries take place once a year, and are published as IMF Article IV Staff Reports: Article IV Obligations Regarding Exchange Arrangements is part of the Articles of Agreement of the IMF adopted on 22 July 1944 saying 'each member undertakes to collaborate with the Fund and other members to assure orderly exchange arrangements and to promote a stable system of exchange rates. In particular, each member shall, among other things: endeavor to direct its economic and financial policies toward the objective of fostering orderly economic growth with reasonable price stability, with due regard to its circumstances.') The IMF (2005) regards South Africa as playing a leadership role in sub-Saharan Africa – what I call, in this book, a sub-hegemonic role. Its reports stress South Africa's 'implementing sound monetary and fiscal policies' so that 'government finances continue to be strong' and 'conditions in the labor market have improved with the introduction of legislation to streamline the arbitration process and allow for more flexibility in employment', so the IMF 'expressed concern about labor market reform'. Even so, the IMF 'cautioned that while higher growth could be anticipated, it was unlikely to significantly affect unemployment and poverty'. In 2005, Anne O. Krueger, First Deputy Managing Director of the International Monetary Fund (IMF), took part in the annual report on South Africa. She too thought that:

> More rapid economic growth is vital to achieve the significant reduc-
> tions in poverty we all want to see. This requires structural reform
> across the economy. The need for labor market reform is especially
> pressing: tackling high unemployment is difficult everywhere and

South Africa is no exception ... A review of labor legislation and regulations and their impact on employment, with the aim of increasing job creation, would help raise employment levels and the rate of economic growth ... So would further trade liberalization.

The World Bank has a limited presence in South Africa, with thirteen loans approved for a total amount of approximately US $302.8 million and eight active World Bank operations with a commitment value of approximately US $15 million. The South African Department of Trade and Industry cooperates with the World Bank Investment Climate Survey to look at South Africa's 'investment climate'. The 2004 survey of 800 enterprises found that 'the investment climate for large formal firms in South Africa appears favorable in many ways, [but] some challenges remain', according to Ritva Reinikka, the World Bank Country Director for South Africa. 'Wages for managers, professionals, and skilled workers are high by international standards, eroding South Africa's competitiveness. Exchange rate volatility makes exporting difficult – and yet for a high growth rate exports are critical.' Therefore: 'Addressing these issues will help towards achieving the target growth rate of 6 percent per annum to stimulate development and job creation' (World Bank 2006b). South Africa is also regularly examined by the New York private bond rating agencies. These have recently cautiously approved of South Africa's changes in economic policy. In November 2002 the economic evaluator Standard and Poor's revised its outlook on South Africa's economic ratings from 'stable' to 'positive'. In August 2002, Fitch Ratings also revised the outlook on South Africa's foreign currency debt from 'stable' to 'positive'. And in November 2001 another agency, Moody's, upgraded the country's long-term foreign currency debt rating from Baa3 to Baa2 and raised the government's domestic debt rating from Baa1 to A2. As the credit rating agencies say: 'The privatisation programme is encouraging foreign direct investment with the future looking bright in this regard' (ibid.). (The problem with these 'bright futures' is that they never dawn for poor people, though the sun always rises to shine on those 'investors' and their 'analysts'.)

The basic premise behind GEAR and recent South African economic policy is that the country lacks the capital for investment in rapid growth achieved by any means, via the satisfaction of internal needs, or through export orientation. Attracting foreign capital means creating the right business climate for private investment. This in turn means adopting neoliberal policies, including 'wage moderation' and 'more flexible labour markets' – so we find former union officials agreeing with the IMF and the World Bank on the necessity of 'internationally competitive' wages. Yet South Africa's unions have a long history of leftist militancy from years of opposition to apartheid which has turned towards demanding higher wages in the strike-prone years since 1994. COSATU along with the SACP is a member of the tripartite alliance with the ANC. Thus, 'creating the right business climate' entails the state, led by the ANC, turning against organized labour, its militant base of support. Indeed, the history of state–labour relations in post-apartheid South Africa can be read exactly in these terms, as the black nationalist side of the ANC comes to the fore, and what used to be a social movement becomes a political party, dominated by the rising black bourgeoisie, the new state bureaucrats, the party functionaries and the cellphone elite, all in league with the IFIs and the 'international business community'. In brief, for neoliberal GEAR-type policies to 'succeed' in their own terms, the state must repress labour and this, in the South African class context, means a generation of internecine struggle. Even so, the IFIs conclude that the economic growth they think might result from these draconian measures is 'unlikely to significantly affect unemployment and poverty'. What is a country to do?

There are alternatives to GEAR coming from positions that express the social transformation perspective. The RDP remains officially in place, with support from significant leftist fractions of the ANC. The trade unions and social movements have their own (Keynesian) development alternatives. South Africa presents an opportunity for what Arthur MacEwan (1999) calls a democratic strategy of development. The core of this strategy, for MacEwan, consists of state investment in social programmes. These meet the basic needs of a wide spectrum of the population; they can be the foundations for direct popular participation; and they contribute to income and power equalities. In a democratic strategy, the main connection lies between education, understood as the transmission of knowledge, information and understanding, together with socialization related to the social organization of the workplace, and economic growth, achieved through resulting increases in labour productivity. Here the essential idea is that capitalists have to be constrained and guided by policies to assure that in enriching themselves they contribute to larger social goals. In particular, the aim should be what Gordon (1996) called the 'high road to economic change', the route lying through technology, productivity and wage growth, rather than the 'low road' through assembly lines, conflict, insecurity and low wages. So, policy should be designed to construct markets so that they move society towards a technological high road, through schooling, investment incentives and the regulation of foreign trade. These measures should be linked with a smallholder programme and land reform to increase local production of food. All this would involve popular participation in the formulation of policy, something that is important in itself, but also something that generates commitment and raises the likelihood of success.

When the ANC took power in 1994, internal conditions existed for this kind of democratic strategy. The liberation of South Africa brought a wave of optimistic commitment to social transformation, a network of highly organized anti-apartheid social movements was in place, while a deep sense of guilt prevailed among the white minority – in short all the conditions necessary for initiating a democratic strategy in the only possible way: tax the rich, invest in the poor. Thus the question underlying this entire discussion must at last be addressed. Why did the ANC shift from its long-held commitment to structural transformation through democratic developmental means towards structural adjustment, using neoliberal economic means? The decade of South Africa's liberation, 1985–95, was marked by an articulation between three discursive positions each signified by academic-institutional-media complexes: (1) counter-hegemony – the ANC and its leftist supporters; (2) sub-hegemony, South African capital with strategic liberal business organizations partly integrated into the ANC; and (3) hegemony, global capital together with development institutions interested in the course taken by a post-apartheid South Africa.

1 Counter-hegemony. The ANC had a fifty-year history of translating popular and widespread resentment against the seizure of land and the imprisonment of people into counter-hegemonic proposals for justice, equality, socialism and development. As the end of apartheid drew near, dissident intellectuals in exile and at universities in Johannesburg, Cape Town and Durban, armed with Marxian analyses, along with SACP members and COSATU officials, formed a series of socialist research groups (ET and MERG most prominently) to produce leftist development documents aimed at guiding ANC economic policy. Under the still-dangerous circumstances of the time, it is doubtful whether institutional or theoretical consistency emerged in a fully organized AIM or a coherent counter-hegemonic development discourse: institutionally the left split into fractions, for example the ANC Department of Economic Planning and MERG, divided by suspicion and jealousy;

theoretically, two main versions of development discourse emerged: a workerist nationalization and state planning discourse, and a left-Keynesian, democratic policy of growth through redistribution, social investment led by a developmental state, and basic-needs-oriented industrialization that formed the main, left content of the RDP. Momentous changes were occurring exactly as the possibility of the ANC assuming state power in the late 1980s intensified. SACP members in particular were disillusioned by the fall of the Soviet Union in 1989. In this context, the leftist discourse on democratic development failed to translate a morally superior stance into a coherent, counter-hegemonic policy position. Leftist development was associated with outmoded ideologies, even by activists who had previously dedicated their lives to its cause. We are speaking here not necessarily about a loss of principle by previously committed radical activists, but a capturing of the sense of political practicality and economic realism among politicians and bureaucrats who retained their commitment to South Africa's oppressed majority, but switched direction in the means of achieving progress towards policy positions they had previously despised.

2 Sub-hegemony. South African capital had long been preparing for the inevitable day when apartheid would end. Liberal business organizations strategically ensured that liberation was finally achieved through negotiation rather than violent upheaval. Encouraged by an increasingly realistic Nationalist government, business organizations invested heavily in scenario exercises exploring redistribution through growth led by the initiative of private enterprise. In these partly home-grown visions, the role of the state would be limited to providing the right business climate for investment and, at most, overseeing limited social redistribution through welfare, education and housing programmes financed by taxation rather than deficit spending. These ideas were effectively disseminated, as a relatively coherent development discourse, by consultants, economic experts and media personalities, in presentations to the elite of South African society, including the upper echelons of the ANC. Most importantly the models proposed by local business organizations were lent legitimacy through correspondence with 'accepted' international economic opinion. Particularly important is the use of 'accepted' forecasting techniques that provide 'quantitative information' about what policies will result in. Well … GEAR made the optimistic forecasts shown in Table 5.1 as part of its claim for a better economy for everyone by following the

149

Table 5.1 Projections versus reality in South Africa

	1996	1997	1998
% growth in GDP (GEAR projection)	3.5	2.9	3.8
% growth in GDP (reality)	3.2	1.7	0.1
New jobs per year ('000) (GEAR projection)	126	252	246
New jobs per year ('000) (reality)	-71	-126	-186
% real private investment growth (GEAR projection)	9.3	9.1	9.3
% real private investment growth (reality)	6.1	3.1	-0.7

Source: Adelzadeh 1999.

policies it proposed. The table compares the forecast with what actually happened. These projections always err on the side of favourability to the argument proposed. Once made, and opinion changed, they are forgotten. And should anyone be nasty enough to remind the 'professional economists' of what they once said, there are lots of easy outs such as 'forecasting is notoriously difficult in Third World countries'. Meantime, power has been claimed on the basis of a guess disguised as a forecast. This might be funny were it not for the fact that several million poor and desperate people suffer from lack of effective discussions of policy alternatives in the plush offices of the economic experts in Pretoria.

We are speaking here of a geopolitical context in which left alternatives to free market capitalism, whether communist or social democratic, have all but disappeared as viable possibilities in the hegemonic world view. As one economist put it: 'Capital is all-powerful; national policy must pay obeisance or pay the cost' (Nattrass 1996, quoted in Smith 1999: 173).

3 Hegemony. Global capital's interests in a country with strategic economic and political significance were directly represented by the IMF, which made several loans to South Africa under well-defined stabilization conditionalities, and the World Bank, which used anti-poverty and job-creation programmes as leverage points suggesting structural adjustment. By the mid-1980s both institutions had fastened on to a standard set of neoliberal means of achieving rapid economic growth in countries like South Africa. My argument is that these policies derived from the capturing of the leading developmental model by ideas stemming from neoliberal, monetarist political economics. This discourse proposes joining the global capitalist system through trading connections freed of

restrictions, with a domestic environment made internationally competitive through deregulation, privatization, wage restraint and prudence in government spending. As the end of apartheid drew near, the ANC came under heavy diplomatic and institutional pressure to adopt policies that accorded with these positions. More significantly neoliberalism became the picture of economic progress that flooded the speculative imaginary on stock exchanges and currency markets locally and around the world. Even the whisper that deviation might taint this idealized vision brought instant retribution, most obviously as runs on the rand, from the bears of the world's financial markets. In contrast with the disarray and disillusionment on the counter-hegemonic left, the interests of global institutions and local business federations were synthesized in a hegemonic neoliberal discourse that has learned to turn a compassionate face on social problems moralized as poverty, illness and ignorance. Acting not in unison, but in parallel, global hegemonic and regional sub-hegemonic forces joined in projecting a discourse seemingly invested with the authority of respectability and truth which captured the developmental imaginary to such a degree that even the model's massive failure to deliver has barely shaken the confidence that eventually unfettered private enterprise will come through. What terror on Robbens Island could not do to Mandela, the 'sympathetic' atmosphere at the Davos World Economic Forum could.

SIX
Counter-hegemony

§ Every year, social movements opposed to neoliberal globalization meet at the World Social Forum (WSF). There, for a few days,
they discuss an alternative 'Southern agenda'. The meeting takes
the form of a festival. But the thousands of people who attend a
week of conferences, panels, workshops, seminars, cultural activities
and demonstrations have the serious intent of producing real social
and economic alternatives to neoliberal globalization. (The phrase
'anti-globalization' movements often used in this context, I think,
concedes globalization to neoliberalism. The WSF is the best kind of
globalization in the sense that it convenes large numbers of people
from movements from all over the world. Social movements representing millions of active poor people represent globalization far better
than a few thousand capitalists and experts at the WEF.) The idea
for a WSF came out of the massive protests against the World Trade
Organization meeting in Seattle in 1999. Three activists met in Paris
in January 2000 to discuss alternatives to contemporary globalization: Oded Grajew, founder of the Brazilian Business Association
for Citizenship (CIVES), an organization of progressive businesses
aligned with the Brazilian Workers Party; Francisco Whitaker, of the
Brazilian Justice and Peace Commission (CBJP); and Bernard Cassen,
chair of ATTAC-France (Association for the Taxation of Financial
Transactions for the Aid of Citizens). Grajew proposed a Social
Forum as an alternative to the World Economic Forum, held each
year in Davos, Switzerland, which convenes leaders of Western states,
CEOs and some NGOs, to discuss the global economy. As we have
seen, the WEF supports neoliberal globalization. Grajew proposed an
alternative Social Forum, held at the same time, to discuss alternatives
to those policies supported by business at the WEF. The idea was to
hold the forum in the global South, preferably the city of Porto Alegre,
Brazil, known for its participatory budget process, and controlled at
that time by the Brazilian Workers Party. The city's agreement was
secured, and the first World Social Forum was held nine months later
with 10,000 people attending. The second forum in 2002 saw 50,000
people show up; the third in 2003 was attended by 100,000 activists;

the fourth, in India, had 120,000 participants; and the fifth, in 2005, in Brazil, registered 150,000. In 2006, a polycentric World Social Forum was held in several places: Bamako, Mali; Caracas, Venezuela; and Karachi, Pakistan. Along with these, many smaller Social Forums have taken place, including the European Social Forum, the Asian Social Forum, the Mediterranean Social Forum, the Italian Social Forum, Liverpool Social Forum and the Boston Social Forum.

WSF alternative principles

After the first forum, a committee formed from Brazilian organizations drew up a Charter of Principles to guide the continuation of the forum. The statement read in part:

> The World Social Forum is an open meeting place for reflective thinking, democratic debate of ideas, the formulation of proposals, a free exchange of experiences and interlinking of groups and movements of civil society opposed to neo-liberalism and domination of the world by capital and imperialism, groups that are committed to building a planetary society directed towards fruitful relationships among Mankind and between it and the Earth. The alternatives proposed at the World Social Forum oppose a process of globalization commanded by large multinational corporations and by governments and international institutions at the service of those corporations' interests. The alternatives are designed to ensure that globalization in solidarity will prevail as a new stage in world history. This will respect universal human rights, the rights of all citizens – men and women – of all nations, and of the environment, and rest on democratic international systems and institutions at the service of social justice, equality and the sovereignty of peoples. (World Social Forum 2006)

Looking at the presentations made at the 2002 WSF, Fisher and Ponniah (2003; also Ponniah 2006) see social movements as taking positions that are anti-corporate, anti-imperialist and anti-hierarchical. Social movements see globalization as the expansion of a corporate, capitalist empire, in which production is guided by the imperative of profit, rather than the satisfaction of people's needs. The economy dominates all other aspects of society, rather than society and social imperatives determining economy. The social movements at the WSF, say Fisher and Ponniah, believe in radical, participatory democracy – participatory in the sense that civil society organizations are engaged directly in government. Movements from the Third World in particular want decisions about debt (to the First World) and debt repayment to be made by civil society rather than states – many activists are in favour of debt repudiation on the grounds that only the elites benefited from the loans. While some movements want to reform the state, many see the Third World state as oppressive, and want local control and participatory democracy, with links among more decentralized communities in a 'Southern Front'. (Networks of movements and activists have emerged in the last few years; many activists find networks to be a powerful instrument for changing the world since they 'anticipate' the features of the new world they want to build – they are decentralized, democratic, coercion free and radically non-hierarchical.) At the WSF, the 'youth camp' is most against hierarchy, centralization and top-down decision-making, whether by states or corporations. They want autonomy from state and capital, following the model pursued by the Zapatista movement among indigenous people in Chiapas, Mexico, whereas other more traditionally left movements want to regulate the state, and the state to regulate capital. Radical social movements are anti-bureaucratic and anti-expert. The movements represent the people, not the experts. Social movements want to 'recover' global society from expert domination and embed society within a collective human universe.

Let me repeat, the WSF is a festival of alternatives rather than a policy-setting body. The ideas presented are visionary glimpses into the WSF theme of 'another world is possible' rather than exact theoretical or policy strategies. These are activists, poets, musicians and intellectuals who want the poor peoples of the world to know that there are others like them, people who have not given up, but are thinking back against oppression. There is also a need, however, for strategizing, theorizing and specifying alternative development. This requires alternative institutions packed with committed, educated, hard-working, activist intellectuals. Here the problem lies not in a lack of good people, nor of basic, alternative ideas, and certainly not a lack of commitment. The main problem is lack of funding to support the further development of alternative theories, strategies and policies. Why a lack of funds for what is probably the most important activity in the world today – devising alternatives to the Washington Consensus? It is because the funding for research comes from people who have money. When the rich give to the poor, they fund charities – such as the Bill and Melinda Gates Foundation – that try, ever in vain, to clean up the consequences of poverty, rather than transform its causes. For good reason, since an over-accumulation of global wealth in the hands of people like them *is* the cause of poverty – you cannot expect the rich to fund their own demise! Somehow the Ford family's money ended up in a Ford Foundation that is supposed to fund alternatives. But the foundation is overcommitted and, in any case, averse to funding alternative development theories and strategies. So counter-hegemonic thinking comes cheap. Most theorists earn their living by working hard – teaching, for example – and think and write, speak and organize, for free and from commitment. No problem – we have a forum, we have commitment and we have support from millions of people in social movements.

UN agencies

What about the UN agencies – UCTAD, UNDP and so on – as sources of counter-hegemonic ideas and policies? Here we need to understand the history of development programmes at the UN. Walden Bello (2002), founding director of Focus on the Global South (see below), argues that the post-war period of decolonization produced a Third World movement for the redistribution of global economic power – away from its exclusively Western, capitalist bases and towards the peoples of the periphery. Structuralism was the dominant view of the majority in the UN General Assembly, where the principle of one country, one vote prevails, and where the world's people meet in the closest thing to a global democratic assembly that presently exists. The outcome was supposed to be a special UN Fund for Economic Development (SUNFED), in which the criterion for loans would be development need, rather than banking rules. Opposed to this movement, Bello argues, First World governments resisted by backing the IMF and the World Bank, where voting is according to capital subscription, and the USA has 18 per cent of the vote. One such response was to set up the International Development Association (IDA) attached to the World Bank as its main 'soft loan window'. Along with creating a chronically underfunded UN agency (UNDP, the UN Development Programme), this derailed the Third World governments' demand for a global development institution that they, representing most of the world's peoples, might control.

Third World efforts at achieving economic reform continued in UNCTAD and through the call for a New International Economic Order. These efforts were increasingly resisted by the USA, with ideas particularly coming from the Heritage Foundation, which as we have seen is a right-wing Washington think tank. The Reagan administration, Bello says, came to power with a mandate not only to roll back communism, but also, at the same opportune moment, to discipline the Third World, including the state-assisted capitalist countries of

South-East Asia. This was accomplished through stabilization loans, structural adjustment and neoliberal reform programmes pushed by the World Bank and the IMF in the 1980s and 1990s. The US response to the East Asian crisis of 1997, he says, should be understood not as helping economic recovery, but as a largely successful attempt at resubordination. Additionally, Bello agues, the pro-Third World agency UNCTAD was effectively replaced by the WTO, founded in 1994. The world, he concludes, is now governed by Western-controlled institutions, by the G7/8, led by the USA, together with the IMF, the World Bank, WTO and OECD. The US position is that the existing global capitalist system is basically sound and that significant reform is unnecessary. And that position is backed by ferocious military, economic and cultural power.

UNCTAD

The United Nations Conference on Trade and Development (UNCTAD) was established in 1964 as the principal organ of the United Nations General Assembly dealing with trade, investment and development issues. The organization's goals are to 'maximize the trade, investment and development opportunities of developing countries and assist them in their efforts to integrate into the world economy on an equitable basis'. UNCTAD has 400 staff members and an annual regular budget of approximately $50 million, with $25 million of extra-budgetary technical assistance funds. UNCTAD says that it does three things: (1) it functions as a forum for intergovernmental deliberations, supported by discussions with experts and exchanges of experience, aimed at consensus-building; (2) it undertakes research, policy analysis and data collection for the debates of government representatives and experts; (3) it provides technical assistance to developing countries, especially the least-developed countries and economies in transition (UNCTAD 2006a). For the most part the documents produced by UNCTAD are bland, polite reports written by overpaid, self-indulged 'international experts'. But for a while, *The Least Developed Countries Report*, put out by UNCTAD, functioned as at least a mild critique of Washington Consensus policies. For example, the 2004 report was an empirical analysis of the relationship between trade and poverty in the least-developed countries (LDCs) – as I have said, increasing exports is the standard neoliberal line on producing economic growth and reducing poverty. The UNCTAD report showed, however, that export growth was rarely associated with sustained poverty reduction in the LDCs during the 1990s. Persistent mass poverty in the LDCs is not due, according to the report, to lack of integration into the global economy, nor to insufficient trade liberalization, but is rather the consequence of a historical process of underdevelopment. In fact, the evidence indicates that the extensive trade liberalization has not thus far resulted in a form of integration that supports sustained and inclusive development. What export-led growth does occur is often 'enclave-led growth', a form of economic growth concentrated in a small part of the economy, either geographically or sectorally, such as manufacturing in export processing zones, tourist developments that rely on imports, mining developments and others (UNCTAD 2004).

The first session of UNCTAD in 1964 established a Group of 77 (G77), consisting of seventy-seven developing countries (membership has subsequently increased to 132 countries). This is the largest Third World coalition in the United Nations. The Group of 77 (2006) articulates the collective economic interests of Third World countries and increases its joint negotiating capacity on all major international economic issues at the UN. At the tenth UNCTAD meeting in 2000, the Group of 77 explored policy alternatives for poor countries. Martin Khor, director of the Third World Network, one of the more effective of the international NGOs opposing the World Bank, the IMF and the WTO, reported on the meeting (Khor 2001). First, he said, a fall in the terms of trade for non-fuel commodities vis-à-vis manufactures between 1980 and 2000 led to massive losses of income for underdeveloped regions – $56 billion in the four-year period 1986–89 for sub-Saharan Africa alone (an amount that dwarfs the 'aid' given 'in return'). To remedy this, Khor suggested a new round of international commodity agreements or, failing this, Third World 'rationalization' of supply, as with petroleum exports by OPEC. Trade liberalization, Khor argues, has negative results for underdeveloped countries and should be resisted or very selectively applied. The WTO, he says, is in serious need of reform, especially in terms of its 'culture of decision making'. Second, financial liberalization has produced turmoil in underdeveloped countries and needs to be curbed through national capital controls, exchange rate management, management of foreign exchange reserves, and other measures that he outlines. Third, proposals for investment liberalization made at OECD and WTO meetings brought into question the whole issue of the effect of FDI on development. Khor argued for the national regulation of FDI and a new international investment regime, presenting several compelling arguments that are now seldom heard in a discourse dominated by neoliberal orthodoxy in which FDI is sacrosanct. In a general conclusion Khor argued for more South–South policy coordination, for example through UNCTAD and UNDP; for democratic global institutions; for rebalancing the relative power of state and market; and reconceptualizing development strategies away from the free market model. The Group of 77 therefore begins to propose effective counter-hegemonic policy strategies.

This kind of counter-expert thinking helps. But it is unlikely to continue in UNCTAD. In 2005, UNCTAD got a new secretary-general, Supachai Panitchpakdi, formerly director-general of the WTO (2002–05), and an advocate of free trade. The secretary-general of UNCTAD then established a Panel of Eminent Persons to look at 'what could be the best strategies for UNCTAD to fulfill its development mission and mandates' and to advise the secretary-general. The panel included: Fernando Henrique Cardoso, former President of Brazil (1995–2002), under whose administration Brazil adopted neoliberal economic policies; Jagdish Bhagwatti, Professor of Economics and Law at Columbia University, the world's most ardent academic advocate of free trade; and Lawrence H. Summers, at that time still president of Harvard University, and before that Secretary of the US Treasury, and before that Vice-President of Development Economics and Chief Economist of the World Bank, and totally committed to privatization, free trade and neoliberalization. The panel submitted a report that criticized UNCTAD, saying that its 'normative work is sometimes characterized by a mindset that leads to rhetorical exercises instead of focusing on pragmatic development solutions' and therefore UNCTAD has been 'excluded from shaping the international institutional framework that has evolved to address development issues in a globalizing world'. Therefore, in the context of an overall reform of the UN, 'the challenge is to change the mentality and "culture" in UNCTAD's normative work' so that it comes up with 'pragmatic development policy solutions ... UNCTAD would do well to extend its future analysis to ways and means of achieving what some have called a "shared success" among countries ... This requires overcoming confrontational attitudes, building trust and creating a comfort zone that nurtures a spirit of development partnership and "shared success"' (UNCTAD 2006b: 8–10, 33). The eminent persons then suggested that UNCTAD construct a network of international think tanks around this spiritual motif. With this they disciplined the one UN institution that dared occasionally to think in terms of a counter-expertise. With this the eminent persons told UNCTAD to 'come in to the comfort zone of shared success'. With this UNCTAD was instructed to neoliberalize and join the Washington Consensus ... or else.

UNDP

The United Nations Development Programme (UNDP) promotes what it calls 'people-centered development' through the production of *Human Development Reports* (HDRs). The HDR, independently produced by a team of leading scholars and development practitioners, wants to shift the development debate away from its preoccupation with economic growth, 'towards a balanced concern for equity, sustainability, productivity and empowerment' – this being measured by the Human Development Index, an alternative to GDP as a measure of development. The UNDP is now heavily involved in strategizing how to reach the MDGs following a 'blueprint agreed to by all the world's countries and all the world's leading development institutions' – 'poor countries have pledged to govern better, and invest in their people through health care and education. Rich countries have pledged to support them, through aid, debt relief, and fairer trade'. The UNDP (2005) produced the main report on the MDGs employing a group of experts headed by Jeffrey Sachs, an expert I mentioned in Chapter 4. The report opens with a brave declaration:

> We have the opportunity in the coming decade to cut world poverty by half. Billions more people could enjoy the fruits of the global economy. Tens of millions of lives can be saved. The practical solutions exist. The political framework is established. And for the first time, the cost is utterly affordable. Whatever one's motivation for attacking the crisis of extreme poverty – human rights, religious values, security, fiscal prudence, ideology – the solutions are the same. All that is needed is action.

In essence, the UNDP and its Sachs-led team of experts want to cut global poverty in half, and save tens of millions of lives, through poor countries producing poverty reduction strategies, like those already crafted for the World Bank HIPC programme, in transparent and inclusive processes that involve increased public investments, while promoting the private sector, all this paid for by greatly increased official development assistance. High-income countries should open their markets to developing-country exports, mobilize support for global scientific research and rapidly increase their level of aid. A dozen MDG 'fast-track' countries and a group of 'quick-win' actions should be chosen to show that aid is effective. Overall, the UN and its UNDP should work closely with the IFIs to improve the quality of technical advice. If only it were this easy. Feel sorry. Give more aid. 'Invest in people'.

With this the UNDP, previously a site of alternative expertise, is

Counter-hegemony

made into an arm of the existing IFI apparatus. This is discipline disguised by sanctimony.

Development NGOs

NGOs are private (non-state), non-profit organizations that raise money through charitable appeals and engage in good deeds like disaster relief and poverty alleviation. With the advent of neoliberalism and cutbacks in government provision of social services, the 'third sector' of NGOs (the other two sectors being the market and the state) expanded rapidly. There are now 3,000 development NGOs in First World countries and perhaps 20,000 in Third World countries, along with several hundred thousand community organizations, with 15 per cent of development aid channelled through the networks formed by this system (World Bank 2005). NGOs are integral parts of the 'development machine', an institutional complex of state agencies, practitioners, consultants, scholars and other experts, producing and consuming knowledge about the 'developing world' (Crush 1995). Two kinds of NGO can be distinguished: NGOs emerging from European overseas missionary societies and charitable bodies, such as Christian Aid; and organizations like Oxfam, CARE, Save the Children and Plan International, often originating as 'war charities' to deal with the consequences of the Second World War, and later expanding to the Third World.

Let us briefly explore the background to developmental NGOs. The new discourse of development in the post-war period offered both an alternative language and a set of practices that extended the notion of charity and relief towards dealing with the long-term causes of poverty. The decade of the 1960s, with its Freedom from Hunger Campaign and UN Decade of Development, marked the turning point. The discourse of development also resolved marketing and fund-raising problems for charitable organizations, as it offered a new way of seeing Third World peoples – 'it was no longer that Africans were "uncivilised". Instead, they were "underdeveloped". Either way, the "civilised" or "developed" European has a role to play in "civilising" or "developing" Africa' (Manji and Coill 2002). The problem was that the discourse of development they drew on, and helped remake, was phrased not in the language of emancipation or justice, but in terms of charity, technical expertise and paternalism. The next turning point came in the 1980s, with a need to put a 'human face' on neoliberal policies, and with the 'good governance' agenda of the 1990s. This led to an increase in government funding of NGOs – in the early 1970s 2 per cent of NGO income came from official donors. By the mid-1990s this figure had risen to 30 per cent. NGOs and NGO networks like BOND (British Overseas NGOs for Development) are now a force to be reckoned with in economic policy and development. The question is, does their origin in charity and their reliance on governments and wealthy donors prevent NGOs from forming an alternative perspective and pool of expertise that counters neoliberal discourse?

Two organizations, each with budgets of more than $500 million a year, dominate NGO development work:

- CARE (2006) says that it works with 45 million people in seventy countries, not only feeding the hungry but tackling the underlying causes of poverty. Tackling underlying causes translates into agricultural programmes, such as training farmers and better seeds, educational programmes, health projects, loans to start small businesses, water sanitation and environmental health. My comment is that these are all worthy projects, but not aimed at fundamental causes, and all are acceptable to the dominant paradigm of development.

- OXFAM (2006) does similar kinds of work. But it also engages in research, and issues thirty to fifty policy papers a year, many critical of existing development policy, and many proposing alternatives. NGOs like Oxfam watch the IFIs closely and criticize them frequently. They form a kind of liberal, critical fringe to neoliberalism, sharing many of its basic premises, such as free trade, except that the NGOs want fair free trade, and debt relief, except that they want more. All this is useful. It is not counter-hegemonic.

There is also a small group of policy-oriented, radical development NGOs:

- The Development Group for Alternative Policies (Development GAP 2006) sees itself as a vehicle for Southern opposition to Northern policies and policy-making processes, such as structural adjustment and trade liberalization. Development GAP basically helps grassroots organizations in the South engage effectively in policy analysis, policy development and advocacy and educates US policy-makers, the media and the public about economic reform measures causing ecological and economic devastation in the South. It tries to outline alternative development approaches that are environmentally, socially and economically sustainable. Support for the Development GAP is provided by foundations, church agencies and individuals sharing the organization's belief that the people of the South must play a role in the formulation

Counter-hegemony

of the economic policies, programmes and projects that affect them.

- The Bretton Woods Project (2006) is an independent initiative by a group of British NGOs to scrutinize the World Bank and the IMF with special emphasis on environmental and social concerns. The project puts out briefings, reports and a bimonthly digest, *Bretton Woods Update*, which monitors projects, policy reforms and the overall management of the Bretton Woods institutions and goes to 7,000 NGOs, policy-makers, journalists, researchers and parliamentarians worldwide. The project tries to move the IFIs away from 'simplistic approaches' to development.

- The Third World Network (2006) is a network of organizations and individuals involved in development, the Third World and North–South issues. It conducts research on economic, social and environmental issues relating to the South, publishes books and magazines, organizes seminars and serves as a platform representing broadly Southern interests and perspectives at international forums such as UN conferences. It is based in Penang, Malaysia, and has offices in Delhi, Montevideo, Geneva and Accra, with affiliated organizations in several other Third World countries.

- Focus on the Global South (2006) is a programme of development policy research, analysis and action, founded in 1995, with offices in Bangkok, Mumbai and Manila. Its basic position is that as wealthy people have progressed economically, the oppressed and poor, especially women and indigenous peoples, have suffered major setbacks in their quest for economic development, social equality and real independence. There has also been a significant and steady erosion of a large portion of people's economic base. This trend is taking firmer root as globalization accelerates and becomes all pervasive. The mainstream paradigms of development are in serious crisis. The 'free market' economic policies of the IMF and the World Bank have crippled the state as an agent of development and protector of the community. Focus on the Global South tries to articulate local community-based and national, regional and global paradigms of change.

- The Centre for the Study of Developing Societies (2006) in Delhi, established in 1963 by a small group of scholars, conducts theoretical and empirical research on social and political processes, mainly in South Asia. Its main source of funding is the Indian Council of Social Science Research. It has about fifteen fellows on its faculty and a supportive staff of about twenty. The fellows (permanent, visiting, honorary and affiliated) form an interacting college of scholars networking with scholars elsewhere. Its current research programme has four foci: democratic politics and their future; politics of cultures and politics of knowledge; politics of alternatives and human futures; and violence, ethnicity and diversity. The Centre participates in the World Order Models Project and collaborates with organizations like the World Future Studies Federation and the United Nations University's World Institute for Development Economic Research (Helsinki), the International Network on Cultural Alternatives to Development (Montreal), the Sustainable Development Policy Institute (Islamabad), the International Centre for Ethnic Studies (Colombo) and the Bangladesh Study Group in Alternatives (Dhaka). The Centre publishes the journal *Alternatives* in association with the World Order Models Project and the International Peace Research Institute, Meigaku University. *Alternatives* is a forum for thinking about alternatives and futures the world over.

Considering that they have small staffs, cramped working spaces and a precarious financial existence, development NGOs and institutes like these churn out huge amounts of ideas and information. Their publications tend to be propagandistic, the ideas not well developed and data patchy or non-existent. In effect, most radical development NGOs have one well-known, but hopelessly overworked, director, theorist and writer (Martin Khor at Third World Network; Walden Bello at Focus on the Global South, and also a professor of sociology at the University of the Philippines; Rajni Kothari, at the Delhi Institute). Radical development NGOs suffer from one outstanding problem: limited funding. Their money is limited precisely because they oppose the global accumulation of capital by rich, possibly philanthropic people in affluent countries.

In addition, several alternative economics research institutes look at economic policy in general, with some work on development issues:

• The Center for Economic and Policy Research (CEPR) (2006) in Washington, DC, conducts professional research and public education. Research is oriented towards filling gaps in the understanding of economic and social problems, or the impact of policies. The public education portion of CEPR's mission is to present the findings of professional research, by CEPR and others, in a manner that allows broad segments of the public to know what is at stake in major policy debates. The goal of CEPR is ensure that the citizenry has the information and analysis that allow it to act effectively in the public interest.

Counter-hegemony

• The Political Economy Research Institute (PERI) (2006) is an independent unit of the University of Massachusetts, Amherst, with close ties to the Department of Economics. It promotes human and ecological well-being through original research and translates this into 'workable policy proposals capable of improving life'. Its main issues are globalization, unemployment, financial market instability, central bank policy, living wages and decent work, and the economics of peace, development and the environment.

Economics research institutes like these tend to be Keynesian in orientation. PERI, for example, has collaborated with UNDP to produce an economic programme for South Africa, whose main proposals are increased subsidies and cheaper credit for labour-intensive economic activities, and a relaxation of the government's fiscal and monetary stance to produce lower interest rates (Pollin et al. 2006). While 'practical', these are mild proposals in a country characterized by massive social inequalities, high unemployment and the continuing effects of apartheid. This kind of research and policy advocacy is confined by the limited set of theories available to economists, even critical ones, who want to be responsible, pragmatic and effective – that is, to propose policies that they think might be adopted within the existing political-economic framework. This kind of work is also confined by attachment to agencies like UNDP. One of the authors of the study tells me that PERI was glad to get this assignment from UNDP, for it gives them 'legitimacy'. But we must add ... legitimacy limits what can 'legitimately' be said.

Counter-hegemonic praxis

This is the part of the book nearest to my heart. Let me begin it differently.

In the autumn of 2005 I received an invitation to attend a conference on Agribusiness and Agrarian Reform in Brazil. I had been to Brazil several times before, mainly because I knew Milton Santos, a geography professor at the University of São Paulo, during his exile in Canada and the USA, in the 1970s. Milton would invite me to conferences and, somehow, pay for my flight. This recent invitation, however, came from the International Rural Geography symposium held in Presidente Prudente, organized by the State University of São Paulo. I am not a rural geographer and I had never heard of Presidente Prudente. But I had also never been in the western part of Brazil – near the Paraguayan border. So I accepted and flew to São Paulo. It turned out that I was part of a small group of 'counter-experts' and that we were first going to the federal agency INCRA (Instituto Nacional de Colonização e Reforma Agrária) which deals with land reform, to evaluate their activities in the state of São Paulo. Their mission is, essentially, to mediate between peasants and farm workers demanding land, the large landowners reluctant to lose it (and demanding compensation), the state and the courts. The day passed in a blur, with speakers explaining the activities of the agency, and me pretending to understand what was going on – I was an 'expert' after all! Late that day we flew west for a couple of hours to the conference site at Presidente Prudente, where I gave a presentation on the making of development policy – the ideas in Chapter 1 of this book. As usual in Brazil, there were several questions, each lasting about ten minutes, which I tried to answer. And that, I thought, would be it.

But the schedule included a 'field trip' led by Bernado Fernandes, professor at the State University, and organizer of the conference. Off we went, in a small bus, for a couple of hundred miles along roads of varying quality, with Bernado standing up (and Cliff Welch translating), holding up maps and lecturing us about the Landless Labourers' Movement (Movimento dos Trabalhadores Rurais Sem Terra [MST]). Reconstructing what he said: founded in 1984, the MST stands for radical agrarian reform – state intervention to reverse historic land concentration in the hands of a few thousand large landowners (1.6 per cent of landowners control 46.8 per cent of the land on which crops could be grown and 3 per cent of the population owns two-thirds of all arable land in Brazil). Since 1985, the MST has occupied unused land, where they have established cooperative farms, constructed houses, schools and clinics for children and adults, promoted indigenous cultures, and supported a healthy and sustainable environment and gender equality. The MST has won land titles for 350,000 families in 2,000 settlements, while 180,000 encamped families currently await government recognition. Land occupations are rooted in the Brazilian constitution, which says that non-producing land should be used for a 'larger social function' – otherwise ownership reverts to the state. The MST has a membership of 500,000 families – at least 2 million people – and operates all over rural Brazil. The MST runs 500 farm co-ops and helps in the areas of production, marketing, credit and technical assistance. It trains its own technicians, militants and leaders. It has redirected government funds to support its administration of 1,800 elementary schools attended by 160,000 students; the MST teaches basic literacy to 30,000 teenagers and adults; it operates its own university. Sixty members of the MST

165

are studying in Cuba to be (medical) doctors. João Pedro Stédile, national director of the MST, sees land reform as the first step in a larger transformative process. The strategic objective of the MST is to end rural structural problems that contribute to poverty and social inequality. The broader political mission is to radically alter property relations and class inequalities in Brazil, one of the most unequal countries in the world, where the richest 10 per cent of the people receive 48 per cent of national income, while the lowest 10 per cent get ... 0.7 per cent (Friends of the MST 2006; Welch 2006).

Bernado stressed that the land had originally been taken in huge blocks (1,000 square miles) by fraudulent means – phoney documents, bribed officials, the brute force of armed retainers and so on. And that it was being protected with brute force by the military police. Even so, this did not prepare me for what we found. Radical intellectuals talk one way, landless people act another. We stopped at several 'encampments' organized by the MST. Encampment means this: several hundred poor, landless workers set up camps along the roads near unused land on large estates (*latifundios*). The encampments are tightly organized by MST militants and by committees elected by the workers. Rice, beans and sometimes chicken are cooked collectively (Brazil has a social wage, meaning enough money to buy the basic necessities of life), the camp is kept clean collectively, a safety committee keeps order and tries to protect the camp, decisions are taken by vote. The camps last a couple of years. People in the local towns are largely sympathetic to the workers – there is widespread resentment in Brazil against a rural owning class that would sooner shop in Paris than visit the merchant in town. Pressure is exerted on the landowner by the mere presence of a couple of hundred angry, landless workers living right next to them. The landowners respond violently, at night. Then the workers move en masse to occupy part of the estate. All hell breaks out – in some cases, the massacre of hundreds of workers by armed guards and the military police. In other cases stalemate, mediated by INCRA and the courts. In still others, capitulation by the landowner, with compensation from the state. The landlords have recently organized themselves into a paramilitary national organization. Each year 100–150 militants are assassinated. Part of the MST leadership (the most militant) is forced to live across the border, in Paraguay. As we were leaving one camp, a worker took me aside. We talked briefly. I told him I was writing a book. He said that he wanted me to tell you (the reader of this book) something. Everything is not perfect in the camp. It is hot in summer, freezing cold in winter, living under plastic sheets. Sometimes there are squabbles, even fights. But this he stressed (he is not a leader, just a poor worker trying to get land to support his family): they are totally committed to the cause, and willing to give their lives for it.

We went to several settlements – Paulo Friere Settlement and Che Guevara Settlement stand out – some run as cooperatives, some as collectives, some with individual farms. We ate lunch at the house of a militant who had taken previously unused land and was farming it – 5 hectares of coffee bushes, milk cows to supply the nearby town and food crops, which he proudly showed us. His two sons were off to an encampment to get their own land. He was happy to have land, a house with running water and electricity. But mainly he was content with the chance to be, for the first time, a productive farmer. This is what 'social transformation' means.

A young organizer took us to an MST agricultural station, where they had tried, with the help of a state grant, to conduct research on new, organically grown crops. We were on the property illegally. Why? Because the landlords had brought suit in the local court in some trumped-up case. Litigation had lasted for years. In the meantime the tractor repair shop and a milk processing plant lay in ruins. A tornado had ripped off the roof. Expensive machinery was rusting away. The organizer said the MST would get it back, one day. His sympathies were with the militant wing of MST. Activists like him rarely survive to the age of thirty. We returned to Presidente Prudente. Stédile asked that we go to the state prison to show support for a militant, Gleison Mendes, locked up there on charges of conspiracy and sedition for organizing an attempt to take over land. We were politely greeted by the warden, who said that she tried to treat prisoners humanely. Gleison was allowed to see us. At first he had been put in a terrible place, full of murderers and drug dealers, where he feared for his life. This place was better. He said that he was even more committed to the cause. Even so, he was miserable. But his wife had come with us. They hugged while we expressed our admiration for him. Bernado wept as he gave a passionate speech of support. Stédile spoke to the local television reporter, who was sympathetic. We left. Gleison stayed. But in January 2006 I received this email:

> I have good news. Gleison Mendes was freed today, through habeas corpus granted by the Superior Tribunal of Justice.
>
> Bernado

Sometimes, occasionally, now and then, justice touches our lives.

The Bolivarian alternative

Latin America has suffered most from neoliberalism and the Washington Consensus formed from it. And it is there that the most conscious, the most organized, and the most active opposition is forming – in the Brazilian countryside, recently in Bolivia, and most conspicuously in Venezuela.

Between 1948 and the late 1970s Venezuela was widely seen as a stable Latin American democracy. For the forty years prior to Hugo Chávez's election in 1998, two traditional parties shared power and competed for control over the country's most important institutions. Inheriting an oil economy from dictator Perez Jiménez in 1958, the social democratic Acción Democratica (Democratic Action Party), and the social Christian Copei, kept the oil wealth circulating within elite circles, while feeding the country a powerful nationalist rhetoric of 'sowing the oil' throughout the country – everyone got a few seeds. Nevertheless, the richest 10 per cent of the population get 37 per cent of national income, the poorest 10 per cent receive 0.9 per cent, and 23 per cent of the people live on less than $1 a day, proportions typical of all Latin American countries.

With the oil crisis of 1973, and increased prices, the state sowed more, particularly because the government formed its own petroleum company, Petroleos de Venezuela (PDVSA), to participate in production and refining in 1976. A 170 per cent increase in state revenue, together with massive foreign lending, led to the expansion of the state and increased employment. But when oil prices began to drop in the 1980s, the government had to increase foreign borrowing to maintain state spending. With less money flowing to the top echelons of society, the clientelistic trickle-down scheme that had sustained social harmony during the boom years proved inadequate. Unemployment rose at the same time as public spending collapsed. Displaced workers entered the informal sector, where they fell outside the depleted state welfare system. The proportion of Venezuelan families living in critical poverty increased to 40 per cent. Social movements based on the principles of participation, equity and social solidarity emerged outside the formal corporate or labour organizational structures. President Jaime Lusinchi suspended foreign debt repayment in January 1989. The next president, Carlos Andrez Perez, of the Democratic Action Party, after two weeks in office, and following a campaign based on anti-IMF rhetoric, announced the negotiation of a US $4.5 billion loan from the IMF. The structural adjustment that followed was described by its author, Minister of Planning Miguel Rodriguez, as consistent with Washington Consensus principles: open markets;

reduction in government regulation; a business-friendly environment; privatization of oil production; increased direct foreign investment; a free exchange rate for the bolivar; abolition of licences for foreign trade; and a general reduction in state intervention, ostensibly to minimize the possibilities for corruption. When bus fares doubled in response to a 30 per cent increase in fuel costs, demonstrations erupted in nineteen Venuezuelan cities. Six days later, at the end of the 'Caracazo', an estimated 1,000–1,500 (287 by official government count) civilians lay dead, killed by the army and police. From then on, street demonstrations, protests and actions became a regular part of public life. As elsewhere, IMF structural adjustment had created a situation that the poor could not tolerate. In 1993 a banking crisis, capital flight and inflation rates of 70 per cent a year pushed four-fifths of Venezuelan families into poverty, half of these living in critical poverty. Venezuela had to accept a second IMF loan with an austerity package labelled 'The Venezuela Agenda'. The state auctioned operating rights in marginal oilfields to private investors. FDI rose to US $5.5 billion. The changed relationship between the Venezuelan state and its citizenry created unrest, especially in poor, urban populations, but also among sectors of the military who, after all, had to do all that shooting of desperate, poor, innocent people (Redman 2006).

Lieutenant Colonel Hugo Frias Chávez's revolutionary project began in the tumultuous 1980s, when he and other army officers met to discuss topics like the role of the state in social development, elite corruption in Venezuela and the participation of civil society in politics. (Chávez himself had been a student radical in the 1970s.) The group contacted leaders of guerrilla movements and others to create an alliance of military officers, revolutionary parties and popular organizations that eventually included leftist intellectuals and students committed to revolutionary change. The new coalition, with Chávez as its leader and main visionary, called itself the Bolivarian Revolutionary Movement (MBR). After being pardoned for leading a failed military coup in 1992 (when he said that he had only failed '*por ahora*' – 'for the moment') Chávez revitalized the Bolivarian movement by spreading the network to rural areas throughout Venezuela. In the late 1990s, the MBR created a new political 'anti-party' named the Movimiento Quinta República (MVR – Movement for a Fifth Republic). Chávez ran as MVR's presidential candidate in the 1998 election and won by a landslide. He was seen by the marginalized majority as the 'best and only voice' against the global neoliberal economic and political forces that were ranged against the poor. The objective of the

Bolivarian movement was participation by civil society in equitable social, economic and political structures in a new participatory and protagonistic democracy. Chávez explicitly drew on concepts originally presented by Simon Bolivar in the struggle for Latin America's emancipation from Spain: the main principles had been democracy, freedom for slaves and indigenous peoples, land reform and education for all. According to Bolivar, liberation would come only when all peoples of South America were united against threats to their sovereignty from outside powers. Chávez connected with continental liberation by calling his political project the Bolivarian Revolution. The revolutionary process, Chávez argued, had to emerge from an organized and conscious people. To build people's capacity to practise self-determination through direct democracy, Chávez envisioned a strong state role in reducing poverty and comprehensively increasing social welfare. The Chávez administration sees poverty and underdevelopment as coming from the inequitable distribution of profits from the country's vast oil reserves. To ensure that revenues from national resources benefited everyone, the government proposed radical wealth redistribution and increased social investment, in direct contrast to neoliberal policies applied elsewhere in Latin America. The key factor is this: Venezuela has the largest proven oil reserves in the western hemisphere (78 billion barrels) and the largest in the world (300 billion barrels) if the Orinoco tar belt is included. The Venezuelan state owns significant downstream refining and distribution. As the world's fifth-largest crude oil exporter, Venezuela sells 60 per cent of its output to the USA, accounting for 15 per cent of US petroleum imports. In October 2004, Chávez raised the royalty tax on companies working in the Orinoco belt from the 1 per cent they had been paying to 16.6 per cent. All the affected companies, except Exxon Mobil, acquiesced. New projects have a royalty rate of 30 per cent. Chávez has energy agreements with China, Argentina and India. He also wants to create an organization – Petrosur – uniting all state hydrocarbons companies in the region, with the goal of excluding the big multinational oil companies from energy development (Wilpert 2003; Weinstein 2005).

Chávez came into office committed to strengthening the role of the state in the economy. He ordered the military to devise programmes to combat poverty and further civic and social development in Venezuela's urban barrios and poor rural areas. This civilian-military programme, 'Plan Bolivar 2000', includes road-building, housing construction, mass vaccinations, land reform, the lowering of infant mortality rates, the implementation of a free, government-funded healthcare system, and a system of free education to university level. Already, by the end of 2001, the Chávez administration was reporting an increase in primary school enrolment of 1 million students. Elections for a new unicameral National Assembly and for the presidency in 2000 resulted in a two-thirds majority for a Chávez coalition and his personal re-election with 60 per cent of the votes. In 2001, Chávez enacted, by decree, forty-nine laws designed to further the process of social transformation. Fedecámaras, a national business federation, and the Confederación de Trabajadores de Venezuela (CTV), a federation of labour unions, linked to the Democratic Action Party, and tied to the political elite, opposed the the new laws and called for a general business strike. The CTV had begun as a progressive union, but had been thoroughly co-opted by the Democratic Action Party. The CTV collaborated with US-directed anti-communist activity in the region and was funded by the American Institute for Free Labor Development (AIFLD), an organization that is officially part of the AFL-CIO, but is funded by US corporations. In the 1980s the CTV had supported neoliberal reform and privatization (Gindin 2005). On 9 April 2002 CTV leader Carlos Ortega called for a two-day general strike. On 11 April 500,000 people marched towards the headquarters of PDVSA, in support of its management, recently fired by Chávez . The organizers redirected the march to the presidential palace, where a pro-Chávez demonstration was already taking place. Violence erupted between two groups of demonstrators, and between the Caracas Metropolitan Police (at that time still under the control of a mayor opposed to Chávez) and the Venezuelan national guard (under Chávez's command). Lucas Rincón Romero, commander-in-chief of the Venezuelan armed forces, then announced that Chávez had tendered his resignation from the presidency. Chávez was arrested and detained at Fort Tiuna, where he sat wondering why he was still alive. The military leaders appointed the president of Fedecámaras, Pedro Carmona, as Venezuela's interim president. (Carmona had previously been to the USA, where he met with President G. W. Bush. The CIA had known previously that a coup would be staged.) The US State Department immediately recognized the new administration. And in an 13 April editorial, the *New York Times* said that the 'resignation' of the 'ruinous demagogue' Hugo Chávez meant that 'Venezuelan democracy is no longer threatened by a would-be dictator'. Carmona reversed the social and economic policies of Chávez's Bolivarian Revolution. But the coup was countered by pro-Chávez uprisings in Caracas. Venezuelan troops loyal to Chávez retook the presidential palace, and retrieved Chávez from captivity. Chávez completely replaced the

171

upper echelons of Venezuela's armed forces, substituting officers more loyal to the democratically elected government. The revolution survived. Meanwhile a new, pro-Chávez union, the Unión Nacional de Trabajadores (UNT – National Union of Workers), is trying to supplant the CTV. Several pro-Chávez unions have withdrawn from the CTV and affiliated with the UNT (ibid.).

In 2003 and 2004 Chávez launched a number of social and economic campaigns: a literacy campaign aimed at providing free reading, writing and arithmetic lessons to the 1.5 million Venezuelan adults who were illiterate; a programme protecting the livelihood, religion, land, culture and rights of Venezuela's indigenous peoples; a programme providing free higher education to 2 million adult Venezuelans who had not completed their elementary-level education; a programme giving remedial education and diplomas for Venezuela's 5 million high school dropouts. In 2003, Súmate, a grassroots volunteer civilian voter rights organization, started by Maria Corina Machado, who had earlier founded an NGO to privatize homeless shelters, presented a petition with 3.5 million signatures to recall the president. This was defeated by a 59 per cent 'no' vote. The Chávez government subsequently charged the founders of Súmate with treason and conspiracy for receiving foreign funds, earmarked for voter education, from the National Endowment for Democracy, a US organization 'guided by the belief that freedom is a universal human aspiration that can be realized through the development of democratic institutions, procedures, and values' – towards which end it has spent $900,000 in Venezuela. In May 2004, a group of 126 Colombians dressed in Venezuelan army uniforms was captured during a raid on two farms near Caracas – the farm was owned by a Cuban anti-Castro exile and a leader in the unsuccessful 2002 coup. In the aftermath, Chávez further intensified his programme of fundamental social and economic transformation. He expanded his land redistribution and social welfare programmes by authorizing and funding 'Bolivarian Missions' involving massive government anti-poverty initiatives, the construction of thousands of free medical clinics for the poor, the institution of educational campaigns and the enactment of food and housing subsidies – these have resulted in marked improvements in the infant mortality rate between 1998 and 2006. The missions involve widespread experimentation with citizen- and worker-managed governance, as well as the granting of thousands of free land titles to formerly landless poor and indigenous communities. In March 2006 a Communal Council Law allowed communities that organize themselves into councils to be given official state recognition and access to federal funds and loans for community projects, bypassing local and state governments seen as corrupt. In September 2006, the new mayor of Caracas, Juan Barreto, an ally of Chávez, ordered the forced acquisition of two golf courses within the city limits to build subsidized houses for 11,500 poor families. (Twenty families can survive for a week on what it costs to maintain a square metre of golf course grass.) Teodoro Petkoff, editor of the daily newspaper *Tal Cual*, and an opposition politician, said that Barreto suffers from 'megalomaniacal delirium' (Romero 2006).

In his second presidency, Chávez placed greater emphasis on alternative economic development and international trade models, much of it in the form of hemisphere-wide international aid agreements. A joint declaration signed by the presidents of Venezuela and Cuba on 14 December 2004 said that neoliberalism acts as 'a mechanism to increase dependence and foreign domination'. The presidents of the two countries, Hugo Chávez and Fidel Castro, called the Free Trade Association of the Americas (FTAA), proposed by the USA, the 'expression of a hunger to dominate the region'. The free trade area, they said, would result in unprecedented levels of poverty and subordination in Latin America. Their joint declaration presents an alternative to neoliberal free trade. It says that economic integration is necessary if Latin American countries are to occupy a prominent position in the world economy. But integration has to be based on cooperation, solidarity and a common willingness to advance to a higher level of development (Cuba–Venezuela 2004). Opposed to a unicentred world, focused on the USA and western Europe, Chávez favours a multi-centred world that provides new political spaces in which people, particularly in the Third World, can organize themselves in ways they themselves determine. In a play on the proposed FTAA (ALCA in Spanish), Chávez proposes the Bolivarian Alternative for the Americas (ALBA) as Venezuela's vision for regional economic integration and social development. ALBA's key supporters (Chávez and Castro) identify it as a 'process which will assure the elimination of social inequalities, and promote quality of life and the people's effective participation in forging their own destiny'. Chávez has articulated the following key strategic elements of alternative integration: (1) mechanisms to overcome disparities among and within nations, building equality between countries in trade negotiations and between citizens; (2) national sovereignty in setting domestic development priorities and policies, diminishing the control of foreign capital over local economies; (3) prioritizing the role of the state in providing basic services such as healthcare, housing and education; (4) protection for agricultural production as part of cultural identities and people's relationships with nature, as well as being critical for food security and self-sufficiency; (5) removing obstacles to access to information, knowledge and technology; (6) and a critique of free trade as an automatic guarantor of higher levels of growth and collective well-being (Cuba–Venezuela 2004).

The basic political-economic principle supporting these strategies is complementarity. The principle of complementarity rests on the coordination of economic activities so that countries derive mutual benefit from trade relationships. Complementarity allows each trading partner to make up for what the other lacks by supplying finance, technology and knowledge for building the other's productive capacity. So Venezuela supplies Cuba with oil, and Cuba supplies Venezuela with medical doctors. Venezuela and Cuba (Bolivia subsequently joined the trade bloc in 2005) also identify solidarity as the 'cardinal principle' by which ALBA must be guided. Their claim is that integration supports domestic development so that each country is more self-sufficient and therefore more sovereign. Latin America cannot be free if countries in the region are isolated from one another (Cuba–Venezuela 2004). Therefore, Bolivarianism is against nationalism to the detriment of other peoples, or restrictive domestic policies that inhibit the construction of regional alliances. In the discourse of ALBA, asymmetries in negotiating power between regional allies are reframed in the concepts of justice, equality and reciprocal solidarity (Cuba–Venezuela 2004). By creating a regional trading bloc, ALBA strengthens individual countries' negotiating positions in the global arena. Instead of countries individually entering into bilateral agreements with powerful countries, a South American/Caribbean bloc would help reduce dependence on US markets and ensure that the region has better leverage in trade and investment negotiations with the USA, Europe and Asia (Redman 2006). In April 2006 the presidents of Venezuela, Cuba and Bolivia signed an agreement for the creation of the Bolivarian Alternative for the Peoples of Our America (ALBA) and a People's Trade Agreement. Article 5 of the agreement reads:

> The countries agree to make investments of mutual interest which could take the form of public, bi-national, mixed or cooperative companies, joint management projects or any other form of association that they decide to establish. Priority shall be given to the initiatives which strengthen the capacity for social inclusion, resource industrialization and food security, in a framework of respect and preservation of the environment. (Peoples Treaty 2006)

Let me give a specific example of Hugo Chávez's interventions in rural Latin America. An agreement concerning technical agrarian cooperation was signed by La Via Campesina-MST and the Bolivarian Government of Venezuela on 26 September 2005. President Hugo Chávez signed the agreement in the name of the Venezuelan government and João Pedro Stédile signed in the name of the MST and La Via Campesina – a syndicate dedicated to improving food and rural life (La Via Campesina 2006). The basic ideas behind the agreement are the defence of the food sovereignty of all peoples, the protection and multiplication of native seeds used in all types of farm production, the revaluing of peasant farming, strengthening of the internal market and a search for agrarian techniques that do not harm the environment and provide high-quality food for people. The further idea was to create an Agro-Ecological Institute with a specialization in Peasant, Indigenous and Afro-descendant Studies, which will train qualified activists for the organization and development of agro-ecology, support relations between technicians and peasant, indigenous and Afro-descendant organizations, and sustain a new ethical paradigm for rural Latin America. Training in humanistic, holistic and scientific values given to thousands of young men and women will strengthen social movements in the countryside, and will promote technology that is enriched with traditional knowledge. The first 250 students (50 per cent women) began training in 2006, in the municipality of Alberto Arvelo, Barinas state. The institute employs a participatory method that combines social practice with school time and community time during a five-year period until the student acquires a professional degree. The pedagogical method focuses on the classics of science, without omitting traditional knowledges and the sociocultural cosmic vision of indigenous and Afro-Latin Americans. It uses ideas from Brazilian theorists, such as Antón Makarenco and Paulo Freire, which hold that every student is the subject of his or her own social project. The institute is supported by the Bolivarian University and the Venezuelan Ministry of Higher Education, and organizations such as the MST that have trained activists for years, and in general all the accumulated experience of the Latin American Coordination of Rural Organizations (CLOC), La Via Campesina and indigenous and Afro-descendant organizations.

Meanwhile, high oil prices enabled Venezuela's economy to grow by 17.3 per cent in 2004 and by similarly high rates since, leading to a decrease in unemployment from 17 per cent in early 2004 to 9 per cent in 2006. In the period 1999–2004, per capita GDP fell by 1–2 per cent, but grew at rates of 18 per cent in 2004 and 10 per cent in

2005, with the poorest sectors of society having real income growth of 55 per cent between 2003 and 2005, and with a sharp reduction in the poverty rate. And to cap it all, in 2005/06, Chávez instructed Felix Rodriguez, the president of Citgo, the US oil company owned by the Venezeulan state, to provide 10 per cent of its refined product to poor people in Massachusetts and the South Bronx, at discounts of 60 per cent off the market price – US Republican Representatives Joe Barton, of Texas, chairman of the House Energy and Commerce Committee, and Ed Whitfield, of Kentucky, chairman of the Subcommittee for Oversight and Investigations, responded to this by asking the CEO of Citgo for details of the company's offer, believing that 'Venezuela's state-owned oil company' was using the programme 'as part of an unfriendly government's increasingly belligerent and hostile foreign policy toward the United States'. In 2005, Pat Robertson, a conservative fundamentalist Christian, and contender for the Republican presidential nomination in 1988, called Chávez 'a dangerous enemy to our south, controlling a huge pool of oil, that could hurt us badly ... We have the ability to take him out, and I think the time has come that we exercise that ability ... We don't need another $200 billion war to get rid of one strong-arm dictator. It's a whole lot easier to have some of the covert operatives [CIA] do the job and then get it over with.' Speaking from Miami in 2004, Carlos Andres Perez, former president of Venezuela, responsible for the Caracazo, and impeached in 1993 for using US $17 million from the president's special secret fund to help Violeta Chamorro's right-wing government in Nicaragua, said in an interview with *El Nacional*, one of Venezuela's main daily newspapers: 'I am working to remove Chávez [from power]. Violence will allow us to remove him. That's the only way we have ... [Chávez] must die like a dog, because he deserves it' (Sanchez 2004). Secretary of State Condoleezza Rice said that the Chávez regime was a 'negative influence' in the western hemisphere, and in a presentation to the US Senate Foreign Relations Committee added that the Bush administration was 'very concerned about a democratically elected leader who governs in an illiberal way'. In 2006, George W. Bush, President of the United States, said of Chávez: 'Sometimes leaders show up who do a great disservice to the traditions and people of a country' (CNN 2006).

The Bolivian alternative

A few years ago, a miracle happened in a place next to heaven: the mountainous country of Bolivia. An unstable economy with very high inflation was 'stabilized' through neoliberal policies, some local in origin, others suggested by the IFIs, still others by Jeffrey Sachs. Within three weeks of taking office, reversing many leftist and statist principles he had earlier championed, President Paz Estenssoro initiated South America's second (after Chile) most radical neoliberal restructuring programme, termed the New Economic Policy (NEP). The actual implementation of neoliberalism was carried out by a coalition of capitalists, technocrats and politicians, and by Gonzalo Sánchez de Lozada (Goni), principal owner of a large private mining company, COMSUR, and highly committed to neoliberalism. The NEP was backed by the IFIs, who provided half of Bolivia's public investment funds, making up about 9 per cent of the country's GDP. The main condition – privatize the Bolivian state-owned enterprises, shut down 'uneconomic' mines and deflate the economy. This brought inflation down from a rate of several thousand per cent a year. But the price of the miracle was paid by the workers. Closing state-owned mines resulted in 23,000 unemployed miners; within a year, 10,000 public administrative employees and almost 25,000 rural teachers lost their jobs, real wages fell by a third and national unemployment soared. An unusually self-critical World Bank report suggested that donor belief in neoliberal principles – that markets are benevolent mitigators of poverty and governments are harmful – was so strong that the IFIs 'deluded themselves – by faith, [that during] the initial years of democracy and several years of reasonable growth ... that they could completely re-invent the country' (World Bank 2004b). Bolivia's neoliberal transition included an important policy innovation: the Social Emergency Fund (Fondo de Emergencia Social – SEF). The World Bank spent $239.5 million over four years trying to limit the NEP's negative social impacts, by supporting hundreds of small projects in areas of economic and social infrastructure and assistance including school feeding programmes. The projects generated thousands of short-term, sub-minimum-wage jobs in construction, an increasing number administered by NGOs. The NEP began to withdraw the state from the economy while privileging the market. A new generation of neoliberal party leaders then completed the neoliberal transformation. President Gonzalo Sánchez de Lozada's 1993 Plan for All (*Plan de Todos*) promoted a market democracy, composed of a minimally regulated capitalist economy, and a smaller, limited and formally democratic state. The largest state-owned enterprises were sold to multinational corporations. The 'Law of Capitalization', signed in March 1994 with little debate in Congress, authorized the sale of the government's oil and gas, telecommunications, airlines, power generation and railway companies, industries accounting for

Counter-hegemony

12.5 per cent of GDP and 60 per cent of state revenues. International private investment in the country's natural resources was vigorously pursued. The plan aimed to 'deepen and broaden' market democracy by altering the role of the state, its relationship to its citizens, and the nature of citizenship itself. The World Bank's commitment to Bolivia's privatization led it to approve $357 million in credits: $126.4 million for political-institutional reforms, $103.6 million for economic reforms (including establishing regulatory structures), $90 million for education decentralization and reform, and $40 million for social investment funds to ameliorate the social costs of structural adjustment. The plan eventually produced economic growth for a few years in the 1990s, but with increasingly unequal income distribution, already skewed in favour of a few thousand rich families. Between the end of 1999 and October 2003, however, Bolivia went from one political-economic crisis to another, as neoliberal hegemony unravelled. Four factors were particularly important: the inability of two successive governments to generate jobs and significant economic growth; an aggressive coca eradication programme that destroyed the regional economy of Cochabamba; the collapse of the Argentine economy, eliminating Bolivia's largest labour market and source of remittances; and the decline in government revenue brought about by privatization of the state oil company (Kohl and Farthing 2006).

Social unrest accompanied each crisis. Two indigenous movements maintained pressure on the government: coca growers from the semi-tropical lowlands east of Cochabamba and La Paz and Aymara campesinos from the highland plateau surrounding La Paz. Their opposition to neoliberal policies focused on the privatization of resources and basic services, forced coca eradication and greater investment in rural Bolivia. Bolivia's indigenous social movements are the most radical and powerful in the Americas. The highland Aymara have fiercely defended their culture for over five hundred years. A new constellation of oppositional social movements emerged: three major 'indigenous' people's groups; the teachers' union that had became the backbone of a much diminished Bolivia Worker Confederation (the Central Obrera Boliviana or COB), in its heyday perhaps the strongest independent labour movement in the world; urban social movements in the nation's largest cities; and ad hoc committees that arose to defend the rights of Bolivians to water and natural gas. Since the mid-1990s, protests have brought together class-based and indigenous resistances into a political party, originally formed by the coca producers, the Movimiento al Socialismo (Movement toward Socialism – MAS), headed by Juan Evo Morales

Ayma, but including members of the Bolivian Communist Party, Trotskyist miners' leaders and others, such as the Bolivian Movement of Landless Peasants (Movimiento Sin Tierra – MST), inspired by the Brazilian movement of the same name. Previously in Bolivia leftist parties were subordinate to the unions. In the case of the MAS, the activist core is indigenous campesinos, rather than miners or factory workers. The party at first had minimal representation in Bolivia's Congress. Instead it took to the streets in a series of water wars and coca demonstrations that saw massive demonstrations, strikes, national mobilizations and roadblocks that cut off La Paz for a week. In early 2002 confrontations grew increasingly violent, culminating in a wave of police attacks on civilians after two officers were beaten to death. Morales was blamed for inciting a riot and 104 deputies from five parties allied to expel him from Congress as the 'intellectual author' of the soldiers' deaths. Morales turned his exile into a presidential campaign. In the 2002 presidential elections, he came in second on the MAS ticket, winning 8 of 27 seats in the Senate and 27 of 130 seats in Congress. Almost 70 per cent of voters supported anti-neoliberal candidates. In 2003 a tax war opposing an IMF-instigated tax increase was compounded by a police strike and violent struggles between the army and the police. A (natural) gas war, aimed at reversing the 1997 gas and oil privatization (Bolivia has the second-largest gas reserves in South America, with low costs of production), led to Goni having to leave the country precipitously for the safer shores of Miami (where he presented himself as the victim of narco-terrorists). Carlos Mesa assumed the presidency, promising to reverse Goni's 1996 hydrocarbons law and raise taxes from 18 to 50 per cent, calling for a referendum on how the country should use its oil and gas resources, and agreeing to a constitutional assembly that would 'reinvent Bolivia'. On the one hand, Mesa immediately came under pressure from the USA, Spain and the IFIs, who warned that reversing neoliberalism and the coca eradication programme would lead to a withdrawal of financial support. On the other, he realized that he had to have the support of rural Bolivia to maintain control. The resulting stalemate steadily increased opposition on the streets until on 9 June 2005 Mesa resigned and Eduardo Rodríguez, president of the Supreme Court, assumed office as a transitional president, with 180 days to call new elections (ibid.)

The resulting 2005 election finally brought Evo Morales and the MAS to power with 54 per cent of the vote in a campaign that was a national referendum on neoliberal policies of privatization, austerity and trade liberalization. Morales announced that he would repeal Supreme Decree 21060, the 1985 law that led to the privatization of state enterprises. Morales used a Supreme Court ruling that invalidated existing contracts with oil and gas corporations, under which they paid 18 per cent of revenues as royalties, to pass a new hydrocarbon law requiring a total contribution of 50 per cent in royalties. He named a cabinet in which fourteen of sixteen ministers come from indigenous groups and women hold portfolios in the Interior, Justice, Health, and Economic Development. A constitutional assembly of elected representatives is rewriting the constitution. In June 2006, MAS released a document called *Refounding Bolivia* outlining its position in the constituent assembly. The document interprets Bolivian history as a process of indigenous-popular resistance to discrimination and poverty, and proclaims the rights of indigenous peoples to self-determination, control over their territories and collective resources, and use of their traditional political and justice systems, consistent with respect for human rights. The MAS vision for Bolivia is phrased in terms of plural, participative, communitarian and representative democracy, based on diversity of peoples, for the elimination of all forms of colonialism, segregation and discrimination. *Refounding Bolivia* proposes a kind of communitarian socialism, in which local cooperativist forms of organization are nurtured by the state, which exercises regulatory control and joint ownership over strategic extractive industries and public utilities, yet allows a private sector to function, often with considerable freedom. The new aspect of the MAS programme involves an overlay of indigenous political forms of consensual decision-making and communal justice on Western-style state institutions (Weinstein 2006).

MAS proposes land reform in a country where 90 per cent of the land belongs to 50,000 families. Land claims have been pressed, unused land occupied and conflicts between owners and occupiers have been endemic, with the Bolivian courts slow to adjudicate claims, although the law clearly states that unused arable land can be redistributed (as in Brazil). In June 2006 Morales went to the opposition stronghold of Santa Cruz in the eastern lowlands to award titles to 24,864 square kilometres (9,600 square miles) of government land to peasants, as the first phase of a plan to distribute 200,000 square kilometres (77,000 square miles) of government land during the next five years. Private agricultural interests responded to the redistribution by threatening a producers' strike and forming armed 'self-defence' forces.

As part of the Peoples Treaty signed by Bolivia, Cuba and Venezuela in April 2006, a non-profit Cuban–Bolivian organization will provide free high-quality ophthalmologic surgeries to all Bolivian citizens lacking financial resources, thus preventing tens of thousands of poor Bolivians from blindness or serious and often crippling limitations to their sight each year. Cuba will supply advanced technological equipment and ophthalmologic specialists and will pay the wages of the specialists, working in six ophthalmologic centres with the capacity to operate on 100,000 people a year (Peoples Treaty 2006).

The most contentious issue, however, is natural gas. Nationalization of gas is opposed by the IFIs, the USA, the European Union and neighbouring countries, especially Brazil, with interests in the country's resources. Nationalization is supported by most indigenous movements, which want an end to 500 years of colonialism and control of resources and a larger share of natural resource rents for national development. Morales's hydrocarbons policy so far amounts not to nationalization but a prescription for majority ownership by Bolivia's state energy company, Yacimientos Petroliferos Fiscales Bolivianos (YPBF), with an increase in royalty rates from 50 to 82 per cent and higher prices. On the whole, foreign producers with investments in Bolivia's gas industry have accepted the new policy and have adjusted by writing down assets, freezing further investment and threatening to take disputes to international arbitration. The major issue is the compensation that investors will receive for assets they surrender. 'Energy analysts' argue that the Morales policy will prevent foreign investment and result in the failure of Bolivia to realize the potential of its approximately 48 trillion cubic feet of proven gas reserves. On the other hand, Brazil is highly dependent on Bolivian gas and Argentina is also a large buyer. And the Russian energy company Gazprom may invest in exploration, exploitation, production and exportation (Weinstein 2006). Thus the struggle to use Bolivia's natural resources for the development of the mass of its people continues. But this time the country has an indigenous president, committed to a new kind of Andean socialism.

Counter-expertise

The counter-hegemonic alternative policies outlined in this chapter are opposed by an aggressively expansionary USA and by the violent reaction of domestic elites. The notion of a popular development that directly meets the needs of the poorest people is anathema to the rich, but a vision to the poor. Opposition to pro-poor policies is such that names like 'Chávez' or 'Castro' cannot be mentioned by the Western news media without a qualification that they are 'dictators' or the implication that they are 'deranged'. Leaders proposing grassroots development are subject to assassination attempts, coups and the ridicule of the world's press. In the hegemonic imaginary, it is 'madness' to build free clinics for peasants and workers, yet 'rational' for multinationals to profit from their labour and resources. The world is upside down. It needs standing on its feet again. Alternative development policy, as exemplified by Venezuela and Bolivia, shows the way. The point is to transform the development imaginary, so that different economic rationalities can be envisioned, and alternative strategies developed. This requires radically critiquing the dominant neoliberal economic discourse, something that has only just begun, presenting a more compelling analysis, and developing an alternative policy regime that is directed by the aspirations of poor people. Third World activist theoreticians are producing the intellectual and practical basis for a new, post-neoliberal globalization.

Clearly I am critical of compliant expertise – knowledge and experience used in the interests of hegemonic power. Some experts believe in the existing political system and share its aspirations for money and status. Other experts go along with it because they are pragmatic. Indeed, they think that to advocate radical alternatives is to be irresponsible – pie in the sky when we need food on the ground. Poverty, they say, needs alleviating now – and that means accepting and working within the existing policy regime. This is an argument I know well, having heard it many times, and thought it myself from time to time. Should policy directives like the Millennium Development Goals bring debt relief and improve health services, then I am all for them. What I do not appreciate is the notion that 'poverty alleviation' and 'better social safety nets' are all that is necessary to patch up a basically neoliberal policy regime – trying to keep up with the casualties, so to speak. Or the use of liberal sympathy for Aids victims, or people sick with malaria, to prevent the critical imagination from going farther into the root causes of poverty. Poverty is structurally determined. Eradicating poverty means eradicating its source. And the source of poverty is inequality. The poor are poverty stricken because the rich are money laden. Poverty cannot be ended by neoliberal policies that deliberately increase inequality by 'favouring the investor'. Poverty can be ended only by policies that transform socio-economic structures. This means income redistribution in a social democratic sense – free services for poor people paid for by very high taxes on over-wealthy people. But it more fundamentally means redistributing productive resources towards the poor, who yearn for nothing more than to be productive in a society of equals – through land reform, government-supported cooperatives, worker-owned factories, community enterprises, resources dedicated to supporting local livelihood rather than making distant profit. Social transformation means states committed to the poor. Everyone returning from Venezuela tells the same story. It is not the financial support which the people appreciate. It is the sentiment that they finally have a government and a president who stands for them.

We have a counter-hegemonic institutional structure that mobilizes millions of people in social movements and as critical individuals. Within this counter-hegemonic movement, I characterize my own position as 'counter-expert' (see also Chang and Grabel 2004). 'Expertise' may sound pretentious, even when employed in this critical way. But I think that expertise, understood as 'knowing as much as I can', the better to critically oppose perverse convention, the better to optimistically propose life-saving alternatives, is a project deserving intellectual commitment and activist support. A counter-expertise serves social movements by reformulating their wants and needs into policy proposals – within an awareness that this too creates power inequalities between people and expert. But another world is made possible only by thinking carefully in advance.

SEVEN
The three neos

Economic policy is one part of a broad range of political-economic powers reaching out from dominant Western, capitalist countries to control the peoples of the world. This outward extension of European power has recently become more active, more assertive and more American. The entire post-Second World War period might be termed 'Pax Americana' – that is, US succession to global dominance, with the demise of the previous Pax Britannica. But, since the late 1970s, and especially since the tragic attack on the World Trade Center and the Pentagon, the USA has assumed a more aggressive stance towards the world, a repositioning of hegemony that might be called 'neo-imperialism'. This is a new form of imperialism in which control is exercised by physical force but also by political and cultural persuasion – militaristic intervention combined with control over ideals. Behind neo-imperial hegemony lie two ideological systems, stemming from somewhat different sources, but tending towards the same ends. Neoconservatism is the more obviously aggressive ideology by which the American state reasserts its politico-military power to spread 'freedom and democracy' to a world that must want them. By 'freedom' the neocons mean the market and the profit motive, and by democracy they mean American-style elections in which people are free to vote for any candidate or party they choose, provided that the election has already been fixed by the need for campaign finance. Neoliberalism is less obviously aggressive. In this ideology, the economies of the countries of the world are 'reformed' to make them available for development. By development, neoliberalism means privatization, deregulation and other policy devices that entail the capturing of the global economy by finance capital. Let me finish this book by deconstructing the three neos that collectively form modern, global hegemony.

Neo-imperialism

'Neo' means new and different. And 'imperialism' has long meant the geopolitical expansion of national power. By 'neo-imperialism', however, I mean something different from, say, the British, French and other European imperialisms of the nineteenth and early twentieth centuries. In the nineteenth century, the aim of imperialism was territorial conquest, including permanent, physical occupation of foreign spaces, with strict control over their peoples exercised by colonial state authorities directed from London, Paris and the other capitals in Europe. American neo-imperialism of the late twentieth and early twenty-first centuries certainly uses overwhelming physical might to conquer territories, and militaristic terror to control reluctant peoples, as with the US invasion of Afghanistan in 2001, and the occupation of Iraq in 2003. But the long-term aim of US neo-imperialism does not envision long-run, direct control by the State Department in quite the same way as the British did through their Colonial Office. Rather the aim is control of spaces, resources and peoples indirectly via multinational corporations, global governance institutions, policy imposition and foreign investment.

American neo-imperialism has the confidence to control, in the long term, after the shock and awe of the bombing, by setting the ideals that people strive for, rather than controlling bodies through violent intimidation. Control the way people think, control their economic, political and cultural objectives, and there is no need for direct control over people physically. The aim of US neo-imperialism is to control global space by conquering the political and economic imaginaries of the world's peoples ... by having them 'share the American dream'. Neo-imperialism takes the form of the expansion of American ideals like freedom, democracy, equality of opportunity, consumption. Neo-imperialism American-style makes the excuses for British imperialism ('bringing civilization to the world') look utterly out of date and hopelessly deficient. American neo-imperialism means spreading consumption, lifestyle, media, voting and all the good things that people everywhere have already shown that they urgently, deeply want! Neo-imperialism is cast as the latest act in a continuing drama of human liberation.

Neo-imperialism as sociocultural and political control is justified as right, and defended as good, by rationalizations so sophisticated that their perpetrators do not know that they speak in ideological tongues. As I have explained, ideology basically entails spreading persuasive ideas in the interests of dominant institutions of power. That power is usually accumulated geographically, in a hegemonic country, such as Britain previously, or the USA today, and concentrated socially, in a class of people, an ethnic group or a gender – such as white, rich, Anglo-American males. Putting the case bluntly, my argument is that US neo-imperialism is supported by ideologies of democracy, freedom and consumptive happiness in the interests of what I have called 'global finance capital'. Obviously the case is more complicated than this – for example, pension funds are now heavily involved in global investment, black Americans willingly participate, women occasionally head up state agencies like the US State Department. Even so, I think I have shown, convincingly except for those who have too much to lose from realizing the truth, that the spread of Americanism, geopolitically, geo-economically, geoculturally, is not some innocent or inevitable diffusion of the technically superior or the inherently good. Instead, the spread of sophisticated ideologies during neo-imperialistic expansion is in the interests of concentrated, committed and coercive power – and by 'concentrated' we mean a few hundred thousand people at most, living in a tiny fraction of world space, and within this group a few thousand super-rich 'investors'.

Neoconservatism

The neocons are known for their aggressive geopolitics – especially the expansion of 'democratic freedom'. In the neoconservative lexicon, 'American exceptionalism' is 'a belief in the uniqueness and the virtue of the American political system that, when translated into foreign policy terms, offers the United States as a model for the world' (Kaplan and Kristol 2003: 64). The 'Americanness' of this exceptionalism is rooted in US liberal democratic principles and its market economy. Rather than the blood-and-soil conservative nationalism of the first imperialism, this second generation of neoconservative neo-imperialists has 'faith in the universal idea of freedom'. The USA, they say, has the ability to defend those principles, and more generally has an obligation to defend the free world against competing ideologies. This Americanness stands in contrast not only to the communist world, but also to the rest of the free (capitalist) world that cannot or will not defend itself. Americans, they say, rightly think that the security and survival of the USA is synonymous with security and survival of freedom in the world. Peace and political liberty can be fostered not by international organizations, such as the UN, but by American power and American-led alliances. The neocon position was spelled out late in 2003 in a book called *The War over Iraq* by Lawrence F. Kaplan and William Kristol in terms of three principles of a Bush Doctrine:

1 Pre-emption. Pre-emption means striking first. In a world standing at the crossroads of radicalism and technology, the USA cannot rely on a reactive posture but must identify and destroy the threats

posed by its enemies before they reach the country's borders. More countries now possess weapons of mass destruction and the means of delivering them than in the past. Hence acts of 'anticipatory self-defence' are legitimate.

2 Regime change. The right to bring about by diplomatic or military means the demise of regimes with which the USA cannot peacefully exist – the ultimate aim being the spread of liberal democracy.

3 Pre-eminence. The USA must prevent potential adversaries from surpassing or equalling its power. American military power dwarfs that of any other nation, in its war-fighting capabilities and ability to quickly intervene in conflicts anywhere in the world. The USA, as the world's sole superpower, commits itself to norms of international conduct – democracy, human rights, against aggression, against weapons proliferation – norms that successful challenges to American power would invariably weaken. Were the USA, through humility, self-abnegation or a narrow conception of the national interest, to retreat from the position that history has bequeathed, the turmoil that would soon follow would surely reach its own shores. A humane future requires an American foreign policy that is 'unapologetic, idealistic, assertive and well funded. America must not only be the world's policeman or its sheriff, it must be its beacon and guide'. (ibid.: 120–21)

In general, the USA must promote a world order conducive to American interests and defend against any threat to that order. Iraq is a case in point.

In his 2002 State of the Union address, George W. Bush, President of the United States, said that America's goal was to prevent regimes that sponsored terror from threatening the USA or its allies with weapons of mass destruction – the cases being North Korea, Iran and Iraq. The President said:

States like these, and their terrorist allies, constitute an axis of evil, arming to threaten the peace of the world. By seeking weapons of mass destruction, these regimes pose a grave and growing danger. They could provide these arms to terrorists, giving them the means to match their hatred. They could attack our allies or attempt to blackmail the United States. In any of these cases, the price of indifference would be catastrophic … The United States of America will not permit the world's most dangerous regimes to threaten us with the world's most destructive weapons … History has called America and our allies to action, and it is both our responsibility and our privilege to fight freedom's fight. (Bush 2002)

The US position was that Iraq illegally possessed 'weapons of mass destruction' in violation of UN Security Council Resolution 1441. As these weapons posed a grave threat to the USA and its allies, Iraq had to be disarmed by force. Under the UN Charter, however, the use of force by one country against another is permissible only under two circumstances: in self-defence against an actual or imminent armed attack; and when the UN Security Council authorizes the use of force to maintain or restore international peace and security. The Bush administration failed to get UN authorization for the use of armed force against Iraq on 17 March 2003, and invaded on 20 March 2003, under the banner of 'Operation Iraqi Freedom'. This invasion was a violation of international law, especially as the argument for a 'grave threat', involving weapons of mass destruction, was unravelled by an admitted US failure to find such weapons. But as President Bush said in 2006: 'The war we fight today is more than a military conflict. It is the decisive ideological struggle of the 21st century' (Kornblut and Stolberg 2006: A1).

Who pays for this? US troops went in in the guise of liberators bringing freedom, under the illusion that they would be met 'liberation of France style' by a grateful citizenry tossing flowers under their tank tracks. The US Army did not protect the munitions dumps they thought they would soon be asked to clean up. Instead, its soldiers have been killed and maimed by a widely supported Iraqi insurgency, which somehow is against the 'universal dream of freedom', using bombs they were told not to worry about protecting. As always, the working class pays the price for elite illusions. Not to speak of six hundred thousand dead Iraqis, and a civil war that shows every sign of lasting for a decade or more.

But there is another dimension to this that has hardly been mentioned even in the acres of commentry on the Iraq war. During the 2004 presidential elections, in a debate with his Democratic adversary John Kerry, Bush said: 'I believe that God wants everybody to be free. That's what I believe ... And that's been part of my foreign policy. In Afghanistan, I believe that the freedom there is a gift from the Almighty. And I can't tell you how encouraged I am to see freedom on the march' (Bush 2004). In his State of the Union address in early 2005 Bush corrected this, somewhat, by saying: 'We go forward with complete confidence in the eventual triumph of freedom. Not because history runs on the wheels of inevitability. It is human choices that move events. Not because we consider ourselves a chosen nation. God moves and chooses as he wills.' Instead, the notion of the USA responding to the transcendental forces of history was shifted to a kind of inherent human ethic: 'The moral choice between oppression, which is always wrong, and freedom, which is eternally right ... Americans, of all people, should never be surprised by the power of our ideals. Eventually, the call of freedom comes to every mind and every soul.' Freedom, Bush said, is the permanent hope of mankind and the longing of the soul. It is 'an ancient hope that is waiting to be fulfilled'. The fulfilment of the eternal hope for human freedom lends history a necessary dynamic: 'history also has a visible direction, set by liberty and the author of liberty' (Bush 2005). The identity of the 'author of liberty' necessarily remains a little murky. But the implication remains that the 'author' is God. For the President, the USA acts in the world as the agent of God's will.

The most dangerous part of this is the assumption that the USA always, no matter what, represents not only God, but good in the world. And that countries the USA designates as its disciples are good too, no matter what they do. So Israel, as it bombed the sovereign country of Lebanon flat in 2006, killing a thousand, making a million people refugees, was doing ... good in the world. This is a dangerous illusion. The illusion that democracy can be forced on people, whether they want it or not, is reinforced by the delusion that the USA responds to God's will, as it illegally invades, threatens and cajoles, all in the name of spreading a freedom that its own people do not have.

From neoconservatism to neoliberalism

Before the neoconservative onslaught, many intellectuals, artists, writers and academics united in a critique of big business as the dominant institution of a rapacious capitalist system. Concerned about the negative consequences of capitalist production – poverty, inequality and environmental destruction - the left wing of a generally progressive intelligentsia wanted to subvert market mechanisms and substitute state regulation. The neoconservatives read this as a 'new class' of public sector scientists and bureaucrats plotting to take over economy and polity in the interests of managing the system themselves. Faced by this critical onslaught, American corporate capitalism was, in neocon Irving Kristol's (1995: 224) words, 'not merely vulnerable ... [but] ... practically defenseless'. Instead, for newly converted neocons like him, the call for increasing public control over the economy posed a threat to American democracy – to the extent that the corporate world might lose its private character altogether. This support for the corporations proved crucial. It resulted in a Kristol-nacht of change. The corporations had found articulate champions, intellectuals who

189

could effectively counter the anti-corporate critique ... because the first generation of neocons, in a previous incarnation as liberals and leftists, had thought up many of its central arguments! A born-again corporate world rewarded them well, with grants and funding for a new generation of right-wing think tanks and progressively conservative publications that spread the word. Domestically, neoconservatism entailed a positive re-evaluation of the values of American corporate capitalism. The new pro-capitalist doctrine argued essentially for removing state controls, and reducing government spending, in favour of allowing capitalist entrepreneurialism to produce economic growth and the good, consumptive life for all.

Whereas old conservatism had believed that the values of society were maintained most faithfully by its traditional elites, neoconservatism found to the contrary: that capitalist opportunity constantly infuses new blood into a class of rich people that is a capitalist necessity, bringing new ideas to a society that has to innovate in order to survive. A free economy with constant social mobility, the neoconservative argument ran, better cures problems of discrimination and inequality than congressional legislation enforced by governmental regulations. Market freedom allows consumers' choices to democratically guide the direction taken by economic growth as people spend their hard-earned money in ways that make them happy. Acquisitiveness and the profit motive, the neocons caution, might not be morally perfect. But selfishness, they say, is a necessary, legitimate and productive fact of life, while capitalism also inculcates bourgeois values such as diligence, frugality and punctuality in order that it may function effectively. Capitalism promotes and rewards imagination and creativity. Capitalist principles of private property and personal freedom are the social bases for political democracy. And capitalism stimulates a range of powerful civil and economic institutions that counter the accumulation of power by totalitarian states. This was an argument for a progressive, socially fluid and democratic capitalist system – democratic in the sense of market freedom. As Kaplan and Kristol (2003: 119) explain:

> American economic precepts of liberal capitalism and free trade
> have become almost universally accepted as the best model for
> creating wealth, and the United States itself stands at the center of
> the international economic order. The American political precepts
> of liberal democracy have spread across continents and cultures as
> other peoples cast off or modify autocratic methods of governance
> and opt for, or at least pay lip service to, the American principles

of individual rights and freedoms ... what upholds today's world order is American benevolent influence – nurtured, to be sure, by American power, but also by emulation and the recognition around the world that American ideals are genuinely universal.

Neoconservatism therefore conjoins an aggressive foreign military policy with support for the spread of a set of economic beliefs that are virtually identical to neoliberalism, despite a somewhat different intellectual pedigree. As we have seen, these beliefs in markets, entrepreneurship and free trade inform not just progressive capitalist thought in the USA, their homeland, but through neoliberal economic policy, enforced by the IMF and the World Bank, they determine capitalist development the world over. The appointment by President George W. Bush of a prominent second-generation neoconservative intellectual, Paul Wolfowitz, to the presidency of the World Bank solidifies this relationship. Neoconservatism is a belief in spreading neoliberal 'freedom' – by policy preferably, but by force when necessary. Yet, whereas mistakes in geopolitical policy kill people by the thousands, neoliberal mistakes in economic policy kill by the millions, every year, babies mostly, kids that never get the chance to become people who can think, and act, for themselves. (Then the charitable component of liberal neoliberalism comes into play.) That is why this book analysed global power through the lens of geo-economics, and looked in detail at neoliberalism, rather than neoconservatism. Make no mistake, however. What we are seeing in the world today is the spread of a complex of political and economic ideologies, together making up neo-imperialism, that extend US power, in the belief that 'we' are at the pinnacle of human achievement, that America automatically represents everything that is good, and that the spread of its values of democracy, progress and individual liberty is willed by God. At her confirmation as Secretary of State, Madeleine Albright (1997) put it all together, saying: 'In the years ahead, we must continue shaping a global economic system that works for America.'

Neoliberalism and its discontents

Shaping a global system that works for America means shaping a system that works for American corporations, shaping a system that returns profit to American banks, and shaping a world system that is good to wealthy people. For a while, under democratic coercion, the post-war institutions of policy formation had to accede to Keynesian policies that entailed intervention by states temporarily inhabited by experts that had learned from the Great Depression to be wary of unrestricted markets. State-regulated capitalism was good for working people, particularly in the social democracies, but even, also, in that pale, liberal version, the United States. 'Good for working people' meant precisely 'not so good for owning people'. At the same time, developmental states in the Third World were constructing economies that could bring justice to peasants and workers. But the Keynesian world system went into a crisis that was wider than stagflation, for it involved the construction of a counter-culture that rejected the affluent lifestyle and a counter-politics that criticized imperial interventionism. This was a crisis of mass conscience as well as mass consumption. From the cultural and political crisis of the 1960s and 1970s came neoconservatism and, eventually, the repeat of the geopolitical mistakes made earlier in Vietnam. From the economic crisis of the 1970s came, too, neoliberalism, an ideology that revisited the glorious days of the late colonial-imperial nineteenth century and somehow found there ... liberty, democracy and the freedom of the human individual. Thus, what has happened over the last few decades is that the dominant, overwhelmingly Republican political and economic class, the people who choose the politicians, the people who fund the think tanks, the people with money in investment banks, the patriots who buy soldier-dads-with-kids to fight and die for them, the people who fund economic research, the people who fraternize at Harvard, Yale, Princeton and Stanford, the people who philanthropize the poor, the people who own and run everything, put into place a neoliberal regime that extends their rule, their hegemony and their discursive and monetary power into every nook and cranny of a shrinking world. And they call it 'development'. But neoliberalism derives not only from 'intellectuals' like von Hayek squinting at history, it is implicit too in classical, neoclassical and mainstream economics, ideologies that lay claim to science the better to disguise their favouring of the entrepreneur. Neoliberalism is merely liberal economics exaggerated. It therefore has a broad base of intellectual and theoretical support that transcends the 'business community'. The global economy is moulded into neoliberal shape through policy prescription. And policy is made at the US Treasury, at the IMF, at the World Bank, at the think tanks, the economics departments of the Ivy League universities and, most importantly, the Wall Street invest-ment banks. This complex of institutions makes up the pentagon of economic power. (Let me add that further work on this would reveal something more like a hexagon of economic power – for the media not only report the news, they also make it. But a pentagon will do for now.) The policy elite circulates within these closely linked institutions, producing a discourse limited to updates to virtually the same policy regime, except that now we have a more liberal neoliberalism that adds global philanthropy to multinational investment.

The world remains highly uneven and riven by conflict. Neoliberal development produces islands of middle-class prosperity in societies that become more unequal overall. Even the alternative, state-led, export-oriented development is met, in China, by 80,000 violent protests a year by excluded and exploited peasants and workers – so China too seeks alternative development. As well as producing US-style affluence for a few, neoliberalism has exacerbated the already miserable conditions experienced every day by billions of people who never had it so bad. And as these billions watch their children die in agony so the world's rich can dine in splendour they commit themselves to social movements that propose alternative development as part of social transformation. In the past, these Third World upsurges of anger and longing were restrained by their forming in countries where the argument could be made, and widely believed, that progress depends on foreign investment … investment from the ruling elite and from global finance capital. In this formation, development could be bought only by bribing financiers with the promise of high returns to compensate for the risk of investing in unequal and volatile societies. Where Third World countries, such as Cuba, persisted in pursuing alternative routes to a different development, the capitalist world under the 'leadership' of the USA did its utmost to overthrow their governments, isolate their economies and denigrate their political systems. But now, in Latin America, the continent that suffered most from the ravages of the Washington Consensus, we begin to see what people who hate neoliberalism can do instead, in the way of education for the masses, doctors freely available to the poor, nationalized industries paying dividends to the people, state-supported cooperative enterprises, liberated golf courses turned into green housing space for the homeless, and all those other 'mad economic practices' that collectively make up alternative development. These experiments are sustained not by foreign investment but by the revenues from oil and natural gas being returned as investments in the people instead of profits to the elite. As the World Social Forum shows, there is widespread, global support for an alternative to neoliberal policies that deliberately and consciously skew economic growth to favour the investor. Even so, the institutional structure of alternative, counter-hegemonic policy formation remains weakly developed. Movements that mobilize millions are represented by theories devised by a relative few, backed by meagre resources and with a precarious institutional

193

existence. To further their end, this book proposes a counter-expertise to produce an alternative development. All that I have managed to do, so far, is to outline the theoretical and institutional structure of hegemonic policy formation, to look at sub-hegemonic subversion of alternative development, and to give some idea of what I take to be the first moments of truly counter-hegemonic developments in Latin America. The really hard work on counter-hegemonic theorization remains to be done. My conclusion is that counter-hegemonic policy formation deserves the thoughts and the theories, the practice and the persuasion, of the world's activists and intellectuals, those who believe in equality, social justice and real democracy, and think that human beings are capable of finer sentiments in building a far better world.

Bibliography

AAUP (2005/06) *The Devaluing of Higher Education: The Annual Report on the Economic Status of the Profession 2005–06*, <www.aaup.org/surveys/zrep.htm>.

Abelson, D. E. (2002) *Do Think Tanks Matter? Assessing the Impact of Public Policy Institutes*, Montreal: McGill-Queen's University Press.

Adelzadeh, A. (1999) 'The cost of staying the course', *Ngqo*, 1: 1–6.

Aglietta, M. (1979) *A Theory of Capitalist Regulation*, London: New Left Books.

Albright, M. (1997) Confirmation Statement before the Senate Foreign Relations Committee, <www.mtholyoke.edu/acad/intrel/albright.htm>.

Althusser, L. (1971), *Lenin and Philosophy and Other Essays*, London: New Left Books.

American Enterprise Institute (2006) *AEI's Organization and Purposes*, <www.aei.org>.

Amin, A. (1999) 'An institutionalist perspective on regional economic development', *International Journal of Urban and Regional Research*, 23: 365–78.

ANC (1987) 'Constitutional guidelines for a democratic South Africa', in W. Esterhuyse and P. Nel (eds), *The ANC and Its Leaders*, Cape Town: Tafelberg, pp. 162–6.

— (1991) Draft Resolution on ANC Economic Policy for National Conference, Pretoria: ANC Department of Economic Policy.

— (1992) *Ready to Govern: ANC Policy Guidelines for a Democratic South Africa*, Pretoria: ANC.

— (1994) *The Reconstruction and Development Programme: A Policy Framework*, Johannesburg: Umanyano Publications.

— (1997) *All Power to the People!: Draft Strategy and Tactics of the African National Congress*, Pretoria: ANC (draft).

Arnott, R., B. Greenwald, R. Kanbur and B. Nalebuff (2003) Introduction to *Economics for an Imperfect World: Essays in Honor of Joseph Stiglitz*, Cambridge: MIT Press.

Association of Research Libraries (2004) <www.arl.org/>.

Ayres, C. E. (1957) 'Institutional economics: discussion', *American Economic Review*, 47: 26–7.

BBC (2005) 'Foreign investment "fails Africa"', <http://news.bbc.co.uk/1/hi/business/4242554.stm>.

Beattie, A. (2003) 'Report casts doubt on FDI incentives', *Financial Times*, 15 October, p. 1.

Bello, W. (2002) *Deglobalization: Ideas for a New Economy*, London: Zed Books.

Bendix, R. (1960) *Max Weber: An Intellectual Portrait*, Garden City: Doubleday.

Bentham, J. (1996) *An Introduction to the Principles of Morals and Legislation*, Oxford: Clarendon Press.

Bergesten, F. (2005) *The United States and the World Economy: Foreign Economic Policy for the Next Decade*, Washington, DC: Institute for International Economics.

Best, S. and D. Kellner (1991) *Postmodern Theory: Critical Interrogations*, New York: Guilford Press.

Beveridge, W. (1942) *Social and Allied Services* (The Beveridge Report), Presented to Parliament by Command of His Majesty, London: HMSO, <www.fordham.edu/halsall/mod/1942beveridge.html>.

Biko, S. (1996) *I Write What I Like*, London: Bowerdean.

Birdsall, N. and J. Williamson (2002) *Delivering on Debt Relief: From IMF Gold to a New Aid Architecture*, Washington, DC: Institute for International Economics.

Birnbaum, J. H. (2005) 'The road to riches is called K Street: lobbying firms hire more, pay more, charge more to influence government', *Washington Post*, 22 June, p. A01.

BIS (Bank for International Settlements) (2004), <www.bis.org/statistics/secstats.htm>.

Bloch, E. (1986) *Inside Investment Banking*, Homewood, IL: Dow-Jones-Irwin.

Blommestein, H. J. and N. Funke (eds) (1998) *Institutional Investors in the New Financial Landscape*, Paris: OECD.

Blumenthal, S. (1986) *The Rise of the Counter-Establishment: From Conservative Ideology to Political Power*, New York: Harper and Row.

Blyth, M. (2002) *Great Transformations: Economic Ideas and Institutional Change in the Twentieth Century*, Cambridge: Cambridge University Press.

Boggs, C. (1976) *Gramsci's Marxism*, London: Pluto Press.

Bollag, B. (2000) 'The new Latin: English dominates in academe', *Chronicle of Higher Education International*, 8 September.

Bond, P. (1991) *Commanding Heights and Community Control: New Economics for a New South Africa*, Johannesburg: Raven Press.

— (1996) 'Neoliberalism comes to South Africa', *Multinational Monitor*, May, pp. 8–14.

— (1997) 'Fighting neo-liberalism: the South African front', *Southern Africa Report*, 12(2): 14–20.

— (2000) *Elite Transition: From Apartheid to Neoliberalism in South Africa*, London: Pluto Press.

Boyer, R. and Y. Saillard (2002) 'Regulation Theory: statis or confirmation of a research programme?', in R. Boyer and Y. Saillard (eds), *Regulation Theory: The State of the Art*, London: Routledge, pp. 45–54.

Bretton Woods Project (2006) <www.brettonwoodsproject.org/>.

Brookings Institution (2006) *About Brookings*, <www.brook.edu/index/about.htm>.

Burchall, G., C. Gordon and P. Miller (eds) (1991) *The Foucault Effect: Studies in Governmentality*, Chicago, IL: University of Chicago Press.

Burris, V. (1992) 'Elite policy-planning networks in the United States', *Research in Politics and Society*, 4.

Bush, G. W. (2002) State of the Union address, <www.whitehouse.gov/news/releases/2002/01/20020129-11.html>.

— (2004) The Third Bush–Kerry Presidential Debate, <www.debates.org/pages/trans2004d.html>.

— (205) State of the Union address, <www.whitehouse.gov/news/releases/2005/02/20050202-11.html>.

CARE (2006) *About CARE*, <www.care.org/about/index.asp>.

Castoriadis, C. (1991) 'The social historical: mode of being, problems of knowledge', in C. Castoriadis, *Philosophy, Politics, Autonomy*, New York: Oxford University Press, pp. 33–46.

Center for Economic and Policy Research (CEPR) (2006) <www.cepr.net/>.

Center for Responsive Politics (2006a) *The Big Picture. The Money behind the Elections*, <www.opensecrets.org/bigpicture/index.asp>.

— (2006b) *Influence, Inc. The Bottom Line on Washington Lobbying*, <www.opensecrets.org/pubs/lobby00/index.asp>.

Centre for Civil Society (2005) 'South Africa: a focus on the basic income grant', Centre for Civil Society

Research Report no. 11, Durban, South Africa, pp. 1–38.

Centre for the Study of Developing Societies, Delhi (2006) *Introduction*, <www.csdsdelhi.org/intro.htm>.

Ceruti, C. (1996) *How and Why the ANC's Nationalisation Policy Changed: Economic Nationalism and the Changing State–Capital Relation*, MA thesis, Department of Sociology, University of the Witwatersrand, Johannesburg.

Chang, H.-J. and I. Grabel (2004) *Reclaiming Development: An Alternative Economic Development Manual*, London: Zed Books.

Chang, H.-J. and R. Rowthorn (eds) (1995) *The Role of the State in Economic Change*, Oxford: Clarendon Press.

Clark, J. B. (1888) 'Capital and its earnings', *Publications of the American Economic Association*, 3, 2.

Clark, R. (2002) 'Jeremy Bentham', *The Literary Encyclopedia*, <www.utilitarian.net/bentham/about/20020915.htm>.

CNN (2006) 'Bush: Chavez doing "disservice" to Venezuela', <www.cnn.com/2006/WORLD/americas/06/07/bush.venezuela/index.htm>.

COSATU (1996) *Social Equity and Job Creation*, Johannesburg: COSATU.

Council for Aid to Education, RAND (2005) <www.cae.org>.

Coupe, T. (2002) *Revealed Performances: Worldwide Ranking of Economists and Economics Departments 1969–2000*, <http://homepages.ulb.ac.be/~tcoupe/ranking.html>.

Cox, R. (1987) *Production, Power, and World Order: Social Forces in the Making of History*, New York: Columbia University Press.

Cronon, W. (1983) *Changes in the Land: Indians, Colonists, and the Ecology of New England*, New York: Hill & Wang.

Crush, J. (1995) Preface, in J. Crush (ed.), *Power of Development*, London: Routledge, pp. xi–xiv.

Cuba–Venezuela (2004) Joint Declaration, <www.cuba.cu/gobierno/discursos/2004/ing/d141204i.html>.

Dean, M. (1999) *Governmentality: Power and Rule in Modern Society*, London: Sage.

De Leon, P. (1997) *Democracy and the Policy Sciences*, Albany: State University of New York Press.

DeParle, J. (2005) 'Goals reached, donor on right closes up shop', *New York Times*, 29 May, pp. 1, 21.

Derrida, J. (1971) 'White mythology', in *Margins of Philosophy*, trans. A. Bass, Chicago, IL: University of Chicago Press.

Desai, A. and H. Bohmke (1997) 'The South African intellectual during the democratic transition', *Debate*, 2: 10–34.

Descartes, R. (1968) *The Philosophical Works of Descartes*, trans. E. Haldane and G. R. T. Ross, Cambridge: Cambridge University Press.

Development GAP (Devleopment Group for Alternative Policies) (2006) <www.developmentgap.org/>.

Dolny, M. (2006) 'Study finds first drop in think tank cites: progressive groups see biggest decline', *Fairness in Accuracy and Reporting*, <www.fair.org/index.php?page=2897>.

Domhoff, G. W. (ed.) (1975) 'New directions in power structure research', special issue of *The Insurgent Sociologist*, 5(3).

— (ed.) (1979/80) 'Power structure research II', special issue of *The Insurgent Sociologist*, 9(2/3).

— (1990) *The Power Elite and the State: How Policy is Made in America*, New York: Aldine de Gruyter.

— (2001) *Who Rules America? Power and Politics*, New York: McGraw Hill.

Donaldson, A. R. (1997) 'Social

Bibliography

development and macroeconomic policy', *Development South Africa*, 14: 447–70.

Dreyfus, H. L. and P. Rabinow (1983) *Michel Foucault: Beyond Structuralism and Hermeneutics*, Chicago, IL: University of Chicago Press.

Dryzek, J. (1982) 'Policy analysis as hermeneutic activity', *Policy Sciences*, 14: 309–29.

— (1989) 'Policy sciences of democracy', *Polity*, 22: 97–118.

— (1996) *Democracy in Capitalist Times*, New York: Oxford University Press.

Dumenil, G. and D. Levy (2004) *Capital Resurgent: Roots of the Neoliberal Revolution*, Cambridge, MA: Harvard University Press.

Dunford, M. and D. Perrons (1983) *The Arena of Capital*, New York: St Martin's Press.

Edsall, T. (1985) *The New Politics of Inequality*, New York: Norton.

Escobar, A. (1995) *Encountering Development: The Making and Unmaking of the Third World*, Princeton, NJ: Princeton University Press.

Esterhuyse, W. (1990) 'The Freedom Charter and the ANC's Constitutional Guidelines', in W. Esterhuyse and P. Nel (eds), *The ANC and Its Leaders*, Cape Town: Tafelberg, pp. 98–110.

Fallon, P and L. A. Pereira de Silva (1994) *South Africa: Economic Performance and Policies*, Informal Discussion Papers on Aspects of the Economy of South Africa no. 7, Washington DC: World Bank.

Faux, J. (2006) *The Global Class War*, New York: Wiley.

Fine, B. and Z. Rustomjee (1996) *The Political Economy of South Africa: From Minerals–Energy Complex to Industrialization*, London: Hurst.

Fischer, F. and J. Forester (eds) (1987) *Confronting Values in Policy Analysis: The Politics of Criteria*, Newbury Park, CA: Sage.

— (eds) (1993) *The Argumentative Turn in Policy Analysis and Planning*, Durham, NC: Duke University Press.

Fisher, H. E. S. (1971) *The Portugal Trade: A Study of Anglo-Portuguese Commerce 1700–1770*, London: Methuen.

Fisher, W. and T. Ponniah (2003) *Another World is Possible: Popular Alternatives to Globalization at the World Social Forum*, London: Zed Books.

Focus on the Global South (2006) <www.focusweb.org/>.

Foucault, M. (1972) *The Archaeology of Knowledge*, New York: Harper and Row.

— (1973) *The Order of Things*, New York: Vintage Press.

— (1979) *Discipline and Punish: The Birth of the Prison*, New York: Vintage.

— (1980) *Power/Knowledge: Selected Interviews and Other Writings, 1972–1977*, New York: Pantheon.

— (1991) 'Governmentality', in G. Burchall, C. Gordon and P. Miller (eds), *The Foucault Effect: Studies in Governmentality*, London: Harvester Wheatsheaf, pp. 87–104.

Frank, A. G. (1979) *Dependent Accumulation and Underdevelopment*, New York: Monthly Review Press.

Freedom Charter (1955) Appendix B, in W. Esterhuyse and P. Nel (eds), *The ANC and Its Leaders*, Cape Town: Tafelberg, pp. 157–61.

Friedman, M. (1958) 'Foreign economic aid: means and objectives', *Yale Review*, 47: 500–516.

Friedman, M. and R. Friedman (1979) *Free to Choose*, New York: Harcourt Brace Jovanovich.

Friedman, S. (1993) *The Long Journey: South Africa's Quest for a Negotiated Settlement*, Johannesburg: Raven Press.

Friends of the MST (2006) *About the MST*, <www.mstbrazil.org/?q=>.

G8 (2005) *G8 Finance Ministers'*

Conclusions on Development, London, 10/11 June, <www.g8.gc. ca/concl_devel-en.asp>.

Gallagher, P. and L. Zarsky (2006) 'Rethinking foreign investment for development', *Post-Autistic Economics Review*, 37, 28 April, article 2, <www.paecon. net/PAEReview/issue37/ GallagherZarsky37.htm>.

Garrett, G. and P. Lange (1991) 'Political responses to interdependence: what's "left" for the left?', *International Organization*, 45: 539–64.

GaWC (Globalization and World Cities Study Group and Network) (2006) <www.lboro.ac.uk/gawc/>.

Gerhart, G. (1978) *Black Power in South Africa: The Evolution of an Ideology*, Berkeley: University of California Press.

Germain, R. (1997) *The International Organization of Credit: State and Global Finance in the World Economy*, Cambridge: Cambridge University Press.

Gibbon, P. (1992) 'The World Bank and African poverty 1973–91', *Journal of Modern African Studies*, 30: 193–220.

Gill, S. (ed.) (1993) *Gramsci, Historical Materialism and International Relations*, Cambridge: Cambridge University Press.

— (2003) *Power and Resistance in the New World Order*, Basingstoke: Palgrave Macmillan.

Gill, S. and D. Law (1989) 'Global hegemony and the structural power of capital', *International Studies Quarterly*, 33: 475–99.

Gindin, J. (2005) 'Made in Venezuela: the struggle to reinvent Venezuelan labor', *Monthly Review*, June.

Gonce, R. A. (2003) Review of I. M. Kirzner (2001) 'Ludwig von Mises: the man and his economics', *American Journal of Economics and Sociology*, 62: 633–6.

Gordon, D. (1996) *Fat and Mean: The Corporate Squeeze of Working Americans and the Myth of Managerial 'Downsizing'*, New York: Free Press.

Government of the Republic of South Africa (1994) White Paper on Reconstruction and Development, *Government Gazette*, Cape Town, 23 November.

— (1996) *Growth, Employment and Redistribution: A Macroeconomic Strategy (GEAR)*, Department of Finance, Republic of South Africa.

Gowan, P. (1995) 'Neo-liberal theory and practice for eastern Europe', *New Left Review*, 213: 3–60.

Gramsci, A. (1971) *Selections from the Prison Notebooks*, London: Lawrence and Wishart.

Granovetter, M. (1985) 'Economic action and social structure: the problem of embeddedness', *American Journal of Sociology*, 91: 481–510.

Gray, J. (1998) *False Dawn: The Delusions of Global Capitalism*, New York: New Press.

Gregory, D. (1982) *Regional Transformation and Industrial Revolution*, Minneapolis: University of Minnesota Press.

Group of 77 (2006) *What is the Group of 77?*, <www.g77.org/>.

Habib, A. and V. Padayachee (2000) 'Economic policy and power relations in South Africa's transition to democracy', *World Development*, 28.

Hajer, M. A. (1995) *The Politics of Environmental Discourse*, Oxford: Oxford University Press.

Halpin, T. (2004) 'Britain wins eight places in world list of 50 best universities', *The Times* (London), 4 November, p. 10.

Harmon, M. D. (1997) *The British Labour Government and the 1976 IMF Crisis*, London: Macmillan.

Harvey, D. (2005) *A Brief History of Neoliberalism*, Oxford: Oxford University Press.

Heckscher, E. F. (1935) *Mercantilism*, 2 vols, London: Unwin Hyman.

Heritage Foundation (2006) *About Heritage*, <www.heritage. org/About/aboutHeritage.cfm>.

Hilferding, R. (ed.) (1981) *Finance Capital: A Study of the Latest Phase of Capitalist Development*, London: Routledge and Kegan Paul.

Hill, C. (1958) *Puritanism and Revolution: Studies in Interpretation of the English Revolution of the 17th Century*, London: Secker and Warburg.

Hodgson, G. M. (1988) *Economics and Institutions*, Cambridge: Polity Press.

Hume, D. (1987) *Essays, Moral, Political and Literary*, Indianapolis: University of Indiana Press.

Hutchison, T. W. (1953) *A Review of Economic Doctrines, 1870–1929*, Oxford: Clarendon Press.

IMF (International Monetary Fund) (1992) *Economic Policies for a New South Africa*, Occasional Paper no. 91, Washington, DC: IMF.

— (2000) *Debt Relief for Low-income Countries: The Enhanced HIPC Initiative*, New York: IMF.

— (2005) *South Africa: 2005 Article IV Consultation – Staff Report; Staff Statement; and Public Information Notice on the Executive Board Discussion*, 19 September, <www. imf.org/external/pubs/cat/longres. cfm?sk=18583.0>.

Innes, S. (1995) *Creating the Commonwealth: The Economic Culture of Puritan New England*, New York: Norton.

Institute for International Economics (2006) *About the Institute*, <www. iie.com/institute/aboutiie.cfm>.

Institute for Policy Studies (2006) *Overview*, <www.ips-dc.org/ overview.htm>.

Joffee, A. et al. (1995) *Improving Manufacturing Performance in South Africa: Report of the Strategy Project*, Cape Town: UCT Press.

Johnston, D. C. (2005) 'Richest are leaving even the rich far behind', *New York Times*, 5 June, pp. 1, 17.

Jones, J. P. and J. E. Kodras (1990) *Geographic Dimensions of United States Social Policy*, London: Edward Arnold.

Jonsson, G. and A. Subramanian (2000) *Dynamic Gains from Trade: Evidence from South Africa*, IMF Working Paper WP 00/45, Washington, DC: IMF.

Kahneman, D. (2003) 'Maps of bounded rationality: psychology for behavioral economics', *American Economic Review*, 93: 1449–75.

Kalaitzidakis, P., T. Mamuneas and T. Stengos (2003) 'Rankings of academic journals and institutions in economics', *Journal of the European Economic Association*, 1: 1346–66.

Kaplan, L. F. and W. Kristol (2003) *The War over Iraq*, San Francisco, CA: Encounter Books.

Kearny, A. T. (2004) *FDI Confidence Index*, Global Business Council, October, <www.atkearney.com>.

Kenis, P. and V. Schneider (1991) 'Policy networks and policy analysis: scrutinizing a new analytical toolbox', in B. Marinand and R.Mayntz (eds), *Policy Network: Empirical Evidence and Theoretical Considerations*, Frankfurt: Campus Verlag, pp. 25–59.

Kentridge, M. (1993) *Turning the Tanker: The Economic Debate in South Africa*, Johannesburg: Centre for Policy Studies.

Keynes, J. M. (1936) *The General Theory of Employment, Interest and Money*, New York: Harcourt Brace.

Khor, M. (2001) *Rethinking Globalization: Critical Issues and Policy Choices*, London: Zed Books.

Kohl, B. and L. Farthing (2006) *Globalization and Social Movements: Bolivian Standoff*, London: Zed Books.

Kohli, A. (2004) *State-directed Development: Political Power and*

Industrialization in the Global Periphery, Cambridge: Cambridge University Press.

Kornblut, A. E. and S. G. Stolberg (2006) 'In speech, Bush warns of risks in quitting Iraq', *New York Times*, 1 September, pp. A1, A6.

Kristol, I. (1995) *Neoconservatism: The Autobiography of an Idea*, New York: Free Press.

Krueger, A. (2005) Statement by IMF First Deputy Managing Director Anne O. Krueger at the Conclusion of a Visit to South Africa, IMF Press Release no. 05/138, 10 June, <www.imf.org/external/np/sec/pr/2005/pro5138.htm>.

Kuczynski, P.-P. (2003) 'Setting the stage', in P.-P. Kuczynski and J. Williamson (eds) (2003), *After the Washington Consensus*, Washington, DC: Institute for International Economics, pp. 21–32.

Lapavitsas, C. (2005) 'Mainstream economics in the neoliberal era', in A. Saad-Filho and D. Johnston (eds), *Neoliberalism: A Critical Reader*, London: Pluto Press, pp. 30–40.

Lasswell, H. D. (1951) 'The policy orientation', in H. D. Lasswell and D. Lerner (eds), *The Policy Sciences: Recent Developments in Scope and Method*, Stanford, CA, Stanford University Press.

La Via Campesina (2006) <http://viacampesina.org/main_en/index.php>.

Lekachman, R. (1959) *A History of Economic Ideas*, New York: Harper and Row.

Leone, R. C. (1996) Foreword, in E. N. Wolf, *Top Heavy: A Study of Increasing Inequality of Wealth in America*, New York: New Press.

Leonhardt, D. (2002) 'Scholarly mentor to Bush's team', *New York Times*, 1 December, Section 3, pp. 1, 12.

Lester, A., E. Nel and T. Binns (2000) 'South Africa's current transition in temporal and spatial context', *Antipode*, 32: 135–51.

Leube, K. R. (1984) 'Friedrich August von Hayek: a biographical introduction', in F. von Hayek, *The Essence of Hayek*, Stanford, CT: Hoover Institution Press, pp. xvii–xxxvi.

Lipietz, A. (1987) *Mirages and Miracles*, London: Verso.

Logan, I. B. and K. Mengisteab (1993) 'IMF–World Bank adjustment and structural transformation in sub-Saharan Africa', *Economic Geography*, 69: 1–24.

Lordon, F. (2002) 'Regulation Theory and economic policy', in R. Boyer and Y. Saillard (eds), *Regulation Theory: The State of the Art*, London: Routledge, pp. 129–35.

MacEwan, A. (1999) *Neoliberalism or Democracy? Economic Strategy, Markets, and Alternatives for the 21st Century*, London: Zed Books.

Magubane, B. (1979) *The Political Economy of Race and Class in South Africa*, New York: Monthly Review Press.

Majone, G. (1989) *Evidence, Argument, and Persuasion in the Policy Process*, New Haven, CT: Yale University Press.

Mallaby, S. (2004) *The World's Banker: A Story of Failed States, Financial Crisis, and the Wealth and Poverty of Nations*, New York: Penguin Press.

Mandela, N. (1990) *The Struggle Is My Life*, 3rd edn, London: International Defence and Aid Fund.

Manji, C. and F. Coill (2002) 'The missionary position: NGOs and development in Africa', *International Affairs*, 78: 567–83.

Manzo, K. (1995) 'Black consciousness and the quest for a counter-modernist development', in J. Crush (ed.), *Power of Development*, London: Routledge, pp. 228–52.

Marais, H. (1998) *South Africa Limits to Change: The Political Economy of Transformation*, London: Zed Books.

Martin, R. L. (1994) 'Economic theory and human geography', in D. Gregory, R. L. Martin and G. E. Smith (eds), *Human Geography: Society, Space and Social Science*, Basingstoke: Macmillan, pp. 21–53.

— (2000) 'Institutional approaches in economic geography', in E. Sheppard and T. Barnes (eds), *A Companion to Economic Geography*, Oxford: Blackwell, pp. 77–94.

Marx, K. (1973) *Grundrisse: Introduction to the Critique of Political Economy*, Harmondsworth: Penguin.

Marx, K. and F. Engels (1970) *The German Ideology*, New York: International Publishers.

Mbeki, T. (1985) 'The historical injustice', in ANC, *Selected Writings on the Freedom Charter: 1955–1985*, London: ANC, pp. 36–50.

Meier, G. (1984) *Leading Issues in Development Economics*, 4th edn, New York: Oxford University Press.

MERG (1993) *Making Democracy Work: A Framework for Macroeconomic Policy in South Africa*, Cape Town: Centre for Development Studies.

Metcalfe, J. S. (1998) *Evolutionary Economics and Creative Destruction*, London: Routledge.

Miliband, R. (1969) *The State in Capitalist Society*, New York: Basic Books.

Mills, C. W. (2000) *The Power Elite*, New York: Oxford University Press.

Mohan, G., E. Brown, B. Milward and A. B. Zack-Williams (2000) *Structural Adjustment: Theory, Practice and Impacts*, London: Routledge.

Moore, M. (2004) *Fahrenheit 9/11*, DVD.

Morgan Stanley (2006a) Emerging Markets Strategy Profile, <www.morganstanley.com/web/verity/webapp/search>.

— (2006b) *About Morgan Stanley*, <www.morganstanley.com/about/index.html>.

Morgan Stanley Institutional Fund (2006) Emerging Markets Portfolio. MSIF Class A Shares Symbol: MGEMX CUSIP: 61744J820, Second Quarter Review, 30 June.

Mosley, L. (2003) *Global Capital and National Governments*, Cambridge: Cambridge University Press.

Murray, J. M. (ed.) (1982) *South African Capitalism and Black Political Opposition*, Cambridge: Schenkman.

Narsiah, I. (2006) *Delusions of Development: Neoliberal Development Discourses and Privatization in South Africa*, PhD dissertation, Clark University.

Nattrass, N. (1994) 'Politics and economics in ANC economic policy', *African Affairs*, 93: 343–59.

— (1996) 'Gambling on investment: competing economic strategies in South Africa', *Transformation*, 31: 25–42.

Nelson, B. (1996) 'Public policy and administration: an overview', in R. E. Goodin and H.-D. Klingemann (eds), *A New Handbook of Political Science*, Oxford: Oxford University Press.

New York Times (2002) 'Hugo Chavez departs', Editorial, Section A, 13 April, p. 16.

— (2006) 'Bonanza on Wall Street', 26 November, p. 2.

Nilson Report (2003) Issue 797, October, <www.nilsonreport.com/>.

North, D. (1990) *Institutions, Institutional Change and Economic Performance*, Cambridge: Cambridge University Press.

— (1995) 'The new institutional economics and Third World development', in J. Harris, J. Hunter and C. M. Lewis (eds), *The New Institutional Economics and Third World Development*, London: Routledge, pp. 17–26.

Obstfeld, M. (1998) 'The global capital market: benefactor or menace?', *Journal of Economic Perspectives*, 12: 9–30.

OECD (Organization for Economic Cooperation and Development) (1988) *The Newly Industrializing Countries*, Paris: OECD.

— (2002) *Foreign Direct Investment for Development, Maximising Benefits, Minimising Costs*, Paris: OECD.

Offe, C. (1985) *Disorganized Capitalism*, Cambridge, MA: MIT.

Oxfam (2006) *About Us*, <www.oxfam.org/en/about/>.

Padayachee, V. (1994) 'Debt, development and democracy: the IMF in post-apartheid South Africa', *Review of African Political Economy*, 62: 585–97.

— (1998) 'Progressive academic economists and the challenge of development in South Africa's decade of liberation', *Review of African Political Economy*, 77: 431–50.

Painter, J. (1995) 'The regulatory state: the corporate welfare state and beyond', in R. J. Johnston et al. (eds), *Geographies of Global Change*, Oxford: Blackwell, ch. 9.

Palley, T. I. (2005) 'From Keynesianism to neoliberalism: shifting paradigms in economics', in A. Saad-Filho and D. Johnston (eds), *Neoliberalism: A Critical Reader*, London: Pluto Press, pp. 20–29.

Panitch, L. (2000) 'The new imperial state', *New Left Review*, NS 2: 5–20.

Patel, E. (1993) *Engine of Development? South Africa's National Economic Forum*, Kenwyn: Juta.

Peck, J. (1998) 'Geographies of governance: TECs and the neoliberalisation of "local interests"', *Space and Polity*, 2: 5–31.

— (1999) 'Grey geography', *Transactions*, IBG 24: 131–6.

Peck, J. and A. Tickell (1994) 'Jungle law breaks out: neoliberalism and global-local disorder', *Area*, 26: 317–26.

— (2002) 'Neoliberalizing space', *Antipode*, 34: 380–404.

Peet, R. et al. (2003) *Unholy Trinity: The IMF, World Bank and WTO*, London: Zed Books.

Peoples Treaty (2006) Text of Peoples Treaty Bolivia, Cuba, Venezuela, <www.tni.org/altregdocs/albatcptreaty.htm>.

Perelman, M. (2006) *Railroading Economics: The Creation of the Free Market Mythology*, New York: Monthly Review Press.

Perkins, J. (2004) *Confessions of an Economic Hit Man*, San Francisco, CA: Berrett-Koehler.

Peschek, J. G. (1987) *Policy-Planning Organizations: Elite Agendas and America's Rightward Turn*, Philadelphia: Temple University.

Piketty, T., E. Hess and E. Saez (2004) 'Income inequality in the United States, 1913–2002', Unpublished paper, updated 2006, <http://elsa.berkeley.edu/~saez/>.

Pityana, B., M. Ramphele, L. Mpumlwana and L. Wilson (1992) *Bounds of Possibility: The Legacy of Steve Biko and Black Consciousness*, London: Zed Books.

Poggi, G. (1983) *Calvinism and the Capitalist Spirit: Max Weber's Protestant Ethic*, Amherst: University of Massachusetts Press.

Polanyi, K. (1944) *The Great Transformation*, New York: Farrar and Rinehart.

Political Economy Research Institute (PERI) (2006) <www.peri.umass.edu/>.

Pollin, R. (2003) *Contours of Descent: US Economic Fractures and the Landscape of Global Austerity*, London: Verso.

Pollin, R., G. Epstein, J. Heintz and L. N. Dikumana (2006) *An Employment-targeted Economic*

Program for South Africa, Amherst, MA: PERI.

Ponniah, T. (2006) *The World Social Forum Vision: Radical Democracy versus Neoliberal Globalization*, PhD dissertation, Clark University.

Poon, J. P. H. (2003) 'Hierarchical tendencies of capital markets among international financial centers', *Growth and Change*, 34: 135–56.

Poulantzas, N. (1978) *State, Power, Socialism*, London: New Left Books.

Powell, L. (2006) ReclaimDemocracy. org, <www.reclaimdemocracy. org/corporate_accountability/ powell_memo_lewis.html>.

Przeworski, A., M. E. Alvarez, J. Antonio Cheibub and F. Limongi (1990) *Democracy and Development: Political Institutions and Well-being in the World, 1950–1990*, Cambridge: Cambridge University Press.

Rabinow, P. (ed.) (1984) *The Foucault Reader*, New York: Pantheon.

Rahnema, M. with V. Bawtree (eds) (1997) *The Post-Development Reader*, London: Zed Books.

Rantete, J. M. (1994) *Facing the Challenges of Transition: A Critical Analysis of the African National Congress in the 1990s*, MA dissertation, Faculty of Arts, University of the Witwatersrand.

Rayack, E. (1987) *Not So Free to Choose: The Political Economy of Milton Friedman and Ronald Reagan*, New York: Praeger.

Redman, J. E. (2006) *The Bolivarian Alternative for the Americas: Negotiating the Role of the Venezuelan State in Development*, MA thesis, Clark University.

Ricardo, D. (1911 [1817]) *The Principles of Political Economy and Taxation*, London: J. M. Dent.

Rich, A. (2004) *Think Tanks, Public Policy, and the Politics of Expertise*, Cambridge: Cambridge University Press.

Roberts, P. C. (1971) 'Oskar Lange's theory of socialist planning', *Journal of Political Economy*, 79: 562–77.

Rodrik, D. (2006) 'Goodbye Washington Consensus: hello Washington Confusion', *Journal of Economic Literature* (forthcoming), <http://ksghome.harvard. edu/~drodrik/papers.html>.

Roll, E. (1942) *A History of Economic Thought*, New York: Prentice-Hall.

Romero, S. (2006) 'Caracas mayor lays claim to golf links to house poor', *New York Times*, 3 September, p. A3.

Rubin, R. (2003) *In an Uncertain World: Tough Choices from Wall Street to Washington*, New York: Random House.

Ruggie, J. G. (1982) 'International regimes, transactions and change – embedded liberalism in the post-war order', *International Organization*, 36: 379–415.

Sachs, J. (2005) *The End of Poverty: Economic Possibilities for Our Time*, New York: Penguin Press.

Samuels, W. (1995) 'The present state of institutional economics', *Cambridge Journal of Economics*, 19: 569–90.

Sampson, A. (1999) *Mandela: The Authorized Biography*, New York: Knopf.

Sanchez, M. (2004) 'Violence needed against Chavez, Venezuela opposition leader says. Dictatorship must follow', <www. venezuelanalysis.com/news. php?newsno=1320>.

Sassen, S. (1991) *The Global City: New York, London, Tokyo*, Princeton, NJ: Princeton University Press.

Scammel, W. (1975) *International Monetary Policy: Bretton Woods and After*, London: Macmillan.

Schluchter, W. (1979) 'The paradox of rationalization: on the relation of ethics and world', in G. Roth and W. Schluchter, *Max Weber's Vision* of *History: Ethics and Methods*, Berkeley: University of California Press, pp. 11–64.

Schneider, V. (1988) *Politiknetzwerke der Chemikalienkontrolle. Eine Analyse einer transnationalen Politikentwicklung*, Berlin: De Gruyter.

Schrire, R. (ed.) (1992) *Wealth or Poverty? Critical Choices for South Africa*, Cape Town: Oxford University Press.

Schumpeter, J. (1934) *The Theory of Economic Development*, Cambridge, MA: Harvard University Press.

Scott, A. (1995) 'The geographic foundations of industrial performance', *Competition and Change*, 1: 51–66.

Sideri, S. (1970) *Trade and Power: Informal Colonialism in Anglo-Portuguese Relations*, Rotterdam: Rotterdam University Press.

Simmons, B. (1999) 'The internationalization of capital', in H. Kitscheldt, P. Lange, G. Marks and J. Stevens (eds), *Continuity and Change in Contemporary Capitalism*, Cambridge: Cambridge University Press, pp. 36–69.

Simon, H. A. (1957) 'A behavioral model of rational choice', in Simon, *Models of Man*, New York: John Wiley.

— (1990) 'A mechanism for social selection and successful altruism', *Science*, 250: 1665–8.

Simon, W. (1979) *A Time for Truth*, New York: Reader's Digest Press.

Smith, A. (1937) *The Wealth of Nations*, New York: Modern Library.

— (1976) *The Theory of Moral Sentiments*, Oxford: Oxford University Press.

Smith, D. (1999) 'Social justice and the ethics of development in post-apartheid South Africa', *Ethics, Place and Environment*, 2: 157–77.

Smith, J. A. (1991) *The Idea Brokers:*

Think Tanks and the Rise of the New Policy Elite, New York: Free Press.

Smith, V. (1994) 'Economics in the laboratory', *Journal of Economic Perspectives*, 8: 113–31.

Soros, G. (1998) *The Crisis of Global Capitalism: Open Society Endangered*, New York: Public Affairs.

South African Reserve Bank (1999) *Quarterly Bulletin*, 211, March, Pretoria: South African Reserve Bank.

Sowetan (1990), 5 March.

Sraffa, P. (ed.) (1951) *The Works and Correspondence of David Ricardo*, Cambridge: Cambridge University Press.

Steil, B. and R. E. Litan (2006) *Financial Statecraft: The Role of Financial Markets in American Foreign Policy*, New Haven, CT: Yale University Press.

Stiglitz, J. E. (2002) *Globalization and its Discontents*, New York: Norton.

Straussman, W. P. (1993) 'Development economics from a Chicago perspective', in W. J. Samuels (ed.), *The Chicago School of Political Economy*, New Jersey: Transaction Books, pp. 277–94.

Strom, S. (2006) 'A charity's enviable problem: race to spend Buffet billions', *New York Times*, 13 August, pp. 1, 21.

Sunley, P. (1996) 'Context in economic geography: the relevance of pragmatism', *Progress in Human Geography*, 20: 338–55.

Sunter, C. (1987) *The World and South Africa in the 1990s*, Tafelburg: Human and Rousseau.

Tabb, W. K. (2004) *Economic Governance in the Age of Globalization*, New York: Columbia University Press.

Third World Network (2006) <www.twnside.org.sg/>.

Tickell, A. and J. Peck (1995) 'Social regulation after Fordism: regulation theory, neoliberalism and the

Bibliography

global–local nexus', *Economy and Society*, 24: 357–86.

Torgerson, D. (1986) 'Between knowledge and politics: three faces of policy analysis', *Policy Sciences*, 19: 33–59.

— (2002) 'Democracy through policy discourse', in M. Hajer and H. Wagenaar (eds), *Deliberative Policy Analysis: Understanding Governance in the Network Society*, Cambridge, Cambridge University Press.

Toye, J. (1987) *Dilemmas of Development: Reflections on the Counter-revolution in Development Theory and Policy*, Oxford: Blackwell.

Tucker, B. and B. R. Scott (eds) (1992) *South Africa: Prospects for Successful Transition*, Kenwyn: Juta.

Turgeon, L. (1996) *Bastard Keynesianism: The Evolution of Economic Thinking and Policy-making Since World War II*, Westport, CT: Praeger.

UNCTAD (United Nations Conference on Trade and Development) (2004) *The Least Developed Countries Report 2004*, Geneva: UNCTAD.

— (2005) *World Investment Report 2005: Transnational Corporations and the Internationalization of R&D*, New York: United Nations.

— (2006a) *About UNCTAD*, <www.unctad.org/Templates/Page.asp?intItemID=1530&lang=1>.

— (2006b) *Report of the Panel of Eminent Persons: Enhancing the Development Role and Impact of UNCTAD*, OSG/2006/1, Geneva: UNCTAD.

UNDP (United Nations Development Programme) (1999) *Human Development Report*, New York: UNDP.

— (2005) *Investing in Development: A Practical Plan to Achieve the Millennium Development Goals*, New York: UNDP.

— (2006) *Annual Report: Global Partnership for Development*, <www.undp.org/publications/annualreport2006/index.shtml>.

United Nations Secretary-General (2006) *International Financial Situation and Development Report of the UN Secretary General*, New York, 12 July, A/61/36.

USA Today (2005) 'Pat Robertson calls for assassination of Hugo Chavez', <www.usatoday.com/news/nation/2005-08-22-robertson-_x.htm>.

Van der Burg, S. (1990) 'The economic argument in favor of negotiation, and the ANC's economic viewpoints', in W. Esterhuyse and P. Nel (eds), *The ANC and Its Leaders*, Cape Town: Tafelberg, pp. 111–23.

Van der Westhuizen, G. (1994) 'The South African Congress of Democrats', in I. Lienberg et al. (eds), *The Long March: The Struggle for Liberation in South Africa*, Pretoria: HAUM, pp. 72–80.

Veblen, T. (1912) *The Theory of the Leisure Class: An Economic Study of Institutions*, New York: Macmillan.

Von Hayek, F. (1945) 'The use of knowledge in society', *American Economic Review*, 34: 519–30.

— (1984) *The Essence of Hayek*, ed. C. Nishiyama and K. Leube, Stanford, CT: Hoover Institution.

— (1994) *The Road to Serfdom Fiftieth Anniversary Edition*, Chicago, IL: University of Chicago Press.

Von Mises, L. (1912) *Nation, State, and Economy*, New York: New York University Press.

— (1932) *Socialism: An Economic and Sociological Analysis*, trans. J. Kahane, New Haven, CT: Yale University Press.

— (1953) *The Theory of Money and Credit*, New Haven, CT: Yale University Press.

— (1983) *Nation, State, and Economy: Contributions to the Politics and History of Our Time*, trans. L. B.

Yeager, New York: New York University Press.

Wade, R. (1992) 'East Asia's economic success: conflicting perspectives, partial insights, shaky evidence', *World Politics*, 44: 270–320.

— (1996) 'Japan, the World Bank, and the art of paradigm maintenance: the East Asian miracle in political perspective', *New Left Review*, 217: 3–36.

Wade, R. and F. Veneroso (1998) 'The Asian crisis: the high debt model versus the Wall Street-Treasury-IMF complex', *New Left Review*, 228: 3–23.

Warf, B. (2000) 'New York: the Big Apple in the 1990s', *Geoforum*, 31: 487–99.

Watkins, K. (1994) 'Debt relief for Africa', *Review of African Political Economy*, 62: 117–27.

Watts, M. (1994) 'Development II: the privatisation of everything', *Progress in Human Geography*, 18: 371–84.

— (2006) 'Empire of oil: capitalist dispossession and the scramble for Africa', *Monthly Review*, 58(4): 1–17.

Weber, M. (1958) *The Protestant Ethic and the Spirit of Capitalism*, New York: Charles Scribner's Sons.

— (1978) *Max Weber: Selections in Translation*, ed. W. G. Runciman, Cambridge: Cambridge University Press.

Weimer, D. L. and A. R. Vining (1999) *Policy Analysis: Concepts and Practices*, 3rd edn, Upper Saddle, NJ: Prentice Hall.

Weinstein, M. (2005) 'Venezuela's Hugo Chavez makes his bid for a Bolivarian revolution', *Power and Interest News Report*, <www.pinr. com/report.php?ac=view_report &report_id=285&language_id=1>.

Welch, C. (2006) 'Movement histories', *Latin American Research Review*, 41: 198–210.

— (2006) 'Bolivia's Evo Morales launches his movement toward socialism into the political trenches', *Power and Interest News Report*, 15 June, <www.pinr.com/report. php?ac=view_printable&report_ id=510&language_id=1>.

Wells, D. R. (2004) *The Federal Reserve System: A History*, Jefferson, NC: McFarland.

Williamson, J. (ed.) (1990) *Latin American Adjustment: How Much Has Happened?*, Washington, DC: Institute for International Economics.

— (1994) 'In search of a manual for technopols', in J. Williamson (ed.), *The Political Economy of Policy Reform*, Washington, DC: Institute for International Economics, pp. 11–28.

— (1997) 'The Washington Consensus revisited', in L. Emmerij (ed.), *Economic and Social Development into the XXI Century*, Washington, DC: Inter-American Development Bank.

— (2002) 'Did the Washington Consensus fail?', Outline of remarks at CSIS, Washington, DC: Institute for International Economics.

— (2003) 'Overview: an agenda for restarting growth and reform', in P.-P. Kuczynski and J. Williamson (eds), *After the Washington Consensus: Restarting Growth and Reform in Latin America*, Washington, DC: IIE, pp. 1–19.

Williamson, O. E. (1981) 'The economies of organization: the transaction cost approach', *American Journal of Sociology*, 87: 548–77.

— (1985) *The Economic Institutions of Capitalism: Firms, Markets, Relational Contracting*, New York: Free Press.

Wilpert, G. (2003) *Venezuela's Mission to Fight Poverty*, <www. venezuelanalysis.com/articles. php?artno=1051>.

Wilson, D. and R. Purushothaman

207

(2003) *Dreaming with BRICs: The Path to 2050*, Goldman Sachs Global Economics Paper no. 99, <www2.goldmansachs.com/insight/research/reports/99.pdf>.

Wolf, E. N. (1996) *Top Heavy: A Study of Increasing Inequality of Wealth in America*, New York: New Press.

World Bank (1981) *Accelerated Development in Sub-Saharan Africa: An Agenda for Action*, Washington, DC: World Bank.

— (1994) *Reducing Poverty in South Africa: Options for Equitable and Sustainable Growth*, Washington, DC: World Bank.

— (1995) *Working with NGOs: A Practical Guide to Operational Collaboration between the World Bank and Nongovernmental Organizations*, vol. 1, report no. 15013, <http://web.worldbank.org/servlets/ECR?contentMDK=204 14786&sitePK=244330>.

— (1996) *South Africa – Industrial Competitiveness and Job Crea-tion*, Project ID ZAPA 48606.

— (2004a) *World Development Report*, New York: Oxford University Press.

— (2004b) *Report and Recommendations on a Country Assistance Strategy for the Republic of Bolivia*, Report no. 26838-BO, Washington, DC: World Bank.

— (2005) *World Development Report*, New York: Oxford University Press.

— (2006a) *HIPC Debt Relief*, <http://web.worldbank.org/wbsite/external/news/0,,content MDK:20040942~menuPK:34480~ pagePK:34370~theSitePK:4607,00. html>.

— (2006b) 'South African investment climate favorable but challenges remain', World Bank news release 2006/198/AFR, <http://web.worldbankorg/ WBSITE/EXTERNAL/COUNTRIES/ AFRICAEXT/SOUTHAFRICAEXTN/ 0,,contentMDK:20753842~menu PK:368082~pagePK:141137~piPK:14 1127~theSitePK:368057,00.html>.

— (2006c) *International Development Association. Private Sector Development*, <http://web.world bank.org/WBSITE/EXTERNAL/ EXTABOUTUS/IDA/0,,content MDK:20189487~menuPK:413823 ~pagePK: 51236175~piPK: 437394 ~theSitePK:73154,00.html>.

World Economic Forum (2006) *Global Competitiveness Report 2005–6*, <www.weforum.org/en/ initiatives/gcp/Global%20 Competitiveness%20Report/ index.htm>.

World Social Forum (2006) Charter of Principles, <www.wsfindia. org/?q=node/3>.

Yergin, D. and J. Stanislaw (1999). *The Commanding Heights: The Battle between Government and the Marketplace that is Remaking the Modern World*, New York: Touchstone.

Index